The Airport

The Airport

Terminal Nights
and Runway Days at
John F. Kennedy International

James Kaplan

William Morrow and Company, Inc.
New York

Library of Congress Cataloging-in-Publication Data

Kaplan, James.
The airport : terminal nights and runway days at John F. Kennedy International/
James Kaplan.
p.   cm.
Includes index.
ISBN 0-688-09247-0
1. John F. Kennedy International Airport (N.Y.)—History. 2. Aeronautics,
Commercial—United States—History. I. Title.
HE9797.5.U52N63   1994
387.7'36'09747243—dc20   93-48715
CIP

Printed in the United States of America

First Edition

1 2 3 4 5 6 7 8 9 10

BOOK DESIGN BY NICOLA MAZZELLA

This book

is dedicated to the memories of

KENNETH OSBORNE CUMBUS

and ROBERT EDWARD KAPLAN.

They flew.

Preface

I am a passenger. I am not, by any stretch, an aviation expert: before I began this book, in fact, I knew far less about airplanes and airports than I know now, which is only a bit. (There was a humiliatingly long time at the beginning of my research when—despite the fact that I'd flown on many 727s, 737s, 757s, 767s, DC-8s, DC-9s, DC-10s, and Airbuses—the only airliners I could identify with any hope of certainty, even from quite close up, were the unmistakable 747 and the Concorde.) I travel by air about as much as anyone does these days: more than some, less than many. Like you, I suffer through turbulence; like you, I have seen my life pass before my eyes not a few times. I have watched the paperback on my lap rise into the air in front of my face and float there for a terrifying three full seconds—*one thousand one, one thousand two, one thousand three*—as my traveling companion crossed herself, when the airliner I was on plummeted into an air pocket. I have been in a plane that was struck by lightning—big bang, white flash—while approaching LAX. ("Oh my God!" a woman across the aisle shrieked. "This is it!") I have missed flights; I have been upgraded, downgraded, and bumped.

The only expertise I can claim is, quite literally, seat-of-the-pants experience: Like you, I have spent thousands of hours wedged into the seats of commercial airliners, and many more thousands waiting, waiting, waiting in molded-plastic chairs in airports around the country. And, probably like you, while I've flown and waited, I've often wondered why commercial aviation is the way it is, why airports are the way they are, and how it all works. It was this wondering, in great part, that led to this book.

No doubt much here will be outdated by the time you read it. Some of the people you'll meet in these pages have since left the airport. Technology changes, fast—although, economics being what it is, the implementation of technology is always another matter. Economics being what it is, airlines die and are born; carriers rise to the top of the heap and slide down; fare wars flare and fade away. Commercial aviation is a cutthroat, volatile business, and is likely to remain so for a long time. This, at any rate, is a constant. As are the discomfort and indignity of flying.

Kennedy Airport will change, but only very slowly. Its rattletrap efficiency; its brazen, almost touching, lack of ingratiation—these are likely to endure. In its ambitious redevelopment programs, it has aspired to the condition of state-of-the-art airports, the chief hallmark of that condition being facelessness. The programs have largely failed, as have Kennedy's yearnings toward conformity. For worse and better, as the third millennium dawns, the airport remains—steadfastly, adamantly, and mostly unapologetically—itself.

Acknowledgments

The original idea for a kind of *The Way Things Work* account of Kennedy Airport came from Rachel Abramowitz, who mentioned it to my brother Peter W. Kaplan when they were both working at the lost and lamented *Manhattan, inc.* magazine. And it was my brother—mainly to his great credit—who blithely suggested I take on the impossible task of portraying JFK International at book length. Peter also served as a crucial razor when I'd finished a first draft almost as big as the airport itself.

I would also like to thank my many helpers, enablers, informants, and hand-holders in dark hours: Lisa Bankoff (for her unreasonably persistent belief); Jim Brady; John Brant; Bill Cahill; Sammy Chevalier; Roger Cohen; Paul Geinberg; Jack Gartner; Peter Horton; Len Klasmeier; John Lampl; Ed McDonald; Tom Middlemiss; George Murphy; *The New York Times* (for its coverage of the crash of Eastern Flight 66); Les Radley; John Seabrook (for his *Manhattan, inc.* profile of Roger Berlind); *Tales of Gaslight New York* (for its piece on the *Colonel Slocum* disaster); Captain Tony Vallillo; my mother, Roberta Wennik-Kaplan (for support both concrete and moral); and Adrian Zackheim (for his persistent belief).

And Sylvia Plachy, for her wonderful photographs.

Nicholson Baker, whom I am proud to call a friend, inspired me. As, of course, did the great John McPhee, with whom I'm proud to say I once ate lunch.

The title came from the esteemed Fred Dannen, who dreamed it.

The author always, not always comprehensibly, thanks spouse and children. Let me try to put a finer point on it: A book has a reason for being only if its author does. And it is to my reasons for being—Karen Cumbus, Jacob Kaplan, Aaron Kaplan—that I tender this volume.

Contents

Thus things proceed in their circle, and thus the empire is maintained.

—Machiavelli

Overture

Begin on a Sunday night in February 1964, when, on the tiny round screen of the cherrywood RCA television in the corner of my grandparents' den in Hewlett, Long Island, New York, Ed Sullivan introduces, with a hint of amused condescension, the Beatles, who have just landed on a Pan American jet at the recently renamed[+] John F. Kennedy International Airport (formerly Idlewild, a.k.a. New York International) in Queens.

It is a loaded juncture, the middle of one of the grimmest winters in the Republic's history. The young president has been dead scarcely two months: the world has been turned upside-down. The nation hardly knows what to do with itself. Here is Ed Sullivan, a marginally consoling figure from the old order of things (the short-hair-and-cigarettes-and-cocktails order, the life-during-Depression-and-wartime order), a washed-up Broadway columnist from radio days who has brilliantly reinvented himself as a TV personality (yet is basically uncomfortable with the medium), throwing out a treat to the kiddies—a novelty act from England, four boys from Liverpool with mop haircuts, who croon about holding hands, in close, slightly off-key harmony. The Beatles have nothing to do with the old order, which is why they seem amusing and freakish to Sullivan and his kind—cops and bureaucrats and soldiers and others of that vintage, including—at first—Frank Sinatra. (A few weeks earlier, on *Life*'s "Miscellany" page at the back of the magazine—the section always devoted to a full-page black-and-white photo of some risible oddment or other—there ran a picture of, simply, the Beatles riding in an open car. Not the Beatles walking on their hands; not the Beatles reflected in distorting glass. Just the Beatles *being*.) The Beatles, of course, are the new order, and they will bury Ed Sullivan.

There was temporary joy in this new era (*We're out!* the Beatles exclaimed, in *A Hard Day's Night,* when they'd escaped the oppressive confines

---

[+] On December 24, 1963.

XV

of their rehearsal hall to cavort in a field), but it was ambivalent fun. The old world dies hard. My grandparents snickered uncomprehendingly, not comfortably, at the Beatles, here in their little frame house on a bluish-white-collar side street in western Long Island, where their lives were punctuated every minute or so by the dire-sounding thunder of the big jets, a few hundred feet overhead, coming into Kennedy.

It was a bad location: it might as well have been next to a freight yard. Nor was there any escape, whereas formerly there had been many. Nana and Papa's ambit had once been extensive; then they lost their money. Now they were confined, along with their plush furniture, to these too-small rooms, and to their memories. Wealthy people from the 1910s until the early fifties, they had traveled frequently; now they were reduced to watching the planes fly over. Once it had been first class all the way, on the great railway trains and ocean steamers of the time and, later, on airplanes.

They flew out of Idlewild often at the beginning, climbed the stairs onto brilliant-skinned prop liners on windy glaring days at the wide, empty airport, days full of ocean light. *Sun on salt water,* the billion-candled god of pleasure. And then, when they were forced to move from the hushed, white-graveled, dense-hedged lanes of Hewlett Bay Park, they settled directly under the approach paths to what had turned, in the unfolding of the end of the twentieth century, from Idlewild into Kennedy Airport—an abstractly, dutifully named place, whose abstraction seemed to reflect, in a sharply focused way, the banalization of the world itself. (Around this same time, postal ZIP codes appeared, as did push-button telephones; and the great old Manhattan phone exchanges—Rhinelander and Butterfield and Waverly—began to turn into numbers.) *Kennedy.* As the airport (and—coincidentally?—the dead president's star) declined, the name came to be spoken dismissively, even contemptuously.

The new world must have appeared, to my once-glamorous grandparents, a gray, bewildering place, a world where jets instead of propellers roared, rather than droned, through the sky, a sky that had once been fringed, in Long Island's arcadian days, with the towering dreamtime clouds of N. C. Wyeth—*Idlewild*—and that now, in the time of jets and expressways, was full of metropolitan soot. A world where every plane coming in at five hundred feet sounded like The End. In a way, it was true. The 707s roaring over at fifty stories seemed to mark the end of grace in the world. *Gone is the romance that was so divine.* Nostalgia is the perpetual state of humanity. And so one of my first questions was, once I was old enough to formulate it, Did the world really used to be better? Or, in aching for the past, do we simply long for an idyllic version of our own childhood, which is itself a lie?

Overture

*

Given the importance and colorfulness of Kennedy Airport, as well as my heritage and continued residence in the New York Metropolitan Area, the idea of writing a book about JFK initially seemed keenly appropriate, yet I will admit I approached the project with something like pure dread. On several levels. Number one: quite simply, it had been planted in my psyche, as you see, that the place was aversive. Those big jets descending over my grandparents' house were not the gleaming silver birds of airline commercials. They were loud, gritty, and menacing. And in my subsequent experience as a traveler, Kennedy had also proved aversive. Important, yes; colorful, yes; but also squalid and pressured and confusing. It seemed a place to escape rather than one to seek out. And given the antiquated and dilapidated road system that served it, escape was never an easy matter.

Second, I was, before this project began, no fonder of flying than most people who are not utterly terrified by it—which is to say that I didn't require clinical or pharmaceutical aid (besides alcohol) to get through the experience, but I had whitened my knuckles with the best of them. Nor, when I first considered this book, had the days since deregulation in 1978 done much to convince me that airline travel was anything more than a fairly dangerous, extremely tedious flying bus ride. Why, then, would I want to write about scary flying buses and the big place where they parked? Why would I want to spend time—a lot of time—at what amounted to (didn't it?) a not very glorified bus station, and an outmoded bus station at that?

Number three, Kennedy *was* big. Too big. It was immense; it was overwhelming. How could a novelist and profile writer work effectively on anything like such a scale (if scale, in this context, was even a comprehensible concept)? How could you profile an *airport*?

But then the more I thought about it, the more it seemed that reasons three, two, and one were also strong reasons *for* doing a book on JFK, the airport. Kennedy's bigness was more than just a matter of size: there were greatness and scope and history and dirt there, all in large measure. And my fears about flying were surely something to be overcome, or at least tempered, with greater knowledge. And then first, last, and deepest: What, really, *was* the source of Kennedy's aversiveness?

I knew—or at least felt—that there had once been something great about the place, and that that greatness seemed to have passed. But was this true, or was I simply indulging in nostalgia (the gist of which is that the old days were better because they were further from our death)? As a child, I rode out to my grandparents' Hewlett house on Robert Moses' jammed and potholed Long Island and Grand Central expressways, and, sitting in traffic, stared at the old

Overture

Y-shaped gray wooden light stanchions along the road, bathed in the white ocean light of the Island, a light that seemed to contain something primeval and profound. Something lost. What was it? It wasn't just Nana and Papa's fortunes, whose fruits I dimly remembered tasting. It had to do with the sea and the vast sky, with the collision of city and country, past and present.

When I first began to go out to Kennedy for this book, I saw that old ocean light again—shining on an airport that was in fiscal and physical and moral peril. Pan American World Airways, JFK International's biggest rent-payer, its mainstay for forty-four years, was just about to go out of business. TWA didn't seem far behind, and prospects weren't rosy for many of the other airline tenants, either. A major airport-renovation project was falling apart. Crime was rife; homelessness—at the airport!—was growing. Investigative newspaper reporters were all over the place like white on rice, turning in hard-hitting exposés that made Kennedy Airport look like an air/bus depot from hell, a sinkhole of civic/aeronautical turpitude.

Was it true? Well, but there was that ocean light! Kennedy/Idlewild was a powerful place, a place of strong history, and that history needed looking into. And whatever the problems—and nobody appeared to deny them—there was the continuing miracle of a great airport, and its city of workers, functioning around the clock, moving eight hundred planes through the place a day, and ninety thousand passengers. Three hundred thousand planes a year; thirty million people.

Thirty million people! And many of them coming through Kennedy Airport, the Ellis Island of our era, to live in freedom for the first time. A little fact we've gotten quite used to, to the point of boredom, and that most of the rest of the world can barely comprehend.

Was the world really better once? Has it, in other words, turned significantly worse? And was JFK, the airport, somehow in this regard a mirror of the world? Early on in my work I had a dream of being able to hold the whole immense airport in my hands. To turn it, examine it, comprehend it. And, once it was in my grasp, of being able to help it—to rescue it, even. Was such a thing necessary? (And who was I, to presume?) I went to spend some time on the cattailed bayside tract that had once flourished under the beautiful dreamy name *Idlewild*—a name that sang with sun and wind and the largeness of a world where retreat was still possible—to find out.

Prologue

Long Ago and Far Away: Jamaica Sea

I n the *very* beginning—ten thousand years ago—the glaciers scraped across the western side of the long island, planing away everything in their path, the trees and hills and boulders, leaving the countryside wide open and almost perfectly flat. It was a region that would come to be known, ninety-eight centuries later, as the Hempstead Plains. Long Island, New York. It dozed for decades in pastoral silence, growing potatoes. On the Fourth of July 1909, far to the west-northwest, in the state's Finger Lakes region, in a tiny farming town called Hammondsport, an authentic American genius named Glenn Curtiss, flying an aircraft of his own design, won the *Scientific American* prize for the first public airplane flight of one kilometer, in a straight line, in the United States. (Aviation had developed slowly since the Wright brothers' 852-foot, 59-second flight at Kitty Hawk, North Carolina, five and a half years earlier.) And less than a week after Curtiss's flight, he pulled up stakes and moved his base of operations to Garden City, Long Island, where he set up a flying school amid the potato fields at the corner of Washington Avenue and Old Country Road, across from the Mineola Fair Grounds.

Why did Glenn Curtiss move? He had a head full of airplane ideas (soon he would come up with one of the most basic and enduring concepts in aviation, the aileron—the movable flap on an airplane's wing used to control the plane's rolling and banking movements), and in the early years of this century, no place on the planet was as perfectly suited for the development and testing of such ideas as western Long Island. The terrain was as flat as it had been for ten thousand years, and virtually as unobstructed. Big parcels of land were available at low cost. The Island was situated roughly halfway between Europe and the Pacific coast, making it a natural starting or finishing point for what was bound to come along sooner or later: transcontinental and transatlantic flight. Also, no place on the Island was very far from water, which made it an ideal venue for the testing and flying of the seaplane—a device Curtiss would invent in 1911. And New York City provided a deep labor pool, and a

Prologue

large, enthusiastic audience for flying competitions and record-breaking flights.✦ Within months of Curtiss's arrival, his airfield was the focal point of world aviation, and new fields quickly sprang up around Garden City and environs. Kitty Hawk may have been the birthplace of aviation, but western Long Island (including Queens and Brooklyn) was its cradle, and would remain so for thirty years.

The country was besotted with airplanes in those days, and this was where it was all happening: races, stunts, endurance tests, parachute jumps, skywriting, midair weddings. (And crashes. Lots of crashes.) The many newspapers of New York provided a ready and hungry publicity outlet for the new art/science of aviation, as did the fledgling movie industry, which, before it moved to Hollywood after the end of World War I, had its world headquarters in Astoria, Queens. Much of early flying had only curiosity value, but then the serious milestones began to come along: The first transatlantic flight (made in a Curtiss seaplane, with a crew of two, between Newfoundland and the Azores) originated from Jamaica Bay at Far Rockaway, Queens, in 1919. The first nonstop transcontinental flight left from Roosevelt Field, a mile east of Glenn Curtiss's old flying school, in 1923. And in the early morning of May 20, 1927, a sober-sided, methodical young airmail pilot, newly famous for having broken a cross-country speed record, also took off from Roosevelt Field, heading into the dawn, and became Lucky Lindy, an international celebrity, by crossing the Atlantic solo, from New York to Paris, for the first time.

In the early twenties, in the midst of this flying frenzy, a boy in knickers was growing up in Springfield Gardens, Long Island, a short bike ride north of a sandy, grassy plot on Jamaica Bay called Idlewild. He would never achieve any celebrity, but in 1973 he would finish his thirty-four-year career as a captain for American Airlines piloting airplanes Glenn Curtiss could never have dreamed of.

Len Klasmeier was an old man when I found him, and though he was not well, on several fronts, his former robustness radiated from him: A big, square-jawed fellow with large, craggy features and a potbelly, he spoke in a gruff voice, in the tough-guy accents of old New York. He was a pilot of the old school, a high-school dropout, who had learned to fly by flying. Now he lived in a little house in Valley Stream with his wife of forty years, a former stewardess, just down the road from his childhood home and directly under the Kennedy Airport approach paths. As the jets roared over, he recalled a sweeter time.

✦ I am indebted to George C. Dade and Frank Strnad's superb *Picture History of Aviation on Long Island, 1908–1938.*

Prologue

*

"What was Idlewild like when you were a boy?" I asked him.

"Back in the early twenties, there was a trolley car line that went along Rockaway Boulevard," Klasmeier said. "And I remember you'd get off at this little road, it was a one-track dirt road, where the cars could get down, and carriages. And we'd walk about a mile down.

"Idlewild—the resort—was not active then. What it was, there was a great big hotellike structure, with a porch all the way around and then a dock, and it had a boathouse and a little lighthouse, and a place down the road a little bit for the carriages."

"Was it dilapidated?"

"No, it was in good shape," he said. "But the owner wasn't there. He might have been in Europe. His name was Ehlers, or something like that. They traveled all over the country, and they had friends all over the world. And the people would come and just idle their time there—the countryside was really wild. And that's where it got the name of Idlewild. And the old man—some relative on my father's side—was a caretaker. And of course when nobody was there, we'd go down. Oh, it was wonderful, you know."

Klasmeier stared out into the middle distance. "I remember—we'd go fishing, go out in a rowboat with my father. And the fish were so plentiful—you'd just drop the line, and you'd pull 'em up. This was in Jamaica, exactly where Kennedy Airport is now. Now, that was all country; there were three houses there. There was nothing between Merrick Road and our house. We used to ride on a bicycle to Merrick Road—I remember there was a gas station, a little tiny place, with a hot-dog stand. The gas was in a portable tank with big wheels on it. That was long ago and far away.

"Up a few blocks there was a golf course on either side of Merrick Road. And walking home—way off the road—the first thing I remember, I hear this roar. The automobiles used to have cowl lights then. And out of the corner of my eye, I saw the lights, and then this guy hit me. I was sailing up in the air and landed on the hood. And he's goin' down the road like this, and finally I rolled over. He hit me so hard, my shoes stayed right where they were. He kept right on going. This other friend I was with, he just got him on the edge and spun him around. The guy must've had a skinful or something."

"What were your first experiences with airplanes?" I asked.

He smiled. "Well, now I'm around nine, ten years old—and P.S. Thirty-seven, where we went to school, was about a mile away. This other fellow and I got into morning school, so we'd be out at twelve o'clock. And every afternoon, we rode over to old Curtiss Field and back again. It was sixteen miles—each way—and we'd spend our time over there. Didn't know anybody. We knew about these fellows Harry Webb and Tom Smith. Pilots. We said hello; they never said hello back again." Klasmeier laughed. "This was over where Roosevelt Field shopping center is now."

"I guess flying was very romantic then," I said. "I mean, there was Lindbergh and everything—"

"No, we were over there before Lindbergh," he said.

I took this in for a moment. "How much before, exactly?"

"Oh, maybe '22, '23. Anyhow, this other group of kids and myself, we were building this airplane—a Heath Parasoar. We were supposed to have a motorcycle engine converted, and we never got it finished. Finally we traded it to another kid for a horse." He laughed. "That was a bad deal, because whether you use a horse or not, he's eatin' all the time. I think that's where I got my appetite from."

"What were they flying at Curtiss Field when you went there?" I asked. "Biplanes? Monoplanes?"

"Oh, everything was biplanes. Curtiss Jennys. JEN 4-Ds. Everything was biplanes. Waco 9s and then later Waco 10s, Stinson biplanes. And then Fairchild come out with this cabin airplane—monoplane. And I used to watch this fellow fly that. I used to admire him so much. Where everybody else had leather coats and helmet and goggles and silk scarf, this was a cabin airplane. This guy flew with a derby, and a blue coat with a black velvet collar and a scarf. Anyway, this fellow's name was Art Capon. And when I finally got with American Airlines, on my first flight—it was in December 1939, to Detroit—the captain was Art Capon."

"When was your first solo? What did you fly in?"

"Well, in the early days, you had to put up a bond of something like fifteen hundred, two thousand dollars to solo," Klasmeier said. "That was impossible. So Jamaica Sea opened—that's where Kennedy is now. And this fellow, I think his name was Bill Gulik—he was flying this Travel Air there. And you didn't have to get an hour—you could fly for eight dollars and fifty cents for twenty minutes. Now, eight dollars and fifty cents, oh, that's fantastic. So, I'd go over there and get a little twenty-minute lesson. I was making twelve dollars a week. I couldn't fly very often, now!"

"How were you making your money?"

He smiled. "One job I had was in the A and P, as an order boy. I'd get five dollars a week in tips. And, I remember I used to like to travel around a lot, so I got this other kid, Walter Purcell, to work for me for two dollars and fifty cents."

"You subcontracted," I said.

"Yeah. So I'd come in on Saturday, and I'd pick up my five dollars, and I'd give Walter his two dollars and fifty cents. And one week I come in there and the manager says, 'Come over here. Are you working here, or is that guy?'" Klasmeier laughed. "What was I talking about?" he asked.

"Your solo."

"Oh yeah. Well, then these other kids, from the other side of town, they got ahold of this airplane that was busted up, and they rebuilt it and repaired it. A Curtiss Robin—a monoplane, and a cabin airplane. And they borrowed an OX-5 engine and they put that in, and they were doing pretty good; they soloed and everything else. Anyhow, one night they had the Robin tied down, and a windstorm come along and blew it away and broke a wheel off of it and some other stuff. So I made a deal with Eddie Harrington that I would pay for the wheel and he would solo me. Eddie was sixteen years old. I was about eighteen. I think it come to about one hundred dollars, a hundred and ten dollars, and I borrowed that off my mother, which I had to pay back. And I thought, oh boy, I sure lucked out on this deal. Eddie's pretty sharp, but I outsmarted him. Well, it wasn't a month ago I looked at my log book—he gave me two hours and five minutes when he soloed me. For a hundred dollars. So I didn't do so great. But I got what I wanted."

"What made you want to fly?" I asked.

"I don't know," Klasmeier said. "It was just one of those things. My father wanted me to be a photoengraver. He didn't know that I was flying, and he found out about it, and I remember he was furious. He said, 'Stay away from those goddamn airplanes or out of the house you go!' Then, as an afterthought, he said, 'Why don't you be like other kids and hang around the pool room.'" He laughed.

"Pilots were nothing then," he said. "You were a bum or you were a pilot, you know. Same thing. Sometimes you make a lot of money and most of the times you're starving to death. One of those things. But when people come down to see an airplane, you were really something."

"What was Jamaica Sea like?" I asked.

"Jamaica Sea," he said, shaking his head. "All the airport was, there was a road going down here to the water, which was about—oh, two thousand feet down. And it was very narrow, and the wind was usually blowing. Now we got pretty good at landing crosswind, because of the fact that you could only land that way. And there was this tin hangar. Just one tin hangar. This fellow Ernie Marcus had an Eagle Rock out there, and he had a transport license. There might have been one, maybe two other airplanes in the hangar. That was it. No asphalt. Just sand and bulrushes."

Prologue

"What about school?"

"I'd gone to high school for a while, at Brooklyn Tech. And I was disappointed. My God—such childish things that they were teaching there—you know, things you couldn't use, about how to get sap out of a tree, and this and that, you know. Half of the time I didn't go. I went back to school later, to Jamaica Evening High, five nights a week. But in October sometimes, you'd get these beautiful moons. . . the hell with school! We'd go out and get in the airplanes, start up, be flying at night, you know. And, there was no lights on the field, no lights on the airplane. We knew where the wires were. And then we landed on the wheels, 'cause you could never see the ground. Never, you had no idea. And you'd fly in on the wheels—see, then it wouldn't stall. Come in like that till you hear it go *wuhwuhwuhwuh.* The wheels rollin'— then you throttle it back. So we did that for a while, we'd fly over town, get everybody, all the kids out. Then some of the other guys, the men, started to take people for rides. Now, they didn't have lights, either. I remember this one night, we come in to land, we throttle it back—suddenly you hear the other airplane, you're looking at exhaust. So we finally put lights on 'em."

"And when did you start to teach flying yourself?" I asked.

"There was this friend of mine, Walter Purcell—" Klasmeier began.

"From the A and P?"

"Yeah. Anyway, when Walter was young he'd been in an automobile accident—got hit in the head—and he got ten thousand dollars. That was a lot of money then. So, when he turned twenty-one he got the money, and he bought a brand-new Dodge, and I also talked him into buying this airplane, a Fledgling, for eight hundred fifty dollars. Two people could sit in it, one in the front and one behind. It was built originally by Curtiss as a training plane for the services. It was a big thing, burned a lot of fuel. And I remember— 'cause we had no money, you know—in the backseat, there was only one half of a seat belt on there. So when you were sitting in the back and somebody else was flying, you better make sure you held on. We never did get the other half of that belt.

"My deal—I was to teach Walter, and other people, to fly. And this fellow Dick Spencer, who was a writer and an artist—boy, he was a good illustrator, too—apparently he commanded a lot of money, 'cause some big papers were looking all over for him. But he wanted to get out of it, and he started this flying school called American Espadrille.

"And I'm sittin' on a fence one day, doing nothing, you know, and Spencer sits down next to me and he says, 'How would you like to fly for me?' I'd had him up in that Fledgling once or twice."

Prologue

Just then a jet, sounding as though it were about to touch down in the front yard, shook the house. We waited a moment till it passed over. "So I said, 'Geez, you know, I don't have a license,'" Klasmeier continued.

"So Spencer said—"

"So Spencer said, 'Well, we'll get you one.'"

1

Arriving

Van Wyck. IAB. The Manager

"At Queens Boulevard, I took the shoulder. *At Jewel Avenue, I used the* median*! I had it! I was there! And then . . . I hit the Van Wyck. They say no one's ever beaten the Van Wyck. But gentlemen—I'll tell you this. I came as close as anyone ever* has. *. . ."*
>   —ELAINE on *Seinfeld,*
>   TV situation comedy of the early nineties

On the kind of early-spring late afternoon when the shadows in Manhattan are long and purple on the brick faces of the old tenements of the far Upper East Side, I hail a cab for Kennedy. The fact that I have no luggage makes zero impression on the driver, nor does the fact that after a block I whip out a reporter's notebook. "Can we talk?" I say, not consciously echoing Joan Rivers. "Sure, why not?" my driver says. Like most cabbies and cops, he is surprised by little, and quite happy to talk, feeling—probably with a good deal of justification—that he has two or three books' worth of material in him. His name, I read on his hack license, is Efthimios Andreadis. My very rough translation from the Greek is "good-spirited man." This Andreadis is. He is an extraordinarily equable cab driver, of philosophical bent—a dark, mustachioed fellow of indeterminate early middle age. "The last time I went to Kennedy?" he says. "Maybe about three weeks ago. The thing about Kennedy, you rarely get a fare back to the city. You look around a little, then you go back empty. Financially speaking, it's not too bad — it works out about the same as cruising in Manhattan. As long as you don't hit traffic."

We turn onto the FDR Drive, which is packed but flowing. We're heading north, toward the Triborough Bridge. "Sometimes it's just luck," Efthimios

1

Andreadis muses. "Every corner you turn, you pick up somebody. Other times, you look and look for a fare. It's funny," he says, turning his profile to me. Whenever I chat with a cabbie, which is often, I have to figure out whether he wants me to make angular eye contact in the rearview mirror—a process that disconcerts me by its indirection—or directly with the side of his face. Andreadis is a hybrid. "Just before I picked you up, I was thinking about what else I might do," he says.

"In your life?"

"In my life. My dream," Andreadis says, "is to maybe get three or four medallions, then lease out the cabs by the week. I could drive, not drive—I'd still be making the money."

Now we're on the approach to the Triborough, Robert Moses' Pharaonic 1934 colossus. I think of Andreadis's dream; I think of Moses, the founder and patron saint of the Triborough Bridge and Tunnel Authority, and his secret funds, and of the male human animal's never-ending scheming toward the making of a buck. Between 1955 and 1965, neither the TBTA nor the Port Authority spent a penny on mass transit in the New York Metropolitan Area, but the two together spent billions on highways that were doomed, from the word go, to be choked. Much of that money went toward improving access to bridges and tunnels *in order that more tolls might be collected.* Tolls, the czars of New York commerce learned very early on, are gold. I have a dim child-hood memory of hearing an official announcement that tolls on one of the Manhattan river crossings would stop being collected as soon as the crossing was paid for. The crossings, and their maintenance, have been paid for many, many times over, and in all the years that have passed, I haven't noticed that anyone has stopped collecting tolls on the Manhattan river crossings. Why should they? This money is gravy! Why do we pay the tolls? Because they're there!

"I'm gonna ask you for the toll now," Andreadis says, as we inch up to the booth. "Since you're a writer, I'll tell you why. Most of the people, if I ask them for the toll when they pay the fare at the end of the ride, they're not happy. Even when I show them on the sign that's the rule. And when they're not happy, the tip is not as high." I give him the $2.50. He pays the man in the tollbooth, who is nodding his head insistently to the beat of a rap song that can be heard clearly in the back of the cab.

"Some guys go out to the airport empty and wait for a fare," Andreadis says, as we swing onto the Triborough's great eastward curve. "Then when things get slow, they jump on the highway and come back to town. I don't see how they make any money, but they must have it figured out. Some guys know the schedules of all the airlines—they know when it's gonna land, what type of people are gonna come out, everything." He shakes his head.

Now we're cruising along in medium traffic on the Grand Central Parkway on this gem-perfect afternoon. A blue-and-white ASPCA car speeds by with its siren blooping and its lights flashing. On the shoulder, two motorcycle cops with a weirdly La Guardia (Fiorello)–era look about them—rakishly squashed-down hats and puttees—are writing tickets for a small line of cars they've stopped. Passing by backward and forward, either overtaking us or being overtaken, are, like the various figures inside Dorothy Gale's cyclone: many Volvo wagons; a red Honda Accord with diplomatic plates; a midnight-blue early eighties Buick Riviera with gloriously slick Armor Alled tires and a no-sideburned young sport at the wheel; a Sikh cab driver yelling out his window at a guy driving slow in front of him; a limo driver gesticulating into his rearview mirror to his passenger; a sinister-looking black Continental with reflecting windows and private plates. The traffic in the opposite, westbound, lane is packed solid, stationary. What could be better than cruising by a traffic jam? "It is not enough that I succeed; my friends must also fail," La Rochefoucauld, or some other witty Frenchman, said. "I better find a place to stay at the airport," says Efthimios Andreadis. "Some guy told me TWA is good between five and six."

Andreadis is talking not about checking into an airport motel but about finding a fare back. The approved method of doing so is to wait at one of the officially sanctioned taxi stands by the terminals. The problem with doing this is that one waits in line, and if it's a slow time of day—as it is most of the day at Kennedy, except between two in the afternoon and about ten at night—a driver can hang around for hours. The much more common and commonsensical, although disapproved, method of finding fares is to cruise the likeliest spots, to linger where arriving passengers are thickest. This practice, known as *loitering to solicit,* is officially illegal, and ticketable, although the law is only sporadically enforced. The law is meant both to control traffic and to control the practice of hustlers—some of the world's most assertive and cunning drivers-for-hire, who, in their unlicensed cars and limos, have been known to drive currency-rich and English-poor Japanese tourists around and around the wilds of Queens, finally depositing them at a motel at the airport's entrance, to the tune of five hundred dollars. (Actually, when insiders talk about hustlers at Kennedy, they may have one of two kinds in mind, the other category being the aggressive freelance baggage handlers known as the Smarte Carte Hustlers, many of whom are former inmates freshly released from Rikers Island—either on their own authority or that of the state—who gather outside the International Arrivals Building and solicit luggage-carrying business using the carts that travelers have rented inside and not returned—not unlike the Woody Allen routine in which Allen's nebbish character gets his shoes shined, *against his will,* by an enormous shoeshine boy, and they're suede shoes. This is New York. It should also be mentioned that the classic kind of hustler is more or less nonexistent at Kennedy, with the exception of the airport motels, where contact with the various escort and massage services of Queens can be made by phone. Or, as Officer Bill Curtis, Port Authority Police—Airport Bill to his friends, and others—says, "Let your fingers do the walking.")

In the case of the automotive hustlers, the PA Police Hack Squad cracks down on as many violators as possible, but no one is very much discouraged. For legit and illegit drivers alike, the tickets are simply part of the cost of doing business at Kennedy.

We merge into the Van Wyck Expressway. Six lanes; four miles. Traffic hell. There may be worse four-mile stretches in the world, but none comes quickly to mind. The Van Wyck—named after the first mayor of the combined boroughs of New York, a man who established a New York mayoral tradition by dying abroad, where he had fled to avoid prosecution for Tammany fiscal abuses—is, appropriately enough, four miles of shame. Robert A. Caro, in his epic biography of Robert Moses, *The Power Broker,* writes with eloquent controlled fury of Moses' refusal, in 1946, even to consider the possibility of acquiring the fifty extra feet of right-of-way through Queens that would have allowed a rapid-transit track to be constructed between the traffic lanes of the Van Wyck. A rapid-transit track that would have significantly alleviated automobile traffic, and that would have allowed a *sixteen-minute trip* between Penn Station and Idlewild. A rapid-transit track that would have cost less than two million 1946 dollars above the thirty-million-dollar price of the so-called expressway, which earned the right to have its name put in quotation marks the day it was finished. One suspects that, for Robert Moses, it wasn't even necessarily the money, but the principle of the thing. Moses appears never to have believed in anything he hadn't experienced himself, and he certainly didn't believe in public transportation in New York City. The automobile was the basis for his conception of the universe, yet he never learned to drive: he sat in the backseat. The greatest city in the world has reaped the rewards.

And here they are. To merge from the Grand Central into the Van Wyck is like trying to insert oneself into drying cement. Although it must be said that the Van Wyck is moving this afternoon. Just. But the VW, besides being look younger, more animated, less pinched. They are dressed in the international costume of travel, which—for the middle class, at any rate—is the costume of leisure.✈ (It's downstairs that you're more likely to see saris and kaffiyehs and babushkas and worldly possessions in plastic shopping bags, and to smell the multifarious exudations of the undeodorized world.) A bald guy with a gold Rolex and an expensive camera slung around his neck wears a black T-shirt that says PROPERTY OF ALCATRAZ. A cute little pair of twin French boys with moussed blond hair and fluorescent Hawaiian shirts run by, and as my eye follows them it is abruptly halted by a rivetingly sexy Asian woman in high heels, holding a foam cup of coffee in one hand and a cigarette in another, waiting for someone. Emphatically not me. Her cheekbones are astonishing, her gaze forbidding. The country and western blares insistently. America!

Back out onto the balcony. Ernesto leans on his broom, staring into deep space. Two beeper-wearing teenagers conspire edgily at a plastic table. A drug deal? The cop voice on the loudspeaker seems to gain new heights of desperate boredom with each recorded repetition: "Do *not* accept solicited rides to the city. Do *not* allow anyone except uniformed attendants to handle your luggage. . . ." There is no amenity in the dim sooty daylight; no glance engages another without hurriedly unhooking. No one is eager to linger in this space. This is New York at the end of the twentieth century, the American century: the greatest city in the greatest country in the world. Where are sunlight, grandeur, beauty, mystery, philanthropy, welcome, awe?

❒

The airport chapel, just in back of Food Court on the second floor of the IAB, is empty. The chapel, a small, shallow, windowless room with a single wall of backlit stained glass in a kind of champagne-bubble/atomic-particle motif, is used interchangeably for Catholic, Jewish, and Protestant services. For example, the Jewish ark—the cabinet that houses the Torah scrolls—is stored in a back room, to be wheeled in when needed. This interchangeability was not always the case. From 1966 until 1988, all three faiths had their own buildings, standing side by side in solitary splendor on a grassy plot in the central terminal area—Trifaith Plaza. The three chapels cost in the neighborhood of

---

✈ A 1950 photograph of the interior of Idlewild's old main terminal on a busy afternoon might as well be a Burberry ad: there is not a single man in the picture without a tie. The sixties changed all that. Even the Beatles wore neckties at first: the remnants of the last age always linger into the next. But then the remnants fade away, and the new age—glistening, squalling rudely—is born. By 1978, year one of deregulation, a relentless informality had already begun to become the way of the world. The athletic warmup suit started to become a kind of universal uniform, cutting across boundaries of age, gender, and economic status. (The polyester leisure suit was the fashion industry's briefly attempted truce with the warmup; and while no one misses the leisure suit, it is hard to find complete satisfaction in the warmup's victory.)

might be seen as a significant drawback for the main port of entry of the greatest city in the world and the most powerful land on earth. This is the building that is, for many, many people, their first sight of America—a building that, in the movies, could pass for a second-tier midwestern airport of the late fifties. (Real second-tier midwestern airports of the late fifties were much smaller. And cleaner.) Is this a function of the Port Authority's sole stewardship? Is it cash that has been lacking, or merely vision?

Still, the IAB is not without its own cozy squalor. The Calder mobile is as beautiful as ever, even if the supposed hugeness it was built to mitigate has, as if in a bad joke, turned into something small and base. The gray light on the arched ceiling is, somehow, the light of 1961. As you ride up the escalator— sorry, the *gleaming* escalator—the mobile is at your back: an odd design choice on the part of Skidmore, Owings and Merrill. A jerry-built-looking series of jogs at the top takes you past a small Citibank branch (a favorite target for robbers) and places you in a dubious interior piazza. An airport sundries store and a magazine shop are on the left; Nathan's and Pizza Hut stands, and Food Court—the Golden Door's fast-food replacement—are on the right.

This plaza, a pseudo-travertine balcony overlooking the Calder and the arched front windows, ought to be the center of the necklace's centerpiece, the focal point of the airport. Instead, it is a dim, stingy, desultory space that reads: *Watch your wallet.* Stunned-looking foreigners with backpacks, and wary-looking foreigners with carry-ons, wander by. A clean-up guy with a name tag that reads ERNESTO shuffles glumly among the tables, picking up napkins and plastic spoons. A public-address announcement warning about limo and baggage hustlers, delivered by a bored-sounding, Queens-cop-type voice, plays again and again, over aggressively perky country-and-western Muzak.

Inside Food Court, a single bank of windows looks out a narrow and uninspiring section of IAB apron: the grand views of the Golden Door appear to have gone the way of the restaurant itself. But then you don't eat here for the view. Or the food. Or the prices. (A tuna sandwich—on a croissant, yet— costs $6.95. This is the basic meal item; prices move upward from there.) You eat here because it's here. A middle-aged French couple clutch their trays of tea and muffins, looking suspicious and grim. I want to rush to them and apologize or explain about everything—but then I remember Charles de Gaulle Airport, outside Paris: more futuristic, but no less alienating. The husband approaches the black woman at the cash register. "Excuse me? *Serviettes?*" The woman shakes her head, uncomprehending. The man mimes—rather well—wiping his lips and hands. The woman smiles and points across the room to a napkin dispenser. The man doesn't smile back.

There are some more French—a planeload must have just come in. These

7

were the beginnings of the first international airport prepared to meet the challenge.✢

The wind blows across the vast central parking lot. The wind always blows at Kennedy, and it blows sweet and sour, fine and foul. Out on the Bay Runway, for instance, on a sunny spring afternoon, the breeze has a fine salty tang, and as the sun glints billion-candled on the water, it is possible to imagine the great old days of leisure here, to recomprehend the majestic poetry in the word *Idlewild*. It is possible, in the bay wind, to remember the great glamorous days of aviation, of silver-skinned planes and men and women in hats and gloves. It is even possible, in this wind, simply to enjoy the present: to watch the great planes (they are still beautiful) roll and land and take off and fly; to come to an unsquinting accommodation with the smog, with the breeze-borne trash, and appreciate what is still good. This is the age we must live in; we have no other.

Yet in the big parking lot in front of the International Arrivals Building—known at Kennedy as the IAB—the wind is assaultive, nothing more, and the present is bitter. It is impossible to draw cheer from acres of perpetually-under-construction asphalt, and as one approaches the great outmoded-looking terminal, one feels more repelled with every step, not by any specific outrage, but only by the sense that *it ought to be better.* Meeting or seeing off friends and loved ones should be sweeter, more mysterious, less aversive. Departing for faraway places should be less prosaic. The building itself should continue to inspire the awe it provoked when it was first built, only forty years ago, in an age when travel itself (and air travel in particular) was awesome. When awe itself still seemed accessible to the human spirit. For has not the experience of awe, which is not at all passive, been replaced by entertainment, which is?

Pass the control tower, cross the dangerous pair of roadways. There's supposed to be a PA cop working Post Seventeen, the loneliest post at the airport, crossing people in front of the IAB. "They used to offer two-to-tens and weekends off to anyone who would work Post Seventeen," a cop told me. "Nobody was buying." Into the IAB, the only terminal at JFK maintained by the Port Authority, the only terminal open twenty-four hours a day. The centerpiece of the necklace of buildings in the central terminal area is in a way Kennedy's worst place, the nexus of all that is wrong with the airport. It is not as blatantly unpleasant as, say, the Port Authority Bus Terminal in Manhattan, but the fact that it utterly lacks glamour, grandeur, character, or welcome

✢ From Geoffrey Arend's *Great Airports: Kennedy International.*

a bad road, is also a scary one: The lanes aren't wide enough and big trucks (usually, it seems, loaded with large pieces of rusty scrap metal) clank right alongside, hub by hub. The legendary potholes often occur in the pitch dark, under tenebrous unlit overpasses, where one of those big pieces of metal might fly off and turn you into a John Chamberlain sculpture before you had a chance to swerve. Popular American orchestral music of the vintage of this highway sometimes has peppy, optimistic, horns-are-honking-but-traffic-is-moving-right-along passages; the proper music for the Van Wyck would be a dirge for springs and shock absorbers.

Then, beyond the fabled Kew Gardens interchange, for no apparent reason, the road opens up. The traffic has thinned miraculously, and we're moving. What joy it is to move! Dear reader, I hope right now you're in a plane, going someplace wonderful, and not just sitting in a room. You will understand. Traffic is death. A clogged artery. We were born to flow. To accelerate, even. To walk, to run, to ride, to fly. To drive to the airport, to emerge from traffic, to walk quickly through the masses, to get on a plane and soar over the clouds—these are transcendent things. No wonder we can scarcely bear to think about them, for their opposites must also be considered. No wonder the airport is full of Muzak, and the chapels are hidden.

❒

The IAB was created to be a showcase of the air age. . . . When the IAB was dedicated with a lavish ceremony on July 31st, 1954, editors grasped for superlatives. The *New York Times* called it "an authentic wonder of the world." Perhaps more accurate is the description that the IAB is simple, functional, and elegant.

Artist Alexander Calder created a sense of human dimension to the hugeness that often overwhelms passengers at the airport, when one of his mobiles was hung from the ceiling of the IAB. The mobile is 40 feet fin to fin, but the sweep of the IAB arch is such that the mobile appears to be of conventional size.

Up gleaming escalators, a first-class restaurant, the Golden Door, opened with an unparalleled view of the runway. From here diners could watch the airliners of the world gather and observe throngs of visitors parading outside on the observation deck. . . .

Outside a magnificent "Fountain of Liberty" complete with ducks in the summer sprayed water high into the air at regular intervals. At night as the airliners came and went, multicolored lights in the fountain created a thrilling and truly stirring spectacle.

Now as aviation prepared to enter the jet age, here at Idlewild

5

mitted to building religious buildings. Somebody could take them to court. But they promised."

The rabbi sighs. "My friends say I'm a very successful rabbi, because after thirty years of service at Bellerose Jewish Center, I got appointed to a *shul* and it was promptly torn down." He smiles wryly. "Listen," he says, "the fact is that the freestanding chapels were a mixed bag. For instance, there used to be a reflecting lagoon in Trifaith Plaza, but the lagoon attracted birds, and you know what birds are at the airport. Also, the old chapels were not easily accessible."

"How's it going now?"

He shrugs. "So-so. Listen, I won't kid you. It's difficult. Transients ask for finanacial aid, out of the blue. Panhandlers ask us for money. There was a Russian Jewish family that parked here and said they wouldn't move until we found them a home. Once I cashed a check for four Hasidim who needed money for a friend who was on his way to Israel. Meanwhile, we have to stay afloat ourselves. And even among our biggest supporters, we're always number two. So, we have to try harder."

❏

"I come here in April of 1961," says Anthony Petrucci, who runs the barbershop upstairs in the IAB—a small, seedy, fluorescent-glary, windowless room just down the hall from the chapel that also doubles as a flower and balloon store, lottery-ticket sales point, and post office. Petrucci is a short, bald, grizzled man in need of a shave, with a hoarse voice and an Italian accent. We're sitting in his office, an even smaller room off the shop; as we speak, he keeps glancing nervously out at the store, where his partner, Frank Sepe, is taking care of what seems like scant business. "My brother was working for Varig, and I just finished beauty-culture school, so I came out here and went to work in the original beauty and barbershop of Idlewild, which had opened in 1959," Petrucci says. "The original shop was in the old Temporary Terminal Building, then it moved into the IAB. Everyone used to be in the IAB—TWA, Pan Am. Everyone. Everyone knew each other in those days. It was like a family.

"I bought my shop in '66," he says. "I lease the space from the Port Authority, but I own the shop. My rent is on a commission basis—the more you make, the more you pay."

I ask if the shop is profitable.

Petrucci leans his head sideways. "Right now we change," he says. "We used to be only a beauty-barbershop. Now you see. We sell the flowers, the lottery tickets, the stamps, the balloons." He shrugs. "Summer is faster. Right now is very slow."

"How has the airport changed since you've been here?" I ask him.

He shakes his head. "A lot of change. The big change is the passengers. Now everybody is flying—used to be people would only fly for an emergency, or maybe a vacation after saving for three years. Who would dream of a trip on the airplane before?"

"Who comes through your shop these days?"

"Men, mostly—the business travelers."

I glance out at the empty barber chair. "Who buys the lottery tickets?"

He looks evasive. "Mostly the lower middle class—the airport workers."

Ernesto, I think, involuntarily.

"These people are very ticklish today—I pay them a lot of attention," he says. "These employees in their dirty shoes and overalls are not very welcome in the duty-free shops. So I make them welcome here. Their money is just as good as anyone else's."

"How much profit do you make on a lottery ticket?"

"Six percent."

"You work hard," I say.

"I work hard," he agrees. "Eight-thirty to seven at night almost every day."

"Is there more crime here than there used to be?"

"You're more scared than you used to be, that's for sure," he says.

"Have you ever been held up?"

He rolls his eyes. "Thank God, no. But you're afraid of these people"—he lowers his voice—"the *residents.* You see them washing their feet in the men's room—how you know they won't go out of their mind? I have my cash box here for Lotto—how you know who's gonna come through here?" Suddenly his face lights up. "Hey, Mike!"

"Tony!"

A bald and very tan older man with an animated, muscular face has come into the room. He and Petrucci hug. The man's name is Mike Bon. He recently retired from American Express, he says, after twenty-five years of working in the company's special-services division, babysitting VIP cardholders as they passed through town. Today he's on his way to see his son, an army colonel in Stuttgart. He's logged a lot of time at Kennedy and, like many others, he feels that the airport used to be more tightly knit.

"I used to know everybody here," Bon says. "Station managers, supervisors, the traffic manager. Now I don't know anybody."

"That's another change," Petrucci says. "The distance between all the buildings now."

"Forget the distance," says Bon. "It's these part-time people. They come and they go."

Petrucci lowers his voice. "How could anybody take a bus here to work for four-fifty an hour and no benefits?"

"That's it," Bon says, nodding. "An airline job used to be a glamour job. You had all the benefits. Now they have no benefits—what do they care?"

Petrucci shakes his head. "Everybody running away from each other," he says. "No good, no good."

Bon shakes his head gravely.

"Still," Petrucci says, "I go to Rome Airport, they treat me like a piece of garbage. Over here, we're still the best—we just don't know it."

❐

Down the gleaming escalator. There are a fair number of escalator accidents in the IAB, I have heard, mainly among citizens of the Third World who have never seen such a device before, and who are more likely than most to wear loose, flowing garments. On the lower level, two Port Authority skycaps named Eric Cumberpatch and Lawrence Green are as underoccupied as the barber. I ask them if the Smarte Carte Hustlers are a problem. They both nod vigorously.

"A definite, definite problem," Cumberpatch says. "I've been assaulted twice—one of them threatened me with a razor. He was soliciting from a passenger, and I told him where to get off. He didn't like that."

"They're playin' the hustler problem like it's the homeless," Green says. "It's not. It's the guys from Rikers."

"Who's saying it's the homeless?"

He leans his forehead down and raises his eyebrows high. "Who do you think?" he asks.

"The Port Authority?"

"You said it, not me," Green says.

"But there are homeless here, too?"

"Oh yeah. Plenty of 'em. But the trouble is, the Port Authority is public, so they can't do nothing about it. The airlines are private, so they can keep them out of their terminals. Not here."

"So the homeless *are* a problem for you?"

"Everything's a problem," Cumberpatch chimes in. "When I go out to work at nine to eleven at night, I'm out there by myself. And if I call about a problem today, they come tomorrow."

Green nods vigorously.

"The Port Authority started up the skycaps forty years ago," Cumberpatch says. "And, times being what they were, it might not have seemed so dignified to so many people. But what we did with it, we turned it into a job. There are two things we emphasize today—pride and dignity.

"But these are hard times. Now they're phasing us out—they're not replacing retirees. The Port Authority retired twenty-five skycaps when they brought in the Smarte Carte concession. Which is a damn shame. The Port Authority skycaps are the pioneers of this airport, and the most honest people on the airport. Working inside there"—he points to the Customs area at the rear of the building—"you get propositioned by all kinds of people, lemme tell you. *All* kinds of people. Everybody wants to sneak somethin' through, if you know what I mean.

"There's never been a skycap arrested for doin' that. Never. People of all the other services here have been arrested. I'm talkin' *everybody*—Customs, DEA, police, what have you. No skycap. Once you become a skycap, that's your *nationality*. I have helped the great and famous. Josephine Baker. James Baldwin. Jack Nicholson. Anything that goes on at this airport, a skycap knows. And we have helped kings and queens from all over the world."

❐

Richard Rowe, Kennedy's general manager, is—despite the archetypally anonymous moniker—anything but a faceless bureaucrat, rather a husky, very light-skinned African-American of indeterminate middle age, with slicked-back hair and a slightly professorial-cum-1940s-zoot air about him. He is affability itself, but his big brown eyes, magnified by his thick glasses lenses, can freeze in a second when his managerial side is evoked. He projects an appealing combination of pride and appropriate humility about his impossible bailiwick: he seems to maintain his sanity by embodying the Scott Fitzgeraldian ideal of holding two directly contradictory ideas in his mind at the same time. He can sigh with the best of them at the airport's insane crappiness, yet, withal, he is somehow able to retain a zest for the place, a yeasty sense of optimism.

He has a big, airy office on the second floor of the Port Authority's laughably humble, 1950s-school-board-modern-style administration building. It's a thoroughly businesslike office, yet by some trick it is utterly lacking in solemnity and self-importance. On the wall are shelves full of aviation books, and large black-and-white aerial maps of Kennedy, La Guardia, and Newark; underneath one long window is a ten-foot array of various hats Rowe has picked up along his career path, including a conical wizard's cap given to him by a former Port Authority director in pointed tribute to the minor magic Rowe has been able to work here, in his chesslike task of moving airline tenants around the airport.

Rowe has seen it all at Kennedy. He began here in 1958 as a technical assistant in the maintenance department, then became assistant to the general manager, and rose through the ranks to become the airport's fourth general manager, in 1983.

"Tell me what it was like here when you first started," I say.

He smiles, and sighs. "I tell you the truth, it was absolutely beautiful," Rowe tells me, in his gravelly voice. "It was a gorgeous airport. It was just starting out then as an international airport, but it was a beautiful sight to behold. The roadway system worked well. The design was working well. It had something we don't have today—beautiful restaurants. We had the Golden Door in the International Arrivals Building. BOAC had the Princess Room. American had a beautiful restaurant. I mean, white tablecloths, silver. People came in from off the airport, people who lived in the area, to have lunch and dinner. You had big windows, you could look out over the tarmac and see the aircraft coming in and going out. And people used to come for dinner at night just to sit there in that kind of ambience."

"It was exciting," I say.

"Oh yeah."

"The beginning of the jet era."

"Right, and it was the ease of getting in and out, and parking. It was no hassle. It was a nice relaxed atmosphere."

"What happened to the restaurants?" I ask.

"Well, I don't know the exact answer," Rowe says. "I'll give you my views on the subject. The airlines found that they weren't making as much money on them as they thought they would. They did in the beginning, but it started to fall off. I mean, when the airport started to get a little more crowded, people started not to want to go anymore—why get in that kind of hassle? And then the airlines found that putting more of their efforts into their real business, which is flying aircraft, made more sense."

"And then that's changed so much since the sixties," I say.

Rowe nods. "Fierce competition," he says. "Market share—see, the market share was regulated then. I mean, the airlines didn't have to go out and fight for it. They knew what they had back then. Each one had its specific share, and it didn't move. The CAB"—the Civil Aeronautics Board—"which was in existence at the time, would tell a particular airline what its market was, and they wouldn't allow special requests. They wouldn't allow more than x number of airlines in any one area. So competition was reduced. Someone owned the Florida market, someone owned the California market, and so forth. And they limited the number of flights. So everyone knew exactly what his particular area was. And planning was easier. You knew how many aircraft you would need, and you would have them on line very easily.

"Today, it's dog eat dog, no question about it. And the more aircraft you can put in the air and the more seats you can fill—on-time performance is the winner. Today, it's anyone's market—you've got to go in there and fight. Some people go into markets where there's six or seven airlines, and still think that they're gonna eke out something for themselves. Sometimes they win, sometimes they lose. There's price wars all the time.

"And they have to shift aircraft around from one market to another, because they use different-size planes for different locations, depending on what the load factor might be in any particular area. It's a very complex management game now, in terms of both aircraft and manpower. I mean, if the peak here in New York becomes nice and high, and TWA doesn't have enough people to handle all the turnaround in terms of maintenance of aircraft, sufficient staff to move people within the building, et cetera, et cetera, they'll fly people up from Kansas City, which may not be at that high a peak.

"So it's really a management game now, in the truest sense. Before, it was laid out, you didn't have to do anything, everything fell into place. But now, the slightest thing that goes wrong can throw the whole schedule off."

"What about managing the airport?" I ask. "How has that changed?"

"I tease one of my predecessors," Rowe says. "Whenever he says, 'You know, I used to run Kennedy,' I say, 'Yeah—but the difference between you and me is that you had nothing to do, and I have plenty to do.'

"He had a regulated environment, no new entrants into the system," Rowe says. "Most of the airlines here had twenty-five-, thirty-year leases, so there was nothing new. I mean, everybody was in place and that was it. Nothing changed day to day. The uni-terminal concept was brand-new to any airport anywhere in the world. It was like having six or seven self-contained airports in one. TWA, Pan American, United, Delta, Northwest, Eastern, National. And it worked well. Then. But the airport was designed for fifteen million passengers per year."

"How many per year today?"

He smiles—slightly. "Thirty-one million every year."

"Ah," I say.

Rowe laughs. "So we're putting twice as much in the same bag," he says. "And today, I couldn't even tell you how many airlines are here at any given time. Mergers, takeovers, you know; new entrants. I have a business division—they have to give me a listing of the new airlines coming in, so I know exactly who they are, you know. We now have Aerovias de Mexico, which wasn't here before. We have all kinds of airlines, particularly from the African countries, et cetera. Everyone has a one-aircraft airline, owned by the government. They fly once or twice a week, you know, and that's about it. But they're here."

"Does the uni-terminal concept have to be replaced?"

"Well, yes, in a sense," Rowe says. "But it's not replacing 'em, it's how to make 'em work better, together. And that's why the development program concept"—he's speaking of the Port Authority's ambitious three-billion-dollar redevelopment plan, called JFK 2000—"is to have a central terminal complex in the middle of the central terminal area, connecting each of the uni-terminals by monorail, people-mover assistance. That way people can move back and forth between terminals with ease, and within a very rapid time frame. Maximum, seven minutes; average, three and a half.

"Today, it's forty-five minutes to whenever. In other words, we do connect the terminals now by bus. A free interconnecting bus that goes around the central terminal area. However, with the roadway system not being able to absorb the traffic during peak—you have double parking, triple parking, plus a large vehicle can't get in to the curb, those kinds of things—you never know when the bus is going to arrive. And two, you don't know how long it's going to take you to get from one point to another.

"For example," he says, "we're here in Federal Circle, which is somewhat removed from the central terminal area. I recall one afternoon meeting a friend coming back from an international flight, connecting to a domestic at TWA, and I wanted to see him on his return, chat awhile before he went to domestic. I left my office here at approximately four-fifteen; his flight was due in at five o'clock. I did not get to the TWA terminal till five-thirty. That's from here to there, because of the gridlock. And so, this is the problem, which we have to cure, and the people-mover system would cure that.

"Plus, the central terminal complex adds another benefit. We have been attempting for many years to convince people to leave their cars at home and take mass transit of one type or another. We've had marginal success."

"There was the Train to the Plane," ✈ I say.

"There was the Train to the Plane," Rowe says. "But most of our traffic doesn't come from Manhattan. The heaviest part comes from eastern Long Island, Connecticut, northern Jersey— a lot of it is limo operators bringing groups of people into the airport. The central terminal complex will encour-

---

✈ A short-lived experiment in which, by agreement between the Metropolitan Transit Authority and the Port Authority, it was possible to take a subway from midtown Manhattan to a stop just outside Kennedy. The fare was a very reasonable $7.50, the trains were reasonably clean and safe, but for some reason—perhaps the necessity of transferring to a bus for the short ride in to the terminals; perhaps the potent anticharisma of the New York subway system—ridership was insufficient.

age that even more, because it'll be a one-stop location. The bus or limo could go in and drop off its passengers; they can disperse by people-mover system to their final destination, whatever airline that might be. The bus then can load up with outgoing passengers and—one shot, out of the airport. Today they have to stop at each uni-terminal. Sometimes they go back around again. You never know when you're gonna get outta the airport.

"In our planning and studying for the development of Kennedy," he says, "I've talked to a lot of focus groups as to what they liked or didn't like about the airport. What they like, for the most part, is the numerous schedules and airlines that they can choose from, to go to just about any destination they wish in the world. People like choice. If one airline doesn't accommodate their needs, another one will. So that is the beauty of Kennedy, particularly for the international traveler, and particularly the international businessperson. Because we have a high level of international business travelers coming from Asia, from Europe, South America, et cetera. And they like the accommodations at Kennedy once they get here.

"The main drawback to Kennedy is getting into the airport and getting out. The focus group that we talked to indicated that the single most negative factor for them was returning to Kennedy from overseas. Long flight, tired, want to get home, and can't get out of this airport."

I laugh. "I've been there," I say.

"In fact, they feel that's more of a negative than trying to get to the airport, 'cause you're fresh coming in, but coming back you want out, you're ready to go, you're thinking about your own bed, you've had enough of hotels—"

"Wife, family . . ." And just then, I find myself looking anxiously at my watch. Kennedy has this effect on people.

Perhaps sensing my restlessness, Rowe sighs once more. "I run the gamut of all kinds of unique—kooky, if you will—management problems that I have to solve."

"Never boring for you," I say.

"Never. We have a huge bird problem here."

"I bet. Seabirds?"

"Laughing gulls, we call 'em." Rowe points to a large aerial photograph of the airport on his wall. "Right out there in the bay is a bird sanctuary. And the feds, we finally convinced 'em to do a study—there's Joco Marsh, right at the end of this runway." He taps the photograph at the south end of runway 4 Left. "Anyway. They did the study. And figured out that those birds are dangerous in terms of possibly getting into the turbine blades of a jet engine, and that something has to be done. So now they're gonna go in—this is the nesting season—and oil the eggs, so they can't hatch. Try to cut down on the growth of the bird population. Some other things are gonna have to be done, too, and they're still studying that, but it's a scary thing to think that a huge aircraft like a 747 or a DC-10 or an L-1011 could be brought down by a small bird."

This is all ringing a bell somehow. "Isn't there somebody here who's specifically in charge of the bird situation?" I ask.

"Well, I have a manager of aeronautical services named Jack Gartner...."

"I should definitely talk to him."

"And he'd be very interesting," Rowe says. "But he has a young man that works for him, Sammy Chevalier, who we call the birdman. The birdman of Kennedy."

2

The Birdman of Kennedy

West of the Wooden Cow

Sammy Chevalier and I are cruising the airport in a battered emergency-yellow Port Authority GMC Sierra pickup with a 12-gauge shotgun mounted below the dashboard, riding along the runways on taxiways and service roads, having a look around. It's a milky-colored day in late March, a thaw day, Kennedy weather. Almost any kind of weather, from the banal to the dramatic, can, of course, be experienced at JFK; nevertheless, I like, perhaps sentimentally, to think there's such a thing as *Kennedy weather:* an opalescent cast to the gigantic, empty sky, light wind, small chop on the bay. Multifarious garbage blowing through the tall grass and cattails. The taller towers of Manhattan dimly visible, as in a dream, to the west. The atmosphere here is marine yet domestic; we are in the lee of the bay. The toppling metallic *Sturm und Drang* of the Atlantic is three miles south, past the protective peninsula of Rockaway. This is the beginning of Long Island, conceivably the most domestic place on earth, a long, flat spit with a stolid history of Indians, seashells, and Dutchmen, a monument to mistaken aesthetics, to development gone wrong. A place where the magic of marine light endures, but—as though some awful error had been made—where that light suffuses mile after mile of bad road and endless shopping strips, where the height of the human spirit is aggressively stifled at almost every turn. Long Island— home of Levittown. Of Billy Joel and Jerry Seinfeld. And of Jay Gatsby, and of Amy Fisher and Joey Buttafuoco, and Judge Sol Wachtler, and Katie Beers.

This is the borough of Queens, the gateway to Long Island, famous for organized crime and its murders at 3 A.M. on high-numbered warehouse streets; for the New York Mets, with their repellent but somehow municipally apt orange-and-blue color scheme; for square mile after soul-killing square mile of brown-brick apartment blocks; for the New York world's fairs of

1939–1940 and 1964–1965, with the Trylon and Perisphere, the Unisphere, all the lost fake utopias; for some of the worst highways in the world; for the airports.

Queens has two airports, and La Guardia came first—1939—and stood alone for almost a decade. But La Guardia is a domestic terminus in more than one sense of the word. It is a collection of buildings on a little bit of land, plus two of the shortest jet runways in the world, runways so short they scare passengers and plane crews alike, runways built on sand and thus unable to support the weight of any airplane heavier than a DC-10—which is always, when it uses La Guardia, a domestic jet. A loaded 747 would sink up to its struts in the macadam there. Thus La Guardia is fated by anatomy to domesticity, and you know this the minute you pull into the curved driveway in a taxi: you have ridden maybe fifteen minutes from midtown Manhattan, you haven't really gone anywhere, and you have business on your mind, what you will do on the plane and what you will do when you get there, and you barely take in the ugly functional brown-brick buildings of La Guardia, the large crescent-shaped central terminal. The outlying glassy frippery of the new Delta and USAir terminals do little to leaven the enterprise. This is flying at its most functional; this is the airport as bus station. Kennedy is something else.

Every airport everywhere around the world has a different feeling, *Flugplatzgefühl.* Mainly they are places to get into and out of as quickly as possible. Places of dim amenity, of failed modernity, of fear or relief. There are many small airports full of charm and a sense of place—Jackson, Wyoming, and Luxor, Egypt, quickly come to mind—but in these cases the charm and the location have specifically to do with the smallness; one is still conscious of the fact that one is getting on or off an airplane. The moment largeness comes into play, so does functionality on a large scale, and distance from the act of flying, and thus anonymity. What is specifically absent from major airports is any sense of place: An airport is a no-place on the way to someplace.

Why should this be so? The great railway depots of the world—Grand Central in New York, Union Station in Chicago, Gare de Lyon in Paris, Alexanderplatz in Berlin—built in the late nineteenth and early twentieth centuries, were magnificent spaces, created to sanctify the success of technology, the romance and awe of travel by rail. They reflected an ample sense of human possibility. It could be argued that modern airports are a sign and symbol of mankind's depression with itself. Not to mention fear of flying. In the early sixties, when the basic elements of modern airport architecture were being laid out, it was just becoming apparent to people that flying was a fairly dangerous business. There were a lot of crashes in those days. The goal thus became to benumb the air traveler, to make him or her forget that airplanes were involved in the process at all. Airports thus became interchangeable, anesthetic places. What differences are there, truly, between LAX and O'Hare and Dallas–Fort Worth and Charles de Gaulle in Paris and Schiphol in Amsterdam? A traveler trudges through long, slick, low-ceilinged corridors lined with unenticing marts, listens to public-address announcements delivered by a female voice (studies have shown that people pay closer heed when a woman is talking), perhaps in a foreign language or accent (slight excitement!), and glances at others much like himself (and so unlike! one's soul protests). Here and there is a grazing eye-flirtation, or the stray sight of a good face, a fascinating, necessary face—never to be seen again. It is all a trudge, sidestepping the issues of love and death.

Especially death. As air travelers, we become particles in a moving solid, components in this odd process designed to make us forget we are traveling by air. We are excreted from a tube into another tube; the second tube takes to the sky, then lands, and we are excreted into a third tube. It was not always thus. And all this is true, to some extent, of Kennedy, yet Kennedy once was something else, and—here and there, now and then—still is.

Heathrow is busier. O'Hare and Dallas–Fort Worth and LAX are bigger. Kennedy moves more cargo, by far—$85 billion worth in 1990—than any other airport, but the difference between JFK and other airports is not quantitative; it is spiritual. Airports generate strong feelings—what a psychologist I know described as "intense emotional valences." Valences such as sorrow at leave-taking, joy at reunion. Fear of death and envy and cupidity and lust, all in strong measure. The pleasure of repatriation, the terror of immigration. But in general, all these are true more through the activity of the airport than through the airport itself. The anonymity of most airports makes us feel, if only out of sheer rebellion.

Kennedy Airport provokes by its very essence. For those who are not traveling from it—its employees, as well as those local citizens who still come to watch planes come and go from and to faraway places (much in the spirit of those who, in the days of the great ocean liners, would gather at Manhattan's Hudson River piers to watch ships arrive and leave)—it stimulates place-loyalty, a kind of awe deriving from its days as a port of glamour in the midst of Queens, a white-glove kind of place in the linen-napkin pre-deregulation days of flying. There are not-so-distant vibrations, in its wide sky and huge expanse, of the early history of aviation on Long Island.

For those who travel through it—including many who are arriving in the United States for the first time—it is a place of the most intense stress. We have seen the Van Wyck Expressway. We have heard from the airport manager himself about the difficulties of moving about Kennedy. Those not defeated by the approaches to the airport find themselves in a place where changing airlines because of a missed or canceled flight is all but impossible; where they are likely to be harassed, threatened, or even mugged by the Smarte Carte Hustlers; where parking a car is difficult, possibly dangerous, and conceivably valedictory.

Once they have been thoroughly processed and examined by Customs and Immigration, foreign travelers landing at Kennedy—especially new arrivals to this country, still in a tender state of disorientation, jet fatigue, and international awe—are likely to be pickpocketed by skilled teams of Colombians, specially flown in by drug cartels to gather seed money for overseas deals. Or, if their wallets survive, there are the limo hustlers. Returning New York fliers who have been bold enough to park a car are likely to find the vehicle absent, or incomplete in an important way. Or perhaps, wonder of wonders, the luggage has arrived, the wallet has not been lifted, and the automobile is present and whole—or you, canny traveler, have chosen to be met by a licensed limo, or you simply grab a legitimate Yellow cab at one of the airport's legitimate taxi stands. You loosen your tie, or other corresponding item of apparel, and your heart leaps ahead to your kitchen, bright and clean in your imagining, where your adoring family beams, transformed by your miraculous reappearance. You distribute gifts, drink a drink, eat something warm. Soon you and your spouse will celebrate your return in a more private way . . . and then you blink out of your reverie and see, just ahead of you, a stagnant river of stationary taillights.

The major cause of death at Kennedy, say the policemen who work there, is the coronary.

Yet Kennedy is miraculous. There is that ocean light, that great dome of sky, cruised by egrets, hawks, gulls, and cormorants. There is the starry history of aviation here, and the ghost (and the furtive, compromised remnants) of glamour. On a clear late afternoon, say in early fall, at the magic hour, when the 747s of many lands stand in a row on the ramp✦ behind the International Arrivals Building, the parti-colored logos on their tails are like the blazons in a medieval tournament, or the savage flags on the farthest caravan of Marco Polo's most distant travels. Yes, the tail logos say, the world is squalid and sad and shrinking and filling in with people (and Kennedy can tell this

---

✦ A confusing but essential airport term. In the not too distant past, a *ramp* was one of those wheeled staircases rolled out to meet airplanes. In many small airports, it still is. Yet most often these days (and in this book) the word will refer not to a staircase or an inclined surface, but simply to a big parking lot for planes —any of the paved expanses just behind (or, as it is said, *on the airside of*) the terminals. A synonym is *apron*. An airplane's, or airline's, own parking space is known as a *hardstand*.

tale better than anyplace), but the world is also wide and mysterious. There are wonders there. And here.

Kennedy is a city. Some 44,000 people work here; this colossal, reedy, asphalty, garbagy plot by the bay is the size of Manhattan, river to river, from Forty-second Street down to the Battery. The airport has a resident homeless population of about 150. There are 9 miles of runway and 22 miles of taxiway at Kennedy, and 7,000 lights and lighted signs on those runways and taxiways. There are, some say, ghosts. At least one man is semilegitimately buried out by the runway side; God alone knows how many less-than-legitimate others lie here in unmarked plots. Kennedy has an electrical system that could serve a city the size of Hartford, Connecticut, and backup systems that can operate indefinitely in case of a power failure. There are 70 miles of underground storm drains that empty into Jamaica Bay; there is a subterranean system of pipes that pumps aviation fuel directly to airplanes at their hardstands on the ramp. There is an animal shelter with pens that can hold (and have held) elephants, horses, lions, and apes, not to mention cats, dogs, and parakeets. A herd of giant Texan jackrabbits lives out in the reeds among the runways. ("A crate fell and broke and a couple of the rabbits got loose, and they multiplied," a PA cop explained. "And these things are fuckin' *huge*. I'm out in my cruiser one night on one of the taxiways, and I see this . . . *thing* in my headlights. I swear to God, it looked like what's-his-name, the giant rabbit in the movie. Harvey. Like three feet tall, including the ears.")

Other animals have also escaped here: a Bengal tiger and an orangutan and a rare white rhinoceros and a cobra, among others. All were caught again, but not without cost (the rhino was sprayed with fire extinguisher foam by a panicked, and now legendary, cop; the animal died). Human animals get loose here, too. In a spectacular 1976 incident, a deranged man with a gun hijacked a Vermont Transit bus, drove it to the airport, smashed the vehicle through a gate near Building 269 (the Port Authority Police headquarters), killed a passenger and threw the body out of the bus, then careened around service roads and taxiways at high speeds, with police vehicles in hot pursuit, until police were finally able to shoot the bus's tires out and subdue the hijacker. Kennedy was also the site of the shoot-out that became the climactic event in the film *Dog Day Afternoon*; it was also home to the six-million-dollar Lufthansa heist, in the eventful year of 1975, that formed the basis for the book *Wiseguy* and its adaptation, the movie *GoodFellas*. The airport was the crime finishing school for John Gotti, as well as for numerous other hoods, many of whom wound up finished here themselves.

At the same time, it is in essence a seaside airport, and the eternal tang of marine salt pervades. Kennedy is a place where a stray whiff of suntan lotion, wafting amid the jet fumes, would not be completely amiss. The seabirds wheel eternally. But their picturesqueness is besides the point. There are more than thirty thousand laughing-gull eggs in nests in a swampy area just south of the airport, and some twelve thousand of them have been coated with a heavy mineral oil to ensure that the chicks within will never hatch. Still, at least eighteen thousand of them will hatch, and fly, and laugh, and if just one of those gulls collides with the windshield of a jet airplane, or is sucked into the plane's turbine, that plane could come down. And Sammy Chevalier is here to do everything in his ability to make sure that doesn't happen.

Chevalier is a kind of legend at Kennedy Airport. A short, trim, quiet man of sixty-seven with a neatly cut gray beard, a military crewcut, and eyes that crinkle impenetrably behind photo-gray lenses, he has a raptor's stoop to his neck that makes him somewhat resemble a wise old bird. The resemblance is not inappropriate, considering that Sammy is in charge of Kennedy's Bird Control Unit. He hails from the ornithonymically apt town of Swanton, Vermont, ten miles south of the international border, and his personality partakes of Green Mountain pungency and Acadian apartness in equal, and sometimes conflicting, measure. For example, he hates his given name, which is Marcel. He has been known to correct official documents that dared to use it, substituting his nickname in a scratchy ballpoint scrawl. He takes an amused, slightly removed view of the world, a view well suited to a man who has spent thirty-five years riding around the airport's far reaches in rattly Port Authority pickup trucks. He has spent half those years, the past seventeen, on bird patrol: mostly scaring off seagulls with amplified noise and shotgun blanks; sometimes killing them. Others have patrolled for birds at Kennedy, but, in a very real sense, the franchise is Sammy Chevalier. He started it.

Sammy was uniquely, almost spiritually, qualified to marshal such an enterprise. He started flying at the age of fifteen, on a single-runway airport amid the hushed maples, pines, and aspens of Swanton (with the seagulls that frequent nearby Lake Champlain soaring portentously by). He soloed at sixteen (in an Aeronca Chief, a vanished marque) and got his commercial and instructor's licenses at eighteen. He spent most of the Second World War training army air cadets, finally becoming a quite untrainable cadet himself— he already knew everything there was to know—just before V-J Day.

After the war, in Providence, Rhode Island, he learned to fly helicopters on the GI Bill; it was virtually the only FAA rating he didn't already have. He held down a series of helicopter-piloting jobs throughout New England, steadily moving south, and in 1952 ended up in New York City, working for the Port Authority. "It was a glorified taxi service for PA executives," he says acerbically today—reflecting, with one raised eyebrow, on both his own then-imminent troubles and those of the Port Authority, which has consistently shot itself in the foot with its self-largess. Helicopters, with their traffic-skirting abilities and thrumming, urgent, impressive presence, have always been a favorite (and pricey) means of transportation among PA higher-ups. Forty years ago Sammy would ferry the executives back and forth from the roof of PA headquarters—then at Eighth Avenue and Fifteenth Street—to various locations around the New York Metropolitan Area, chiefly the three airports. Then, one day in 1955, disaster visited Sammy Chevalier.

He still doesn't like to talk about it. Northern Vermonters aren't long on chitchat to begin with, and on this one subject, Chevalier is particularly mum. He crashed, is the long and short of it, and no one was killed but a helicopter was destroyed, and there is an implication in Sammy's tone that what happened was his own fault. After a little while he began to fly for the Port again and continued for almost two years, but then he stopped, unable, in his own mind, to go on. He was reassigned to Idlewild.

He had flown for more than half his life. Suddenly he was a bureaucrat: a duty supervisor, a roving representative of the airport manager. He spent his days driving around the runways and taxiways, checking for broken lights and crumbling pavement, watching the planes come and go. He thought about flight. All kinds. "When fate or God's will took away my ability to fly," Sammy says, "my interest in birds rose." Idlewild, he gradually discovered, was built directly underneath one of North America's four major flyways. Every manner of migratory bird went overhead, and not a few dropped in. "In 1965, a fellow who was to become my friend and I caught a snowy owl," Sammy says. He began doing birdbanding for the U.S. Fish and Wildlife Service, sending the information he culled to USFWS headquarters in Laurel, Maryland, so that the service could determine the migratory routes, longevity, and age and sex classes of the birds that passed over Jamaica Bay.

But bird activity at an airport was of more than ornithological interest. On October 4, 1960, Flight 375, an Eastern Lockheed Electra four-engine turbo-prop, had taken off from Logan International Airport, run into a flock of starlings, plunged into Boston Harbor, and exploded. Sixty-two people were killed. It was the first crash of a commercial airliner in Logan's thirty-year history. Three weeks later, the Federal Aviation Administration sent a telegram to airport operators around the country, asking them to take "all necessary action" to reduce the danger of birds along airplane flight paths. Yet at the same time, a *New York Times* article reported, the Civil Aeronautics Board said "none of the pilots and other witnesses of the Boston accident reported seeing any birds at the airport at the time of the crash. The board has said that

27

it had never, in twenty-one years of air crash investigations, found a fatal accident that was caused by birds." The end of the article, under the ominous subhead "Not a Problem Here," reads, "A spokesman for the Port of New York Authority, which operates New York International, La Guardia and Newark Airports, said yesterday the agency had considered various means for ridding runways of birds, but that 'basically we don't consider it a major problem.'"

On November 12, 1975—less than five months after Kennedy's most calamitous air disaster, the thunderstorm-caused crash of Eastern Flight 66—at about 1:10 in the afternoon, a DC-10 owned and operated by the charter line Overseas National Airways, bound for Saudi Arabia, started its takeoff down Kennedy's runway 13 Right. Ten crew members and 129 others, all Overseas National personnel on their way to work pilgrimage flights to Mecca, were aboard. The weather was cool and drizzly. (Sammy Chevalier was away, vacationing with friends in the hills of eastern Pennsylvania.) Thirteen Right, also known as the Bay Runway, is 14,572 feet long—at almost three miles, Kennedy's longest—and runs in a roughly northwest-southeast direction parallel to Jamaica Bay. Airport runways everywhere are numbered by the first two digits of their compass heading: That is, if 13 Right were a compass needle, it would point to 130 degrees, 5 degrees north of southeast. (Taxiways are named alphabetically rather than numbered, according to the old military telephony style, from Alfa to Zulu.✦)

However, confusingly enough, 13 Right is also 31 Left, for planes landing or taking off in the other direction. Thus Kennedy, which has only four physical runways, actually has eight—each runway being both itself and its compass reciprocal—so that a plane can land or take off north, south, east, or west, according to the direction of the wind, the aim being to move either directly into or across the prevailing air current. Head winds are great; crosswinds are OK. Airplanes, landing or taking off, don't like tail winds. Or birds. Three quarters of the way down the runway, as the Overseas National DC-10 neared its takeoff speed of 178 miles per hour, the pilot, Captain Harold Davis, sighted a flock of gulls on the plane's right (bay) side just an instant before a bird or birds were ingested into his number one engine (on the

---

✦ The alphabetical designations (sheer, breezy, swaggering, airily synesthetic poetry) currently mandated by the International Civil Aviation Organization and accepted worldwide, are:

Alfa	Golf	Mike	Sierra	Yankee
Bravo	Hotel	November	Tango	Zulu
Charlie	India	Oscar	Uniform	
Delta	Juliett	Papa	Victor	
Echo	Kilo	Quebec	Whisky	
Foxtrot	Lima	Romeo	Xray	

plane's left side). The turbines clogged and shuddered; the engine vibrated, harder and harder, then burst into flame and fell off the wing, severing the fuel lines leading to the wing tanks.

Meanwhile, Captain Davis had stood on his brakes, leaving huge skid marks on the runway as the plane veered sharply to the left. The detached engine, as well as the broken landing gear, showered sparks that ignited the leaking aviation fuel. The number three engine continued independently along the ground in a northeasterly direction, traveling at 178 m.p.h., minus ground friction, spewing flame, and finally coming to rest alongside Building 298, a runway-side utility shed then used by Pan Am for trucks and tools. The DC-10 came to rest on taxiway Juliett, near the end of 13 Right (and just short of a twelve-foot-high, solid-steel blast fence), with its damaged landing gear stuck in the sand off the pavement. The flames from the wing tanks spread rapidly to the plane's body as the pilot deployed the inflatable emergency chutes. As the Port Authority fire and rescue vehicles sped up, the 139 Overseas National employees exited the plane in a quick and orderly fashion and slid down the chutes. This expeditiousness was critical: Everyone was off the plane by 1:15 P.M., five minutes after the aborted takeoff had begun. At 1:18, when a New York City fire company arrived, the aircraft was completely engulfed in terrifyingly hot, jet-fuel-fed flames: thirty thousand gallons' worth, an inextinguishable conflagration. Soon afterward, the fire and a series of explosions finished off the twenty-million-dollar jet. Not a single human was killed; there wasn't even a serious injury. The surface of 13 Right was, however, littered with seagull carcasses.

❐

For humans, at any rate, the Overseas National crash was an extraordinarily lucky event. Unlike the Logan Electra, which made its bird strike six seconds after takeoff, the DC-10 hit its flock in its last two seconds on the ground. It was therefore a half-million-pound runaway truck, rather than an airborne, but no longer aeronautical, object. The concept of brakes was still applicable. Also, the plane carried nobody but airline employees, all steeped in emergency procedures. This would scarcely have mattered to the unfortunate passengers of Eastern Flight 375, many of whose seats and seat belts failed upon impact,✛ but it stressed an important concept: Given correct emergency procedure, many crashes are survivable. Perhaps the most important result of the

---

✛ Airplane crashes, ghoulishly enough, are aviation safety's main path of progress—if only through the financial disincentive of decreased business, and lawsuits by the aggrieved relatives of victims, in an accident's aftermath. (It is fair to assume that the Christmastime 1988 explosion of Pan Am Flight 103 over Lockerbie, Scotland, was in no way incidental to the airline's demise.) We may be sure that, as a result of many fevered late nights in testing labs, neither seats nor belts will ever again fail precisely the same way

29

crash for Kennedy, however—and certainly the most important result for Sammy Chevalier—was a sudden and dramatic spike in bird awareness.

"Immediately after the Overseas National crash," Sammy tells me, as we drive alongside the very runway where it happened, "the government agencies all descended on us like a cloud of mosquitoes." He has a country directness, a predilection for rural imagery, and a soft, lilting, halting voice, a country voice, filled with columbine hushes and punctuated by the glottal stops of northern Vermont. What the swarming agencies discovered was what Sammy already knew: Seagulls liked 13 Right. Gulls are garbage-eating birds, and in 1975 there were two active landfills in reasonably close proximity to that runway, one—called the Fountain Avenue Dump—ten thousand feet to the southwest of the south end of 13 Right, and the other, the Edgemere Dump, sixty-seven hundred feet to the southeast of the north end. "Gulls like to eat garbage," Sammy says. "It's easier than dropping clams on the ground to get the meat out. So the gulls would eat the garbage, then come sit on the runway. They like a warm surface to digest their food." When Sammy talks about gulls, it is with a fond, slightly irritated condescension, as if he were speaking of poor relatives: he has an almost eerie ability to think, as it were, *with the birds.*

We turn left onto a service road. "After the 1975 accident," Sammy says, shifting into rhetorical style, "the FAA ordered a dawn-to-dusk bird patrol, to be part of John F. Kennedy International Airport's operating certificate. It was the first such patrol in the country. It would consist of two eight-hour tours, and it would be staffed by people whose sole responsibility was, and is, to

---

they did on that awful October 1960 afternoon in Boston. At the same time, airline-seat technology still leaves much to be desired, especially in terms of flammability. And in terms of impact safety, nobody has yet come up with a cogent argument against the elegant expedient of simply turning the seats around to face backward, as is done in some military planes.

After the 1975 crash of Flight 66, Dr. Michael M. Baden, then New York City's deputy chief medical examiner, performed autopsies on many of the crash's victims. Baden said, "If these people were sitting backwards, I think a lot of these injuries might have been diminished, because in this particular crash, they didn't die so much of smoke inhalation, suffocation, burns, or weren't impaled on tree branches after having been ejected from the plane. They died within seconds of impact injuries." Baden cited the case of a young Norwegian sailor whose liver had been torn along the lines of his seat belt: "He probably would have survived if he rode backwards, or had a shoulder strap." Both the FAA and the National Transportation Safety Board, however, demurred, citing lack of clear evidence and pointing to the 1972 crash, in Albany, New York, of a Mohawk F-227, one of the few commercial planes to have some rear-facing seats. In that crash, rear-facing passengers suffered little injury—but so did the forward-facing passengers sitting nearby.

Even if it seems logical that rearward seating would reduce impact injuries in crashes, spokespeople for the airline industry have steadily maintained that the public wouldn't accept it, for psychological reasons. What this *really* means, of course, is that *neither* the airlines *nor* the public would like it: It might somehow pierce the Muzak-y bubble of what passes for atmosphere (corporate kitsch at its worst) aboard American carriers. And then there would be the cost of reconfiguration.

seek out any flocking tendency of birds, and to take measures to disperse them.

"Gulls were and are our main problem," Sammy tells me. "There are three species out here over the year—ring-billed gulls, herring gulls, and great black-backed gulls. Then, for half the year, we have laughing gulls."

"Ah, the laughing gulls," I say.

The nesting ground of the laughing gulls, Joco—appropriately pronounced *joke-o*—Marsh, Sammy explains, is located on a spit of land jutting south into Jamaica Bay about a quarter mile off the approach end of runway 4 Left, which crosses the Bay Runway near its south end at a right angle. "The laughing gull had been extirpated as a nesting species on Long Island at the end of the nineteenth century," he says. "They were shot for decorative feathers for women's hats and clothing.

"But in 1979, they came back. Twelve nesting pairs took up residence in Joco Marsh, and increased exponentially each year. Today there are eight thousand nesting pairs in the marsh, and they present a serious hazard to this airport. In 1984, I proposed destroying the nests, and I had to fight every year until 1989 to get anything done. The problem is, the National Park Service owns Joco Marsh—it's part of Gateway National Recreation Area. And the National Park Service didn't want to be in the business of destroying bird nests."

We're tooling north, between the two 4-22 runways. "In the summer of 1989," Sammy says, "a blue-ribbon panel of four international bird experts met on the issue, and gave their recommendations. The result is that the next summer I started going out and oiling laughing-gull eggs. It prevents air from getting into the egg—the egg becomes nonviable, and you eliminate one generation of laughing gulls. The result is that the gulls go nest elsewhere."

This result is, at present, theoretical. The factual present is that although the Fountain Avenue Dump was closed in December 1985, and the Edgemere Dump was closed in June 1991, ring-billed gulls, herring gulls, and great black-backed gulls still practice their second-favorite food-gathering method —plucking clams from tidally exposed mud in Jamaica Bay, dropping them from on high to the Bay Runway below, then alighting to dine there. (The preferred cuisine of laughing gulls, who are not shell-droppers, is beetles, crickets, and brine shrimp.) On Midway Island, in the South Pacific, the U.S. Air Force tried for years to get rid of the indigenous albatross population, which was interfering with the operations of its air base there. Nothing worked. Finally the air force gave up, and made the albatross a kind of island mascot. Could the laughing gull become the mascot of Kennedy?

"Well before the Overseas National accident, I was aware of the potential hazard of having all these gulls loafing on Thirteen Right," Sammy says, as though the birds were reprobate teenagers, in neatly cuffed jeans, in a Norman Rockwellesque sweet shop in far-northern Vermont. "There had been several incidents of 747 engines being fouled by birds. Oddly enough, it was technological progress that brought this whole problem on. Metal propellers were a formidable weapon against birds. But now, with jets, and with the high-bypass-ratio engine, what you have mounted on planes is a giant vacuum cleaner. And it doesn't digest very well what it picks up. Even one large-sized gull could knock out a jet engine.

"The engine manufacturers—Pratt and Whitney, General Electric, Rolls-Royce—are constantly trying to improve the metallurgical qualities of their product to the point where it can withstand the impact of a four-pound bird," Sammy says. "Aircraft have been wiped out by the impact of a bird hitting the windshield. Strikes have even occurred after dark, with planes running into migrating ducks or geese flying at altitude, at three or four thousand feet. After one of those strikes, the FAA decreed bird sweeps at *night*." He turns and gives me a wry birdy look behind the thick gray lenses. I don't get it.

"What is a bird sweep?" I ask.

"I or my agent drive up the runway," Sammy says. "You use whatever means necessary to chase 'em—you can drive at them blowing the horn, or play the tape—"

"Tape?"

He indicates a cassette player mounted below the truck's dashboard. The player has a bargain-basement look to it, and the cassette protruding from it is labeled in a broad blue scrawl that I can't quite read. Sammy hands me the tape. GULL DISTRESS CALLS, the label says.

"Gull distress calls?" I say.

Sammy pops the cassette into the player and suddenly, as we drive along a taxiway, a sirenlike whoop emits from the speaker mounted on top of the truck cab. But *sirenlike* is wrong, implying, as it does, an electronic consistency of sound. This noise is more deeply alarming—primal, hair-raising, melancholy. Repetitive. Gull distress. Sammy ejects the tape. "Or," he says, "we can use pyrotechnics." He pats the shotgun.

"You shoot birds?"

"Mostly we use blanks. We do have a permit from the Fish and Wildlife Service to occasionally shoot gulls when necessary—"

"They're not protected?"

"All species of birds are protected, except for house sparrows, starlings, and pigeons," Sammy says, patiently. The reference to starlings, which caused the 1960 crash at Logan, is not lost on me. "That's why we need the permit. If you shoot one gull out of two hundred, it's deadly for the one gull, but not for the rest. And you may save an airplane, not to mention the two or three hundred people on board."

All this bird talk is making my head swirl, but I grasp the dangling thread. "So you don't do sweeps at night?"

He shakes his head scornfully. "Nonmigrating birds *nest* at night," he says. "Typical bureaucratic bungling." We're driving along the outskirts of the airport's five thousand acres, through a lonely, grassy area by Rockaway Boulevard, roughly equidistant from the feet of runways 22 Right, 31 Right, and 22 Left. Nearby, a foul-looking finger of Grassy Bay called Thurston Basin runs parallel to the boulevard for several hundred yards. This is an unlucky corner of Kennedy, a place of airplane crashes: here is where Eastern 66 smacked down; not far away, in 1959, a BOAC Comet coming in for a landing on the old 25 Left, Idlewild's first jet runway, caught the orange-and-white steel blast fence that Sammy is showing me right now, taking out two landing-gear-shaped chunks. Miraculously, the fence, and not the landing gear, gave way, and the Comet landed safely. On a snowy night in 1961, an Aeronaves de Mexico DC-8, whose wings had been de-iced but had then quickly re-iced, took off from the old runway 7 Right (which was, of course, 25 Left in the other direction) but then failed to gain sufficient altitude, and clipped the same blast fence. The plane exploded in the marsh on the far side of Rockaway Boulevard: astonishingly, 101 of 106 on board survived. In 1964, a Pan Am 707 attempting to take off from 4 Right ended up spraddled over Thurston Basin, its fuselage cracked in half. In February 1984, an SAS DC-10 with a malfunctioning automatic throttle, coming in for a landing on 4 Right, touched down at sixty knots faster than normal landing speed, more than halfway down the runway (which is only eighty-four hundred feet to begin with), and went into the basin nose first. A day later, as the plane still sat ingloriously dipped, an SAS team came and painted out the airline's tail logo with white paint.

The gouged-out section of blast fence is long gone, as is any need for the fence itself, which was built to shield cars on Rockaway Boulevard from the report of turbine engines on jets departing on the no-longer-existing 25 Left. Now we've crossed runway 4 Right and pulled up by a dilapidated gray wooden shack in the tall grass in the northeast corner of the airport. The control towers and terminals shimmer far away in the pearly light. The sky has clouded over. The wind whips the dry grass.

"Would you like to see my pigeons?" Sammy asks.

The interior of the shack, which used to be the engineering field office during the construction of 4 Right, is Early Henhouse. Several field mice

33

scurry for cover as we enter. Behind a chicken-wire screen perch three pigeons, white and mottled gray. They turn their heads slightly; one lifts its wings and ruffles its feathers. "Hello, fellas," Sammy says. "I left these guys with my friend Baldy while I was on vacation recently," he tells me, dropping a tantalizing clue about his personal life. "They had to stay in an ASPCA box for a whole week. So now they're enjoying their freedom again."

The pigeons pace their enclosure, looking the pigeon equivalent of concerned. "Hi, guys!" Sammy says. We stand for a moment and watch them. The birds strut, burble, and fluff their feathers. The limits of the pigeon repertoire, not to mention those of conversation with and about pigeons, quickly become apparent. Sammy, who foists his avian enthusiasms on nobody, is sensitive to my unfascination. "See you later, guys," he tells the pigeons. "This building is officially abandoned," he tells me, pointedly, as we leave. "This is an unofficial activity."

We drive out again. It looks like rain. We head down the Major Bill Carter Highway, a service road alongside 4 Left. The road, which is marked by a small, official-looking, white-on-emerald-green metal sign, is named for a former army corporal who in civilian life became a construction supervisor during the building of Kennedy—then New York International—in the late forties. Carter, who shared the fierce autochthonous love for this place of many longtime assignees here, asked before he died in 1984 to be buried at the airport. And—in the unofficial activity of unofficial activities (the runway was closed to traffic, for "repairs")—Carter was obliged (and, in a final grace note, promoted), in a solemn secret ceremony, complete with bagpipers and twenty-one-gun salute. And here he lies, *hic iacet*—or his ashes do, at any rate, out among the blowing runway grasses. Sammy slows down for a second so I can see the simple concrete marker.

One of the two Motorola radios in the truck (one is tuned to the control tower, the other to the Port Authority all-facility band) squawks. "Go ahead, Speedbird Oh Oh Two," a voice says. "That's the British Airways Concorde," Sammy says. "It'll be taking off on Twenty-two Right."

"Speedbird—that's what they call the Concorde?"

"No, that's what they call all BA planes," he says.✈ "Want to watch it go?"

I do. Very much. We cross the field on taxiway Zulu and stop near the end of 22 Right. The extraordinary-looking white stork of a plane, its flexible nose pointed down so that the crew can better see the runway during takeoff, seems to sit still for a moment in the pullulating heat waves rising from the runway.

✈ In fact, the name is a ghost of the swooping logo that used to grace the tails of BOAC planes.

THE AIRPORT

"Better close your window," Sammy says. I close it. The plane creeps, then hurtles down the tarmac toward us. "Better hold your ears," says Sammy. I do. The Concorde rises over the truck—I swivel my head, fingers still stuck in my ears—and reappears in front of us, its exhaust ports burning white-hot in the gray air. If there is a kind of terrifying boredom or blankness to modern urban life, the fire of these exhaust ports sears through it. The plane's crackling, rocketing roar, even through stopped otic canals, is tremendous: It enters the solar plexus and simply *moves the body around.*

"Wow," I say, quite involuntarily.

"It's a beauty, isn't it?"

We drive on. There are other wonders out along the runways and taxiways, nestled in the Queens-dirty grass: mortarlike propane cannons along 4 Left and 31 Right, triggered electronically at random intervals to scare off pesky gulls. One of the cannons fires as we drive past—BANG!—and I jump in my seat. There are orange metal fog detectors; over here is a wind shear detector. It looks like nothing more than a little airplane silhouette, complete with spinning propeller, mounted atop a pole. This small thing might have prevented the crash of Eastern 66. Kennedy now has six of them, two in the center of the field and one each at the airport's northeast, northwest, southeast, and southwest corners. A computer in the tower constantly receives data from all six, and assesses the differentials between them. "A classic case," Sammy says, "of closing the barn doors after the cows have gotten out." And, speaking of cows, here one is, near the west end of 31 Left. A wooden cow, that is; or, rather, a white box, on four two-by-fours, with a couple of black spots painted on it and a rope dangling at one end to represent a tail. "Oh, that," Sammy says. "We catch bugs in it, to study what the resident field birds are feeding on."

I'm still thinking about Eastern 66, and about crashes in general, and wondering, in particular, how I might get Sammy to discuss his own. Suddenly there's another squawk on the radio. "Call three-three," I hear a voice say.

"What's a three-three?" I ask.

Sammy listens for a second. "That's an anticipated emergency," he says. "Three-three is the highest priority."

He stops the truck. We're back next to the Bay Runway—the very runway of the Overseas National crash—and just west of the wooden cow. We lean down toward the radio. "We have a Pan Am✈ Airbus with a control-surface problem," a Queens-accented male voice says, from the tower. "A sta-

---

✈ Pan American, Juan Trippe's grand dream, America's flagship overseas carrier, and one of our proudest businesses for decades, went into swift financial decline after the Lockerbie crash, and blinked out forever in December 1991, almost three years to the day after Lockerbie, and after the bulk of the research for

bilizer is stuck in the cruising position. The aircraft is five miles west and approaching Thirteen Right."

I do calculations in my head. Three hundred miles an hour on approach—say two hundred miles an hour; say just one hundred miles an hour. One hundred miles an hour means a mile and a half a minute.

A police car, its roof lights flashing, shoots down the runway, followed by several chartreuse emergency vehicles, lights also flashing.

Oh my God, I think. *I'm going to see a plane crash.*

The Airbus appears out of the clouds to the southwest. It's a big, fat plane, worthy of its prosy name. With the foreshortening of approach, it seems to be floating rather than flying.

It occurs to me at this moment that Sammy and I ourselves are not out of harm's way. It also occurs to me, all at once, that Kennedy's three-letter airport code was changed several years ago from KIA to JFK, the former, after Vietnam, having unfortunate associations. Bureaucracy detests the subconscious. I look over at Sammy. He's hunched down, his raptor's neck creased, as he stares out through the top of the windshield. "Should we—?" I start to say. I stop. The Airbus is coming down, down, down. The gray air is grainy with mist. The howl of the engines builds. The plane wags slightly on the diagonal. This motion, I will later learn, is called *crabbing.* Beautiful word. The airport is full of beautiful words. And crashes, of all sorts.

this book was completed. I will try, wherever possible, to avoid anachronisms—although the dizzying pace of the airline business makes this nearly impossible—but since Pan Am was a central part of New York International and Idlewild and Kennedy for forty-four years, as well as during two of the more than four years I spent going to the airport, I will sometimes refer to it just as though its departed shade were still alive. *Hic iacet.*

3

Euphemize

Lighting The Fuselage

The Airbus, of course, did not crash. (Pan Am itself was another story.) I say "of course" because the vast majority of planes—the amazingly great majority—don't go down, and if this one had, you would've known about it. But if I had you worried (or titillated) unfairly for a second, I apologize: I only did it so you could experience my own momentary suspension out there next to 13 Right, and to illustrate the preoccupation of nearly everybody—including both those who fly and those who refuse to—with plane crashes.

This has to do, I suspect, not only with the truly sad and shocking refutation of the giddy miracle of flight (and, perhaps, the Icarus-like confirmation of man's hubris) that any crash represents, but also with a certain secret, all-too-human delight at the macabre in general (as long as perfect strangers are involved), and particularly with the pungent intrusion of Death into the holiday medium of travel. Not to mention the fact that *there simply used to be more crashes* than there are now. Just as anyone can be blasé about stepping onto a plane these days, anyone of a certain age remembers growing up with the black headlines: AIR FRANCE (Air Chance, some used to call it). AVIANCA. EASTERN. The incredibly calamitous midair collision, in fog over Staten Island in 1960, of a United DC-8 en route to Idlewild from Chicago and a TWA Super Constellation bound for La Guardia from Columbus, Ohio.✦ The starling crash of Eastern Flight 375 at Logan that same year was just one of a series of Lockheed Electra disasters around that time—which in turn were a subset of the rotten air-safety picture in general. No wonder the bird question was overlooked for a long while.

✦ There were 134 dead: all on both planes and 6 on the ground in Brooklyn. The piquancy of the two types of planes involved, and the year, should not be neglected: it would be cold, but not entirely amiss, to call the crash a collision of the nascent jet and moribund propeller ages.

37

Thus I was startled when a knowledgeable source[*] reminded me that while the world might be trundling hellward in the same old handbasket as always, in the case of air safety, things are actually getting (somewhat) better. Today's airplanes (and the planes of yesterday that are still flying today) are far safer than they used to be. Avionic technology and radar and air traffic computers—particularly the devices responsible for preventing midair collisions—have advanced at the same rate as the technology for human destruction. Yet pilots still make mistakes. And so do machines.[**] Science—that great shibboleth of human progress from the eighteenth century, until 1918 and 1945 *gave us pause*—today makes any thinking person walleyed with ambivalence. This is as true at the airport as anywhere else.

In 1949, the first year the National Transportation Safety Board started keeping statistics, you were 25 times as likely to be involved in a commercial airline accident, and 10 times as likely to be involved in a fatal accident, as in 1990. By 1960, the year of the Staten Island/midair and Logan/starling crashes, things had gotten better—somewhat: You were 13 times as likely to be involved in an accident, and 6.5 times as likely to be involved in a fatal accident, as in 1990.

By 1975, the year of Eastern Flight 66, you were 2.3 times as likely to be involved in an accident as in 1990, and a tiny bit *less* likely to be involved in a fatal accident.

But let's take a closer look at exactly what these statistics mean. In 1949, when men and women wore hats, when cars and planes were rounded at the edges, and when my grandparents, at the peak of their fortunes, were apt to run out to Idlewild on a moment's notice to jump on a Stratocruiser[***] for

---

[*] Dr. Louis Abelson, a remarkable man: physician, pilot, soldier, former champion swimmer, curmudgeon; co-founder (in 1947) of Kennedy's Medical Facility; present at almost all the airport's disasters. More on him shortly.

[**] *Our* Airbus didn't crash, but a remarkable number of A320 Airbuses have been going down in Europe over the past couple of years—they seem to be this era's version of the Lockheed Electra. Consumer experts say never to buy the prototype of any gizmo: you'll just get all the kinks that R&D will work out later. Do they ever say this about flying in new planes? My own personal practice is to avoid flying A320 Airbuses—or any other model that seems to be working itself out at the public's expense—until further notice. You can do this, too. When you make your plane reservations over the phone, just ask, casually, "What's the equipment?" They tell you right away. And if you don't like what you hear—well, you're the consumer.

[***] The fabled Boeing B-377, the last great ocean liner of the sky. A converted B-29 Super Fortress bomber, the big Strat was known as the "airplane that opened Idlewild"—mainly because it was the first plane too heavy to use La Guardia's runways. "In Pan Am's configuration," writes Geoffrey Arend in his picture history *Great Airports: Kennedy International,* "the Strat featured 68 day seats, 18 berths, 25 night seats (today called sleeperettes) plus 14 seats downstairs [via spiral staircase] in the lounge. From flowers in the lounge of the BOAC flights to an all-night snack bar aboard the Pan Am Clippers, the order of the day aboard the Strat was service. Newlyweds and romantics could even reserve the private Bridal Suite."

Havana for a few days of sun, fun, and gambling, Nana and Papa's chances of crashing were 138 in 1,000, or almost 1 in 7. (Talk about gambling! While their fortunes crashed, however, they themselves never did.) And their chances of being involved in a crash in which someone, not necessarily they, died were 15 in 1,000, or roughly 1 in 70. (They both died *in bed,* as the saying goes, seven years apart, my grandfather of Lou Gehrig's disease and my grandmother of disappointment. Provide! Provide!)

By 1960, when Nana and Papa moved to the frame house under the Idlewild flight path (my grandfather, eternally optimistic, worked on a secret scientific project, said to be a solution to the problem of perpetual motion, in the basement of that house), and as John Kennedy's face and the swept-back contours of the Boeing 707 imparted to the world a cosmetic, mostly illusory sense of renewal, your chances of crashing had halved, to 71 in 1,000. Seven percent. Not too bad. Not so great. Your chances of being in a fatal air accident had gone down to 9 in 1,000.

By 1975, when my grandparents had gone on to the Florida condo, bought by their two sons, that would be their last home together, air travel was starting to look like a fairly safe proposition. The odds of being in a crash were 13 in 1,000, or less than a *fifth* of their level fifteen years before. Fatal crash statistics were a ninth of what they'd been in 1960: 1 in 1,000. It looks wonderful on paper.

Then again, there was Eastern 66, with its 113 extremely unlucky passengers.

By 1990—with the advent of wind-shear detectors, bird patrols, improved ground radar, the low-altitude warning signal (an electronic *whoop-whoop,* under a man's recorded voice that cried, with robotic urgency, "Pull up! Pull up!"),[+] and tightened rules about flight-deck chitchat during approach and landing[++]—things seemed to have gotten, air-accident-wise, almost as good as they could get. Your chances of being involved in some sort of crash, even a relatively minor mishap, were now 5.5 in 1,000. Half a percent. The odds of a fatal crash were 14 in 10,000. Much lower, the FAA always loves to remind us, than the comparable statistics for automobile travel.

[+] The direct result of a 1974 crash in which a TWA jet hit the top of a fog-shrouded mountain in Virginia as it approached Washington, killing all ninety-two people aboard.

[++] The direct result of *another* 1974 fog crash, fatal to seventy-two, in which the flight crew of an Eastern DC-9, according to the NTSB report, "engaged in conversations not pertinent to the operation of the aircraft that were distractive and reflected a casual mood and lax cockpit atmosphere, which continued throughout the remainder of the approach and which contributed to the accident." In short, the DC-9 slammed into the ground three miles short of the Charlotte, North Carolina, airport because the crew, busy shooting the breeze, had failed to keep track of the plane's altitude.

Isn't this good? Isn't this nice? If you can avoid wing icing, terrorists (an entirely separate question, on which more later), aged or simply defective aircraft parts that fail in flight,[*] or—still, at this late date—freak wind conditions,[**] why then, you're practically golden. Your chances of being in a serious plane crash these days are minuscule. (The astounding actuarial fact is that your lifetime chances of being killed in a plane crash are 1 in 20,000, as opposed to 1 in 100 for being killed in a car wreck, or 1 in 7,000 for being alive at a time when the earth is struck by a giant asteroid.)

But that it happens at *all,* cry the fearers-of-flying, is too horrible! Make the chances zero! The monumentally neurotic among us, girded with shaky scientific optimism, point to superconductor technology, which, sometime in a *Jetsons*-esque future, may allow *engineless planes* to zip over the earth, held aloft by powerful magnetic fields, like those toys in which a small iron disk hovers. No engines, no fuel; no fuel, no fires. Not to mention far fewer moving parts to fail. Not to mention—eeriest of all—utter silence. The prospect of winding up, in my own grandparenthood, in a house under the landing path of noiseless, ghostlike flying machines gives me ambivalent pleasure.

*

[*] The bolts attaching the engine-mounting pylons to the wings of some 737s have been known to come loose, causing, in several cases, the near loss of an engine in flight. And recently, the same plane has had difficulties with the ground-sensor switch, which enables the deployment of the reverse thrusters, the anti-skid brake system, and the spoilers on the wings that rise to resist air upon landing; the result has been some hairy landings for 737s. Yet the remarkable thing, given the millions upon millions of miles put on their planes by American carriers, is how seldom parts *do* fail. This is a tribute to the quality of both airplane manufacture and airline maintenance—sensational TV-magazine reports about cut-rate airplane-parts service contractors notwithstanding. Fly Boeing and McDonnell Douglas jets on major American airlines, and your odds of surviving the flight are excellent. And then there is the skill of pilots, which is almost always sufficient to compensate for very rare parts failures, even in extreme situations, such as a well-known near mishap with a TWA 727 over Detroit in 1979. A TWA pilot described the incident to me:

"There was a lot of publicity—they were trying to put the blame on the pilot. But he got the airplane on the ground and there were no fatalities. His name was Hoot Gibson, same as the cowboy movie star. I mean, he kind of had the flavor of a cowboy in the first place, but this thing really cemented it. I flew with him the other day. He's still living on the reputation of that incident that happened a dozen years ago.

"A flap panel, they think, blew off of the airplane, which put it into this vertical spiral. Gibson said they were actually coming straight down, supersonic. And doing vertical spins at, like, six a minute. He had given the whole thing some advance thought—there was a fatality in earlier years when the same thing happened. And when he read about that he said to himself, I wonder what I would do if that ever happened to me. And what they think happened is, he threw the landing gear out. Now they were going down supersonic—the shock wave of a supersonic airplane is beyond the controls. You actually have no controlling devices. So when Hoot threw the gear down, plus the fact that they were getting into the heavier atmosphere—it moved the shock wave forward to the point that he had some control over his elevators. And he pulled it up. I mean, they fell, like, thirty-six thousand feet in forty-some seconds."

Whew!

[**] United Flight 585, a 737 that crashed near Colorado Springs in 1991, may have encountered a *wind rotor*—a kind of sideways tornado—as it descended over the Rockies.

THE AIRPORT

My father was, like his own father, a great technophile. Even if human history, as he believed, was going demonstrably downhill, human technology produced marvelous gadgets. He cherished gadgets. Airplanes were included in the category. He traveled somewhere around a million air miles in his life: on business, for pleasure, in the service of his country. There is a photograph of him, circa 1946 and soon to graduate from West Point, standing, grinning (he looks about seventeen; he was in fact four years older), with one foot up on the wing of an army biplane in which he had recently soloed. He piloted Cessnas and Pipers; he flew as a passenger in them, too. Safety statistics for private planes are staggeringly worse than statistics for commercial airlines. He had near-misses in them (just barely hinted at, out of earshot of my flying-phobic mother), but no crashes. He rode as well in Douglas DC-3s and 7s; McDonnell Douglas DC-8s, 9s, and 10s; Boeing 707s, 727s, 737s, 747s, 757s, and 767s; Lockheeds of all varieties, including, often, the ill-fated Electra. (To his regret, he never flew on the Concorde.) Hundreds and hundreds of flights: he was a traveling salesman for a time. He flew all around the United States, and to Europe and the Far East. He had no fear of flying, none that he spoke about anyway, and he never crashed.

Actually, that's not true. He was in a crash once, landing in a DC-3 in Altoona, Pennsylvania. He alluded to it but wouldn't be drawn out. Unlike Francis Weed, in the great John Cheever story "The Country Husband," who went home to a family utterly uninterested in his story of disaster, my father would have had an all-too-attentive audience in his worried wife and (by sympathetic vibration) worried sons. My father flew often when I was a child, and I was convinced, virtually every time he did so, that—*something would happen.* I have a sharp, thirty-year-old memory, forever associated with the partially cooked yolk of a fried egg over easy—the breakfast that my digestive tract held in midtransit when I spied an envelope from a life insurance company on the mail table in the front hall. My father was away on one of his frequent trips. And I saw this envelope and knew, in my gullet, that there was something my mother wasn't telling me. Of course, he had *left* only the day before—life insurers should only fork over with such alacrity, I would later learn. And Freudians will delight in the Oedipal implications of my half-cooked fantasy. But psychology aside, *that was what was in the air in those days.* Those black headlines. Planes crashed. Often.

Not too long after this, one of my father's few friends in the business world was killed, along with 111 other Americans in a tour group, in the 1962 crash of an Air France 707, in Paris. It was a beautiful spring Sunday morning when my father read the news, outside, in our backyard. He betrayed little emotion, besides a certain grim set to the mouth that I was used to: this was the soldier's way. Or, at least, *his* soldier's way. Air Chance, he would say from time to time after that, acknowledging the event and warding it off at the same time, with black soldier humor. Thirteen years later, his West Point classmate and friend Saul "J. R." Horowitz, a rich, handsome, urbane, cocky man, stepped on board Eastern Flight 66 in New Orleans, bound to John F. Kennedy International Airport. There were no jokes after that.

I think there was another reason, besides the fear of worrying his family, that my father never talked about his own plane crash: it had betrayed his faith in technology. Momentarily. After all, he had a choice after that—he could have somehow changed his life, could have decided never to fly again. He elected to go on. He flew hundreds of thousands of miles afterward, without serious incident. Maybe he believed he had paid his dues, that nothing more could happen to him. In the end, it wasn't technology, but biology, that betrayed him: he died in bed of leukemia, at age sixty-six. Too early. *Requiescat in pace.* He had a lot of flights still in him—had, in fact, made his last trip not a month before. United from Newark to Chicago, early morning flight. United back to Newark that same afternoon. Business done, for the day at least. Piece of cake. On home.

❐

When George Murphy was a choirboy at St. Patrick's Cathedral, Father Duffy used to bring him and his fellows out to Idlewild to watch the planes take off and land.

Murphy, who grew up in the Bronx, took the test and became a police officer in the Port Authority pool—the lowest of the low, the ones who get transferred, as needed, from bridge to tunnel to airport, but mostly to the most hated post of all, the Port Authority Bus Terminal on Forty-second Street, where cops have to rouse, move along, and occasionally confront the some-times diseased, sometimes demented people who make the place their home. After a while Murphy rose to detective at La Guardia; then another promotion brought him to Kennedy. "I got into the emergency garage pretty much by accident," he says. "When I got promoted here, I fell in love with the place. JFK is the hub of the world. The center of the International Arrivals Building is the center of the universe. The level of activity is like nothing else. You get the Dalai Lamas coming through here, the Grand Rabbis."

Murphy and I are standing outside the Port Authority Crash and Fire Res-cue Training Facility, just off the nexus of runways 31 Right and 22 Right. "Sorry I forgot to shave," he says, palpating his jowly face. It is a good face, an Irish face—small nose, bushy salt-and-pepper mustache, and blue eyes full of a fierce sentimentality, all under a balding dome. Gray sideburns. A fireman's face. *Pompier.* Murphy shrugs and takes out a big jingly key ring. He has the underdog air of an honest precinct cop, layered in with a prickly sense of his own worth, a slightly cynical view of How the World Works, a restless urge to tell long stories, and a love for all the earth's children and small animals. The latter being fortunate for you, for if your plane crashes at Kennedy, Murphy, or someone trained by Murphy, will very likely be the one who tries to pull you out.

"You gotta promise not to laugh at the Facility," Murphy says, as he unlocks a padlock and opens a metal door. The Facility is a long, white, corrugated-metal house trailer mounted on cement blocks. The interior is dim and cozy between dirty linoleum and dropped ceiling, with the fluorescent-and-tobacco charm of an auto mechanic's office or a firehouse lounge—the latter of which, in fact, is closer to the truth. The elite core members of the Port Authority police force, some 117 strong (about half of the department), are trained both as policemen and firemen. George Murphy is in charge of the latter, and he does his classroom instruction here. On a table next to a deeply stained chair, whose color appears to be somewhere between green and orange, sits a pile of copies of *Fire Command* magazine. Sitting on Murphy's wood-grained steel desk, among sundry other objects, are a very grimy fax machine, a gas mask, and a large can of institutional Lysol. Hanging on the wall, among sundry other artifacts, are a cut-out magazine picture of a crashed and burned jet ("Alert 3—a 727 in the dirt" reads the caption), a Mets schedule for 1987, a Guinness stout St. Patrick's Day poster of four busty young women dressed in scanty emerald-colored costumes over the caption "Get Your Irish Up," and a plain white card on which is printed the single word EUPHEMIZE.

It is easy to forget, amid the wry shaggy-dog comforts of George Murphy's trailer, the reality of his job, which is rescuing people from burning airplanes. All of us who fear flying, whether vaguely or starkly, tend to fear it abstractly. How can we bear to think of the awful smell and unbelievable heat of combusting aviation fuel, of the hellish screams of crushed and burning people, people neither saintly nor evil, but precisely like us? We can't; we prefer not to take it much further in our minds than sweaty palms and turbulence, or an interruption in our in-flight meal. EUPHEMIZE. Whatever the Jesuitical humor, it's an important concept in George Murphy's business. "We've been at crashes," Murphy tells me, shaking his head. He's leaning back in his desk chair, in holding-forth posture. "Stress is a terrible factor. There was Flight 5050, at La Guardia," he says, speaking of the September 1989 incident in which a USAir 737 skidded off the end of a runway and tilted into Flushing Bay. "Even though only two people got killed there, a crash is a crash. You

43

make mistakes. It's the spelling-bee concept—you keep going until you get it wrong. Then you lose."

We talk for a while about the teaching Murphy does along with his partner, Sergeant Jimmy Smythe. "We don't think we do very good training," Murphy says, "but we do the best around." Just then the door to the trailer opens, letting in bright, inappropriate sunlight and two not-so-young trainees —a short black woman and a tall white man with a mustache. The woman, who is in police uniform, has her hair tucked up under her hat. The man, who looks like a lesser villain in a cheap movie, is in jeans, a bowling jacket, and a plastic mesh baseball cap. His face is pale and deeply pockmarked. Neither the man nor the woman appears to be especially happy to be here; their eyes wander around without making contact. Murphy greets them without much warmth and bids them take a seat. The woman and the man sit as far apart as it is possible to sit inside the narrow trailer. Sergeant Murphy hits the lights, turns on a television and a videocassette recorder in front of the room. "Have you seen these?" he asks the trainees and, politely, me. "We got the fire-fighting errors, and the, uh, Delta crash in Dallas." No answer from the trainees. Murphy pops in the first tape. "This is things you should never do," he says, over the sprightly educational-film music at the beginning of the tape. "The following are all actual incidents, filmed at the time of their occurrence," the narrator intones. "No disrespect or criticism of the victims is intended; this record is offered for educational purposes, in the hopes that others might avoid these errors, thus saving lives in the future."

We proceed to watch a kind of Bellocian catalog of catastrophes, as fire fighters and rescue workers pick up live wires and are thrown to the ground, move in their hoses too close to burning fuel and are blown back, crawl over burned-out roofs and fall through. "This guy had his rib cage crushed by the concussion; he didn't make it," Murphy says, of the blow-back victim. *Good God*, I think. *This is a film of a guy buying it.* Of the fireman who touched the live wire, rose into the air, and landed in a heap: "This guy survived, believe it or not." Who took these films? There is a pornographic edge to them, a horrific whiff of slapstick: How can we watch these intimate events, death and maiming, with equanimity? We watch. The second tape is of the rescue work in the August 1985 crash of a Delta L-1011 at Dallas–Fort Worth (DFW) International Airport. Wind shear was the culprit. Detectors were later installed. One hundred thirty-seven died. The rescue went as well as could be expected. The tape shows black smoke billowing furiously from the fuselage, rescue vehicles speeding to and from the crash site. "Crispy Critters," Murphy says, shaking his head. "Sometimes you go to these crises," he says, "and think they're a great endorsement for rail transportation."

THE AIRPORT

*

At the airport's northeast corner, near the foot of runways 22 Left and Right, just a couple of hundred yards south from the spot on Rockaway Boulevard where Eastern Flight 66 crashed in June 1975 (wind shear; detectors were later installed), sits a burned and rusted metal cylinder with dummy engine pods mounted on its sides. This cylinder, meant to simulate a section of the fuselage of a downed airliner, and known throughout the airport as simply "The Fuselage," is periodically set ablaze by the Port Authority police.

This is an unpopular activity. It is relegated to this distant edge of the property for good reason. Environmental groups charge that the aviation fuel used for the fires is soaking into the ground and compromising the water table. Air traffic controllers in the tower and pilots don't like having to divert takeoffs and landings because of the thick, billowing smoke. Passengers in terminals, and in planes both on the ground and in the air, become alarmed. Black smoke spooks airline passengers, for many of whom the line between artificial relaxation—the clinking ice cubes in the plastic cocktail glass—and direst panic is thin indeed. A bump, a whiff, a glance, can turn the balance. Knowledge helps, and gaining concrete knowledge about aviation and airplanes is the substance of Fear of Flying courses, but most people would no sooner understand all the details of what gets them aloft and keeps them that way and lands them again than they would care to contemplate the niceties of their own vascular systems; they would just as soon pretend to believe in the passenger's version of the kabuki of commercial flying—drink the drink, smile at the attendant, eat the meal, watch the movie, sweat out the bumping insult of landing, then *get the hell off the plane.*

Black smoke is, however, precisely what PA police undergoing crash and fire rescue (CFR) training must learn to eat, and this is why George Murphy is here this sunny afternoon with seven trainees, six men and a woman. The Fuselage stands in a dark pool of aviation fuel (500 gallons) brought in earlier and dispensed by tanker truck. A spanking-new chartreuse PA Oshkosh F-29 fire pumper—one of the vehicles that sped out to meet the imperiled Pan Am Airbus, and that would have gone into action had the plane not landed safely—filled with 3,750 gallons of water, as well as 410 gallons of AFFF foam (also known as light water or "product"), stands by, with its operator, Sergeant Teddy Nizwicki, a bespectacled bull of a man. Murphy and the trainees are all dressed in those big black flame-retardant fire coats trimmed in Day-Glo green, and black fire pants and big rubber boots. Each trainee holds a yellow helmet, which has a silvery cloth flap behind and a clear visor in front, and a pair of what look like silver oven gloves. The afternoon is what the TV weather people call unseasonably mild; the clothes are sweaty. Mur-

45

phy's open coat reveals, remarkably enough, a pair of red suspenders holding up the waderlike trousers, as well as what looks like the top half of a pair of long johns. The shirt is soaked. Murphy regards his charges—who stand before him in roughly semicircular array, chatting desultorily or staring off into space—with a certain amount of paternal anxiety. These are grown-up young people who have fired pistols on a training range, who have made arrests, who are growing into the trappings and attitudes of authority—and yet where fire is concerned they are absolutely green; they have no idea what smoke and flame are all about, what a sudden and dire effect they have on the animal inside the human spirit. George Murphy knows all these things all too well. This is the essence of the fireman's sadness.

The first order of business is to learn to man the hose. Trainees at The Fuselage use water instead of foam, because putting out an aviation fuel fire with water is more basic and much more difficult. It is a form of initiation into the ancient form of fire fighting. The hose is big, canvas-coated, rubber-lined fire hose, and it takes two people to handle it; it kicks like a mule when the water comes through. Murphy selects two trainees to start. They pick up the hose and put it over their shoulders. "If you've ever fired a shotgun," Murphy tells his charges, "this has more pressure behind it. It's constant—you have to lean into it.

"The driver won't give you water till you give him a thumbs-up," he says. "Now, I want you to use the distance between you and the flame, then start coming in with sweeps. All right? First we practice without the fire." He points at the head hose-handler, who gives Nizwicki a thumbs-up. The pumper starts to grind, then a second later a pillar of water emerges from the front of the hose. The two trainees buckle slightly. They start moving forward over the grass toward The Fuselage, first just pointing the stream, and then, as they get closer, playing it back and forth to create clouds of flame-quenching mist.

The trainees practice two by two as Murphy watches. The planes departing on 4 Left roar low overhead, full of weight in the air, their underbellies glistening. It's just after 1 P.M., the beginning of rush hour at Kennedy. Maximum incoming and outgoing air (and ground) traffic will continue until about nine at night. "All right," Murphy calls, when his pupils are through. "Does everybody know what we're doing? Now comes the fun part." He closes his coat, dons his helmet and gloves, and lights a flare. Then he walks up to the black pool of aviation fuel and tosses it in.

The fuel doesn't ignite all at once. Murphy moves back. The flame travels across the liquid's black surface toward The Fuselage for a moment, and then there is ignition inside the metal cylinder, a bulging belly of fire, a thick black tree of smoke rising into the milky placid sky. I stare at the fire. It is redder than orange, alive, ravening, billowing. Avid. It makes any cozy domestic flame—a hearth, a barbecue—seem like water, or perhaps skim milk. This is a fire you never, ever want to see. This is Tophet, the eye of hell. And this is just a taste of what a real aircraft fire would be like.

The trainees go in again, in pairs. The pumper grinds into action, its moronic whine converted into a song of beneficence. The mass of flame crackles and shimmers triumphantly. The smoke has become a low-lying black cloud. Twenty stories overhead, a Lufthansa 747, its unpainted underbelly gleaming in the metropolitan sun, breaks through the pall and heads north. The novice fire fighters shoulder the hose in carefully, raking the stream across The Fuselage. The flame licks and sputters reluctantly, becomes obscured by smoke. Then it's all smoke. A TWA L-1011 passes over, a thousand feet or so to the east of the Lufthansa plane's path. The pilots are starting to avoid the smoke. One imagines the passengers' necks craning, the carefully constructed equanimity of the cabin shot to hell. On-board liquor sales will be brisk this afternoon.

The lone female trainee, Officer Mariann Baumbach, a veteran of two and a half years on the force, stands with her coat open, her helmet cradled in her right arm. She's a handsome woman, solid, blond, with nice skin and practical eyes. She's sweating rivers. "This is not fun," she says, shaking her head. "I wanted to be a police officer. I didn't want to be a fireman."

"Don't get hot," George Murphy instructs his pupils, after the fire has been set and put out for the fourth time. The pronouncement has the force of a proverb. Murphy lets the wisdom sink in for a second as he scans his charges, then he says it again. *Don't. Get. Hot.*

"Run away! Run away!" one of the young men chimes, in a gym-class-needler falsetto.

Murphy smiles thinly and, in the finest pedagogical tradition, acts as though nothing had happened. "These coats aren't fireproof," he says. "Nothing's fireproof. Steel melts. Don't try to be a Superman or a Superwoman out there. At the DFW crash there were enough volunteers so that nobody had to go in twice. Nobody should have to go in twice." ✈

✈ The Greens have won: On December 31, 1993, the Port Authority stopped using aviation fuel to torch The Fuselage. The PA plans to switch to propane sometime in 1994, placating the environmentalists but, conceivably, leaving crash and fire rescue crews more prepared to fight a fire in a mobile home than one in an airliner.

4

JFK 2000

A Story Interrupted

*Y*esterday's Technology—Tomorrow's Demands, reads the unintention-
ally mordant, unwittingly prescient title of the slick brochure I carry
with me when I go to talk to Edward O'Sullivan, assistant director of
what is left of the JFK 2000 redevelopment project. Now that the project has
finally been derailed due to lack of funds, the brochure has become that most
embarrassing of corporate artifacts, an overoptimistic prediction in cold type.
And what I want to ask O'Sullivan is, What happened to JFK 2000?

When first built almost 40 years ago [says the brochure], New
York International Airport at Idlewild represented a unique concept in airport design with a main central terminal surrounded by
individual terminals, each housing a major commercial airline
with its own distinctive architectural style.

Since then, the convenience of air travel, the introduction of
wide-body jets and improvements in air traffic control have
prompted a vast increase in commercial passenger and air cargo
flights. As more people chose to fly, the number of travelers to
pass through what is now John F. Kennedy International Airport
doubled and tripled.

Most airline terminals at JFK have expanded to meet passenger
demand. Taxiways and runways also have been lengthened and
improved. However, the airport's central terminal area and the
roadways connecting travelers to individual terminals have essentially remained as when first built. Today, the airport's loop of
roadways, intended to handle the traffic of 15 million travelers
yearly, is often jammed with the vehicles of more than twice that

49

number of airport patrons. Buses, which transport passengers to inter-connecting flights, are frequently stalled in the airport road congestion and require more time to reach their destination than it would take to walk. Luggage transfer, too, is a slower process at Kennedy than at most airports.

As the safety and comfort of flying increase, the number of travelers to use JFK International Airport is expected to grow to 45 million by the year 2000.

A DESIGN FOR THE FUTURE

The JFK Redevelopment Program, or "JFK 2000" as it is called, is designed to ensure the airport's continued status as the premier international gateway to America. The Port Authority of New York and New Jersey's airport modernization project is planned to facilitate passenger and baggage movement in and around JFK, as well as increase and improve services to travelers, international and domestic.

A multi-functional Central Terminal Complex, a new air traffic control tower, an automated "People Mover" system, a high-speed baggage sorting and distribution network and an expanded and streamlined roadway configuration comprise the massive redevelopment program. . . .

O'Sullivan, I sense, is about to give me the company line about why the airlines have declined to lend their crucial financial support to the central terminal building—a mammoth, $1 billion, atriumed cylindrical structure, out of I. M. Pei through Piranesi, which was to have contained restaurants, shops, a so-called Meeters and Greeters Hall, and an omphalic ticketing office for all of Kennedy's airlines—and to the $126 million people-mover monorail, which would have taken the theoretically happy, ticketed, met and greeted, non-traffic-jammed, well-fed-and-supplied-with-consumer-goods passengers from that building on to the individual airline terminals for takeoff.

The central terminal building, the linchpin of the JFK 2000 concept, would have been a marvel. In its gigantic, cylindrical, atrial expanse, passengers would have strolled easily, warm and dry, from airline to airline, from hotel to boutique to restaurant. Such, at least, was the theoretical version, that world view based on the kind of architectural drawing in which people are seen as small, smooth Giacomettis, faceless and manageable and clean.

THE AIRPORT

(Show me an architectural rendering with homeless people in it and I will show you a builder with *vision*.) Then the central terminal building went the way of the Brooklyn-Battery Bridge and the Times Square Victory Arch, into the archives of The City That Never Was.[*]

The airlines kiboshed it, by simply refusing to pay the gigantic leases that would have been levied on them. Why, in the face of declining revenues,[**] should they underwrite a new design for the airport that would make it easier for people to switch carriers? Delta[***] delayed? American overbooked? United overpriced? Report to the central ticket office! A nightmare scenario for airlines, which have been known to remove magazines from their planes to save weight—therefore fuel, therefore money. No, they liked things just fine the impossible way they were. If you missed your flight on American at JFK, to skip over to United was so complicated by car and potentially perilous on foot that it really didn't pay to do anything other than sit around and wait for the next flight on American. Thus the airlines assured that Kennedy would remain what it always has been and seemingly always will be: a loose affiliation of decaying structures, connected by a dangerous, impenetrably complex roadway system.

One of my chief informants on the central terminal fiasco was Stephen L. Berger, the departing executive director of the Port Authority when I met with him, a bearded, high-octane, cigar-smoking, piercingly intelligent, witheringly cynical *über*-bureaucrat, who, on the crucial date of May 9, 1990, released the following masterpiece of press-statement ambiguity:

> We are pleased that our recent discussions with representatives
> of the airline industry on the significant changes in their business
> environment and investment strategies over the past several years

[*] See the wonderful book of this title by Rebecca Read Shanor, a great testament to the eternally optimistic folly of New York civic construction.

[**] The fiscal relationship between Kennedy and the airlines that operate out of it, in the post-deregulation environment, is a complex and tetchy minuet. Alternately, it might help to think of the airport as a grand old Park Avenue apartment house. On the one hand, the carriers lease their terminals (or, in the case of smaller airlines, such as Ecuatoriana and Air Nigeria, the square-footage their offices in the International Arrivals Building take up), from year to year in some instances, and may, like rowdy tenants, be asked to move (or even leave), depending on their solvency and the Port Authority's plans for the space.

On the other hand, the leases and gate user fees the airlines pay contribute substantially to Kennedy's operating budget, and this gives them power—the power to shut down plans for the central terminal, for example.

[***] The occupant, at time of writing, of what were, at the start of my research, Pan Am Terminals A and B.

have enabled us to arrive at a consensus to proceed with several key elements of the John F. Kennedy International Airport redevelopment program.

As a result of these discussions, work on several previously authorized elements of the program will be accelerated. This includes construction of the new internal roadway system, the new air traffic control tower, the new parking garages opposite the International Arrivals Building (IAB), a hotel, and the reconstruction of the utility systems servicing the entire airport.

We have agreed with the airport's major airlines to begin work immediately on design and construction of a new exclusive roadway for buses and other high occupancy vehicles that would serve each of the airport's nine terminal buildings. This new roadway will mean a faster, more reliable trip for passengers using buses and other shared-ride services to get to and from the airport, and will aid our continuing effort to persuade air travelers to leave their cars at home.

As a result of our discussions, we have also agreed to postpone construction of the planned central terminal complex until a later phase in the redevelopment of the airport. The major airlines serving JFK have argued that the best way to improve service to air passengers in the near term is to invest in modernization and expansion of the airport's existing terminals. Several U.S. carriers are prepared to commit several hundred million dollars each to renovation of their own terminals.

Additionally, the Port Authority, in cooperation with several foreign-flag carriers, will now commit similar sums to renovation and expansion of the International Arrivals Building, and to the former Eastern Airlines Terminal, which was recently vacated by Eastern as part of its reorganization in bankruptcy.

The JFK redevelopment plan will continue to reserve space for the planned central terminal, and we expect that construction will begin as soon as the growth in airport traffic and our tenants' space needs require it.

By the end of this year, we hope to reach conceptual agreement with City and State transportation agencies on the development of a new off-airport transit connection and each agency's role in that project. At the same time, the changes in the shape and timing of the JFK redevelopment plan will require some major changes in the design of the automated on-airport "people mover" system, construction of which we had planned to begin this summer. We have already begun to discuss these changes with our contractor, and expect to have the design issues resolved also by the end of this year.

In sum, we expect that the airport development will proceed without interruptions, recognizing that some of the components will be different, some re-phased, but that all of the functions and conveniences to the traveling public that the original plan promised will be retained.

AIRPORT OVERHAUL AT KENNEDY IS OFF, the *Times* trumpeted two days later. "Under pressure from financially pressed airlines [the article continued], the Port Authority has put off construction of a $1 billion central terminal and monorail system at Kennedy International Airport.

"Port Authority officials said they had decided to back off from the centerpiece of a $3 billion airport renovation because airline executives argued that it was unnecessary and that they could not afford it. . . ."

By that July, Berger had announced his decision to leave the Port for that even greater gravy train, the *completely* private sector.

Edward O'Sullivan is a shortish Irishman in his mid-forties with a good-sized gut and a hard-looking moon face. Blue bullet eyes, blank. A former marine captain, Vietnam. Former counterterrorism expert for the Port Authority. A flat bureaucratic voice, with that cop way of inserting unnecessary polysyllables to avoid emotion. Long into the discussion about bond issues and the height of the new control tower,✦ I get fed up and ask him about his own personal experience of the airport. O'Sullivan blinks once, but is happy enough to change the unfruitful subject. He used to come to visit as a boy in the early fifties with his father, he says. He flew in and out of it as a marine.

"My most traumatic experience here was in 1975," he begins, unbidden, matter-of-factly, as though he were about to describe lost luggage—and then out tumbles (in the same flat voice) the story of his experience with Kennedy's worst disaster, the crash of Eastern Flight 66. O'Sullivan claims he was the first airport person on the scene. "I had been to Vietnam, with all the carnage there," he says, still flat, "and my first reaction was how inappropriate this scene was here."

I hear the hum of the fluorescents. "I found a little girl," O'Sullivan says,

✦ At 321 feet, quite an impressive erection. The tallest control tower in the United States, it was designed to maintain a required three-to-one height ratio over the planned central terminal complex. Which, of course, will not exist. Now the tower stands in lonely splendor, tall for tallness sake, and—as of this writing—still unused.

his voice even. He pauses a moment. "Maybe seven years old," he continues. "Only I didn't know it was a seven-year-old girl till later. This was a charred · body, still alive. Hairless. She was rocking on her hands and knees. When I touched her, her skin came off in my hand." Those flat, blue bullet eyes.

"Did she make it?" I ask.

O'Sullivan shakes his head.

5

June 24, 1975

Air, Water, Earth, Fire

A t ten minutes to four o'clock on an early summer Tuesday afternoon, Eastern Airlines Flight 66, a silver-and-blue Boeing 727 that had taken off three hours earlier from New Orleans, descended from the eternally perfect day of the middle atmosphere into a dirty cotton batting of cloud floor as it began its final approach to John F. Kennedy International Airport in New York.

There were 115 paying passengers aboard, and a crew of 8 headed by Captain John W. Kleven of Manhattan, an eighteen-year Eastern veteran. The passengers, smiling and chatting or just finishing their drinks as the clear afternoon sun shone on them, included Wendell Ladner, a handsome star forward for the New York Nets basketball team; Saul Horowitz, Jr., the patrician-looking chairman of HRH, a giant New York construction firm; the bulldog-jawed Right Reverend Iveson B. Noland, the Episcopal bishop of Louisiana; Edgar Bright, the socially prominent former president of the New Orleans Cotton Exchange, and Mrs. Bright, a grand old Crescent City doyenne; Dr. Theodore Drapanas, the chief of surgery at Tulane Medical School; Mr. and Mrs. Joseph DiSpenza, Baton Rouge restaurateurs, and their two young daughters, Sandy and Tina; nineteen Norwegian sailors going home on vacation from the vessels *Fernwave* and *Nopal Tellus;* Gregory Georakis, a nineteen-year-old Greek seaman on his way back to Athens; Helen Polk Berlind, the wife of Roger Berlind, vice-chairman of the New York securities firm Cogan, Berlind, Weill and Levitt, and three of their four children, aged six through twelve; and a two-month-old infant (let him be nameless) in the arms of his mother. Although forty-four of the passengers on board were from Louisiana, it was otherwise a remarkably heterogeneous planeload: Greece, Norway, Denmark, Italy, Syria, Lebanon, Colombia, Venezuela, Argentina, and Mexico were all represented. Eight children, in all, were on the plane. Since a ticket had not been bought for the two-month-old, he was not listed in the manifest, but he breathed, his eyes gleamed, he was as alive as anyone else in the plane, and his presence brought the total number of people aboard Eastern Flight 66 to 124.

It was not good flying weather in New York. Summer had come on fast: the high temperature that day had reached a New Orleansian 93, under sooty skies. But by midafternoon, hooky-playing beachgoers began streaming home—many of them along Rockaway Boulevard, at Kennedy Airport's northeastern edge—as the wind, shifting to east by northeast, swept in thick black clouds and pelting rains. Accordingly, the Kennedy tower was now routing all incoming traffic to the eighty-four-hundred-foot-long runway 22 Left, just south of the boulevard. The tower made this decision for two reasons: First, since 22 Left runs roughly north-south, landing planes would be coming across the easterly winds (tail winds are inimical to takeoffs and landings; head winds are most desirable for both but—given the complex requirements of Kennedy's noise abatement rules and landing-takeoff flow pattern—are not always available). Second, 22 Left was—and remains today—Kennedy's most fully equipped ILS (instrument landing systems) runway, and instruments were in order in these conditions.

Conditions that were worsening by the minute. Captain W. Bellink, the pilot of a KLM Boeing 747 five planes ahead of Flight 66 in the landing queue, reported heavy thunderstorms as he guided his big aircraft down the electronic guide slope of the ILS. Then, suddenly, at three hundred feet, an eerie thing happened: The tail wind the 747 had been riding was no longer there. The plane's airspeed dropped so sharply that Captain Bellink had to gun his engines frantically to keep from plummeting to earth. And the air he had descended into was virtually solid water—the rainfall, several pilots would later say, was of African intensity, worse than anything they had ever seen. Visibility was all but nonexistent. But then, through the pounding water below, the Dutch pilot saw white lights.

The centerline approach lights of 22 Left were horizontal bars mounted on twenty rugged, 25-to-30-foot-high steel stanchions and spaced about 200 feet apart in the marshland just north and south of Rockaway Boulevard. What a pilot saw from behind and above, however, was not individual fixtures but a 14-foot-wide stripe of light leading to the center of the runway. Condenser discharge lights in the centers of the bars flashed in precisely timed sequence, giving the effect of tracer bullets shooting down the center of the stripe toward the landing surface. The Dutch captain may have breathed a sigh of half-relief: The 747 had held the glide slope; now it was time to set down. The 350-ton plane's main landing gears bumped the concrete runway, then there was a second bump as the nose gear struck. The reverse thrusters roared. The passengers—who had felt the heart-stopping free fall of the downdraft, heard the crescendo of the engines, seen the black water painting their windows—sighed and glanced at their watches. They could breathe again, think once more about love, money, appointments, coffee. It was 3:55 P.M.

The next plane in line was a Flying Tiger DC-8 cargo jet, piloted by Captain Jack Bliss. As the DC-8 descended, a vicious downdraft, even worse than the one that had seized the 747, jerked the plane out of the glide path, toward earth. Unlike Captain Bellink, Captain Bliss decided to abandon his approach. He pulled back the throttles to full—but couldn't get his plane to rise. The glide path was unreachable. Witnesses saw the jet dive out of the rain in a 20-degree bank and hit the runway first on one main gear and then the other. There are times, not often, when a pilot has to summon every flying hour of all his years of experience. Somehow Bliss was able to right his plane and land safely. It was 3:58.

But Captain Bliss couldn't bring himself to think relieved thoughts; he was angry at what he had just been through. As he turned onto a taxiway near the end of 22 Left, however, he radioed the Kennedy tower and spoke with a restraint that epitomized the cool canons of air traffic interchange. "I just highly recommend that you change the runways and, uh, land northwest," Bliss said. "You have such a tremendous wind shear down near, uh, near the ground on the final."

The local air traffic controller✦ who received Bliss's message—and who, in any case, had no authority to change runways on his own—disagreed, but with an Oriental subtlety that hewed to the cool canons. The controller, who had twenty years' experience pushing tin (controller slang for moving airplanes), was named Rudolph Arnold. "OK," Arnold told Bliss. "We're indicating wind right down the runway at fifteen knots when you landed."

Bliss's instant response violated the canons. "I don't care what you're indicating," he snapped. "I'm just telling you that there's such a wind shear on the final on that runway you should change it to the northwest."

At this time, in the middle of 1975, *wind shear* was still an aviation term of art, having not yet entered the popular vocabulary. (It was just about to.) It is a beautifully descriptive phrase that refers to a deadly phenomenon, usually caused by heavy weather precisely like the weather that had suddenly rolled in this June afternoon. It is, according to the National Weather Service,

---

✦ Local controllers, who handle final approaches, work in the Kennedy tower; approach controllers, who handle all approaches, up to final, into the three main New York airports, work in another building at Kennedy.

"a change in wind speed and/or direction in a short distance, resulting in a tearing or shearing effect. It can exist in horizontal or vertical direction, and occasionally in both." Wind shear turns an aircraft from a miraculous piece of technology held aloft by the Bernoulli effect (air currents set into rotation by the shape of the wings create a vacuum over the wings' surface, holding tons of metal and subtle electronics, as well as cargo and snack trays and lousy airline food and living human flesh, aloft) into a falling building. It was, indeed, wind shear that Captains Bellink and Bliss had encountered, yet at this point in history the phenomenon was like a microbe that had been identified but lacked a treatment protocol.

As the winds snapped and shunted that black afternoon, the doomy signs, unbeknownst to any single person, were mounting up. Besides Bellink and Bliss's near-misses, there were:

- a radio call from the weather bureau to the Kennedy tower, forecasting possible gusts as high as fifty miles an hour
- a duplication of that warning on an automatic writing machine in the tower
- a radio call to the tower from another traffic control facility across the airport, saying, "You're going to get one hell of a gust in about twenty seconds."

But this last alert came precisely as the KLM 747 was landing, and three minutes before the Flying Tiger DC-8 touched down, and as such had no precise relevance to the work at hand.

Moreover, it was the peak of the 1 P.M.–to–9 P.M. rush hour at Kennedy, and all hands in the tower had as much work as they could handle. Controller Arnold couldn't relay Captain Bliss's urgent suggestion to more influential authorities, for the simple reason that he had another plane to guide in, an Eastern jumbo L-1011, just one minute behind the cargo jet. All at once, however, Captain C. L. Nickerson, the pilot of the 1011, was requesting permission from Arnold—permission that, in this case, the controller was empowered to give—to divert to Newark International Airport.

At 4:01 P.M., as the 1011 flew on to Newark, Captain Nickerson described to the approach controller guiding him in what he had just encountered at Kennedy:

NICKERSON: We had a pretty good shear pulling us to the right and, uh, down. And visibility was nil—nil out over the marker . . . correction . . . about two hundred feet. It was nothing.

CONTROLLER: OK. The shear, you say, pulled you right and down?
NICKERSON: Yeah. We were on course and, uh, down to about two hundred and fifty feet. The air speed dropped to about ten knots below the bug. And our rate of descent was up to fifteen hundred feet a minute. So we put takeoff power on, and we went around in a hundred feet.

The bug is an indicator on a plane's airspeed gauge that a pilot sets manually to show himself, with graphic urgency, his absolute minimum safe speed—about 130 knots for landing. Having heard on his radio about the travails of the KLM and Flying Tiger pilots, Nickerson had given himself a 20-knot cushion of extra airspeed as he approached. But then, as the 1011 reached 250 feet, the wind shear caused it to plunge like a stone: Its airspeed dropped from 150 to 118 knots in two seconds. Nickerson then put on full power and, at one hundred feet above the ground, as in a Warner Brothers cartoon, was able to pull out of free fall and move on to safer skies. "A change in airspeed is not uncommon," he would say later. "But to have it stay there and not move, and not be able to move it, is something I hope never to experience again." His inertial navigation system had indicated a stream of air moving—straight down—at a speed of 60 to 80 knots.

Even so, diverting to Newark was a decision Nickerson couldn't have made lightly. Commercial aviation is, above all other things, a business; diverting, while perfectly justifiable from a safety standpoint, cost Eastern money and the 1011's passengers time.✦ No doubt there was grumbling in the cabin that afternoon; there might well have been displeasure, too, in Eastern's corporate offices, had the day turned out differently.

After the jumbo jet flew on to Newark, the pilot of the Finnair DC-8 that was next in line encountered twenty- to twenty-five-knot drops in his airspeed, but was able to put on enough extra power to land safely at 3:59 P.M. And then an eight-passenger private propeller plane (Kennedy, through its General Aviation terminal, is also a major private airport) landed on 22 Left without incident.

The Beast, it appeared, had moved on.

Aboard Eastern 66, Captain Kleven had heard the transmissions between the pilot of the diverted Eastern 1011 and the approach controller. The same

---

✦ This—the time pressure that airlines put on their pilots—is no joke. In the fatal crash of USAir Flight 405, in March 1992, several of the surviving passengers reported seeing substantial amounts of ice on the Fokker F-28's right wing before takeoff, while the copilot said he saw a clean wing. Could his vision, perhaps, have been affected by scheduling considerations? The Fokker's pilot, who was killed in the crash, had often complained to his wife about his employer's ceaseless demands to *keep things moving.*

controller now advised Kleven to change his heading to avoid the wind shear, and Kleven complied. The controller then told him that he was ten miles from touchdown, and that he was cleared to make an approach to 22 Left.

"OK," Kleven said. "We'll let you know about the conditions."

At this point the approach controller handed radar control of Eastern 66 to Rudolph Arnold, in the Kennedy tower. Captain Kleven decided that, even given his new heading and the apparent letup of the severe conditions, he should employ an extra insurance measure: he would put on nine to twenty knots of extra airspeed in landing, to counteract any downdrafts he might possibly encounter.

The Eastern 727 had spent the past ten minutes descending through the heavy overcast that lay over Kennedy. As the passengers fastened their seat belts and returned their seat backs and tray tables to the upright position in preparation for final approach, the outer fringes of the cloud layer began to trail over the aircraft's windows, and the light in the cabin changed—subtly at first, as the pure high-altitude sun dimmed; then dramatically, as the plane sank into the thick of the weather. Even though the summer solstice had just passed, and the sun wouldn't set for four and a half more hours, it was dark enough in the plane that the copilot, First Officer William Eberhart, flipped the toggle switches that turned on the cabin lights. Now the plane began to bump vigorously as it encountered the storm winds. The 116 passengers, many of whom were experienced fliers, dealt with the turbulence in various ways: Some gripped the arms of their seats and gazed straight ahead; some chatted overbrightly with their neighbors; some stared at the pages of their books and magazines; some glanced for reassurance at the calm faces of the flight attendants, who had just strapped themselves into their jump seats. The two-month-old, who had none of these means at his disposal, and for whom even his mother's face and arms and smell were of limited comfort in extreme circumstances, screeched, making things worse for those of his fellow passengers whose nerves were on edge in the first place. The bumps came harder and faster now: glass and silverware rattled in the galleys. The cockpit door, insecurely fastened, swung open, and the first-class passengers had a glimpse of the flight crew at their stations. Through the soaked windshield, the air looked black. The first-class attendant unstrapped herself momentarily and closed the door.

Roger Berlind, the vice-chairman of Cogan, Berlind, Weill and Levitt, arrived at Kennedy in plenty of time to meet his wife and three children, who had been due to arrive on Flight 66 at 3:45. He went down to the luggage carousel to wait. An Eastern employee told him the flight was delayed, took him to a private lounge, and offered him a drink. Twenty minutes later Berlind was offered another drink.

At 4:05 P.M., in the Kennedy tower, controller Arnold radioed simultaneously to Captain Kleven and to the crew of the plane directly behind Flight 66 that "the only adverse reports we had about the approach is a wind shear on short final, and no braking reports. The approach end of the runway is wet."

At the moment Captain Kleven and his crew heard this message, it must have seemed bitterly ironic: They were now smack in the middle of the self-same wind shear, their three Pratt and Whitney engines roaring impotently as the plane dropped toward the ground. Flight attendant Robert Hoefler, who was sitting in the rear of the cabin, later remembered, "Suddenly I felt the plane vibrate back and forth real fast. At first, I thought it was a bad landing. Then I realized it was more than that." "My first recollection is that the plane rolled to the left and full thrust power was applied," flight attendant Mary Mooney, who was sitting across from Hoefler, recalled later. "We lifted up, then we leveled out and hit. It felt like we were going over a rocky road."

Eight seconds after controller Arnold's radio transmission, the 727, having failed to regain the glide path, struck the third, and then a second later the fourth, of the steel approach-light towers north of Rockaway Boulevard (providentially, the street, which had been packed with cars an hour earlier, was nearly empty) slightly to the right of its intended course, creating a huge white electric arc that gave several eyewitnesses the erroneous impression that the plane had been struck by lightning. Captain Kleven struggled to pull up and was able to get his plane to rise over the fifth light tower. It was the last moment of control, the last moment the uniquely powerful commercial order of America in the late twentieth century still held. The design of a plane's interior, the protocol of commercial flying, the image of an airline, including its logo, slogans, and jingles—all seem as solid and sustaining to us as the tutelary gods seemed to the ancients. We believe. Then, in one awful second, *the jurisdiction shifts*—the control of the plane passes from the airline and tower to Eris, the goddess of Chaos. Too badly damaged to regain altitude, the 727 demolished the next four towers and the chain-link fences surrounding them, embedding one landing gear and breaking off parts of the horizontal stabilizer as it went, before it plunged to the left, flipped over, and exploded.

It was 4:06 P.M.

The force of the crash was horrific. The passengers' upper bodies snapped forward with such velocity that skulls burst, wrists and forearms shattered. A two-month-old infant, clutched however desperately before impact, became a twelve-pound projectile. Tightly fastened seat belts crushed and ripped internal organs. The seats themselves, both with and without their occupants, exploded from the plane and littered the landscape; some strapped-in passengers landed, upside down or right side up, in the foul, brackish water of Thurston Basin, a finger of Jamaica Bay that hooks between Rockaway Boulevard and runway 22 Left. And then there were the billowing, ravening flames, flames that did unspeakable damage to human flesh and tissue, inside and out: In the vicinity of the plane, in the crash's immediate aftermath, there was no air to breathe, only fire, and many of those still breathing inhaled hell.

The approach to 22 Left—the muddy ground just north and south of the boulevard, as well as the street itself—was a kind of Gethsemane, scattered grotesquely with the broken, mangled, and burned bodies of what had been the passengers of Flight 66, as well as with shards of the skin and innards of what, seconds earlier, had been the ambivalent marvel that is a modern jetliner—seats, luggage, cargo, galleys, floors, newspapers, magazines, Eastern-logo cocktail napkins, partially consumed meals. The only recognizable remnants of the 727 were a section of the underside of the fuselage that lay just short of Rockaway Boulevard, and a section of wing and rear fuselage on the south side of the street. The rear boarding stairs, which had popped out on impact, hung horribly down what had been the plane's side. The rain still poured down, and for an endless minute after the crash, all was silent—all except for the retreating thunder, the crackling of the vicious, jet-fuel-fed flames, the screams and moans of the few injured, and, in the distance, sirens.

Flight attendants Hoefler and Mooney, seated in the rear of the plane just seconds earlier, found themselves, somehow, outside and running—to where, they didn't know; just away.

It was the airport people, the crash-and-fire-rescue-trained Port Authority cops and miscellaneous employees, who sped up first. In the next few minutes, they performed the urgent tasks of putting out the fire and locating the few survivors. Wearing asbestos suits that let them approach within five yards of the terrific flames, the PA cops used fire-fighting foam to extinguish the main part of the blaze. The NYPD and the Fire Department of New York—which was not equipped with foam and would have had trouble finding a hydrant hookup in the vicinity anyway, not that water would have done any good on so much burning aviation fuel—arrived soon afterward, and Port Authority ambulances, as well as several fire trucks pressed into litter service, removed fourteen of the sixteen survivors to Jamaica Hospital. A city policeman took the other two, attendants Hoefler and Mooney, to South Shore Division Hospital of Long Island–Hillside Medical Center. Hoefler had broken ribs; Mooney, cracked vertebrae. Both were in shock; neither, however, had been burned. They were the only ones on the plane to escape the flames.

After waiting a half hour in the Eastern lounge, Roger Berlind grew impatient, and stepped out to find the main floor of the Eastern terminal overrun with policemen, rescue workers, and reporters. Television lights glared in his eyes. Berlind was told that Flight 66 had crashed, and that fourteen people had survived. He would wait five hours to learn that his wife and children were not among the fourteen.

And that it should have happened *after:* after the lunch served on the plane, after the plates and utensils and bottles were put away, the garbage bagged, the food begun to be digested; at the end of the flight, when every mind on board (except, of course, the infant's) was set on arriving—had, more or less, arrived—this was, somehow, cruelest of all.

The life of the airport had changed forever; at the same time, things went on, of necessity, just as though nothing had happened. Kennedy was reopened to traffic at 4:53 P.M. For the next several hours in the muggy, darkening air, as the jets once again flew overhead—life goes on!—Rockaway Boulevard and 22 Left were overrun by what seemed like all of humanity: more and more fire and police units, EMS crews, the Salvation Army, priests, print and television and radio reporters. The mayor. The police commissioner. Frank Borman, the flinty-eyed, strong-jawed former *Apollo* astronaut and recently appointed president of Eastern Airlines (a company that was one billion dollars in debt as his watch began), inspected the wreckage. Inside the Eastern terminal, looking grim and choosing his words carefully, Borman told reporters that it had been "a very bad crash," accompanied by "a severe fire." He declined to speculate on what had caused the accident. He went on his way. There was, after all, little he could do.

"Why is the good life which men have achieved in the twentieth century so bad that only news of world catastrophes, assassinations, plane crashes, mass murders, can divert one from the sadness of ordinary mornings?" writes Walker Percy in *The Message in the Bottle.*

Why did the young French couple driving through the countryside with their baby, having heard the news of a crash nearby of an airliner killing three hundred people and littering the forest with bits of flesh, speed frantically toward the scene, stop the car, and, carrying the baby, rush toward the dead, running through thickets to avoid police barricades? Did they have relatives on the plane?

In Queens that afternoon the amateur curious of all ages, but mostly young, arrived almost immediately after the crash. Many kids came by bicycle. The spectators had gathered on a little hill overlooking what used to be a garbage dump north of the boulevard. But the rescue made poor viewing. The cops and ambulance crews had quickly covered the corpses with white sheets. All that remained was a lot of sad shards, and a big yellow plastic tent marked MISSING PERSONS SECTION, which soon became the morgue. Many of the kids left again soon after they came, some hanging on to the ambulances that sped away, scolded by angry cops. Most of the reporters proceeded to the hospitals to try and talk to survivors. Most of Flight 66's passengers weren't doing any talking. The bodies were burned so badly that for a long time the police were able to make only three positive identifications: the pilot, John Kleven; Wendell Ladner; and Saul Horowitz. The colorful phrase used by rescue workers and reporters to refer to burn victims, living and dead, is *Crispy Critters*. The phrase has two uses: For the ones who have to undergo the horror of seeing those so burned, it alleviates stress; for the ones who have never undergone such a horror, it has the zesty, forbidden thrill of dead-baby jokes. The problem with the term is that for the victims themselves, or for those who know or knew them, it lacks both palliative capacity and humor.

And what did a two-month life mean?

The only children to survive the crash were the daughters of Joseph and Connie DiSpenza of Baton Rouge, nine-year-old Sandy and seven-year-old Tina. Joseph DiSpenza also survived; his wife did not. Joseph, Sandy, and Tina DiSpenza were all massively, unspeakably burned. This was hell visited on the undeserving, the pleasure of having a body inverted into inconceivably comprehensive pain. Tina DiSpenza would succumb to her injuries after two days.

In the marsh, all was mud, stench, and horror. The rain continued on and off; mosquitoes swarmed. Rescue workers slapped at themselves and swore. Everybody was in someone else's way. What rapidly became apparent was that *nobody was in charge*. This hadn't been planned for. Precinct captains argued with Port Authority police. Airport security men contended with city fire lieutenants. Rockaway Boulevard was choked with official and unofficial vehicles (radio news of the crash had drawn many cars; many other drivers had been forced from the beach by the storm). The accident had had the misfortune to have taken place both on and off airport property, thereby slipping between jurisdictional bounds. Some weren't above taking advantage of the confusion. In the early evening, two men, one carrying a doctor's bag and wearing a white coat and one wearing a city fireman's coat, hat, and boots, were arrested for impersonating rescue workers. Of course their motives were never discovered: they may have been ghoulish or simply practical. Disaster sites—part of whose horror lies in the sudden, gross, and profligate exposure of all that the living hold closest to the vest—are, to some, fields of opportunity. Joseph DiSpenza, who would somehow survive his injuries, would later discover that nearly $15,000 of $22,000 in cash his wife Connie had been carrying in her purse disappeared in the accident's aftermath.

Emergency, as Walker Percy noted, takes human behavior from the doldrums to the extremes. In both directions. As with any calamity, numerous incidents of altruism, even heroism, followed the crash of Flight 66. Civilians directed traffic on Rockaway Boulevard. Two city firemen, wearing heavy coats and equipment, went deep into filthy Thurston Basin to pull out Gregory Georakis, the nineteen-year-old Greek seaman, upside down and underwater, still strapped into his blown-out seat unit between two strapped-in corpses. Peculiarly enough, the very deadliness of the crash had eased the proceedings. Mass death simplifies triage. Had there been many more survivors with bad injuries, the lack of a disaster plan that transcended jurisdictions might have killed as effectively as fire and explosion.

In the end, jurisdiction assumed greater and greater importance—in the crash itself as well as the rescue. In the accident's aftermath came the predictable progression of newspaper articles, as the novelty of horror wore off, from detailed analyses to terser postmortems to the small items about lawsuits. In the end, the lawyers pick over the bones.

In 1904, a not dissimilar New York calamity riveted the national attention: On June 15 of that year, the *General Slocum,* a wooden sightseeing steamboat, burned and sank in the East River while on a picnic cruise with thirteen hundred people—mostly German-Americans from Manhattan's Lower East Side, and mostly women and children—aboard. One thousand and twenty perished, burned and drowned. The illustrated journals of the era had a field day. This sold papers! The photographs of white-shrouded corpses laid out on the East River shore are eerily similar to the photographs in *The New York Times* of June 25, 1975.

It turned out in the aftermath of the sinking that the *General Slocum*'s crew "consisted of a medley of truck-drivers, laborers, and dockmen . . . absolutely unskilled in the task of protecting the boat and its passengers from fire. . . ." That the boat's fire hose was made of flimsy two-thread linen, with no rubber lining. That the crew had no idea how to launch the lifeboats, and that the life rafts were wired to the deck. As were the life preservers, which in any case were filled with dried-out granulated cork whose buoyant properties were nil. In the December 1904 issue of *Munsey's Magazine,* Herbert N. Casson wrote of the *Slocum* disaster, "One thousand and twenty human lives destroyed by greed and criminal negligence, and yet no one has been made to suffer, no one will be made to suffer, the penalty for this unspeakable crime!"

No such thumping outrage was possible seventy-one years later. For one thing, the regulatory and litigative mechanics of society had become far more intricate. Culpability could be sliced a hundred ways to Sunday. With the death of the one hundred and twelfth victim, on June 30, Flight 66 became the worst single-plane disaster in the history of American aviation. And finally, the issue that volleyed back and forth, like an Alexander Pope shuttlecock, was the question of blame. Who was at fault? Should Captain Kleven have refused, as was his right, to land on runway 22 Left? Should the FAA—which administers the Kennedy tower—have changed runways? Should the Port Authority—which alone had the authority to close the airport—have done so? In an editorial on June 26, the *Times* wrote:

> Even at this early stage, one question emerges insistently: Why was Kennedy Airport open to receive planes under the extremely bad weather conditions in New York City last Tuesday afternoon? ... In the adverse environment with which the pilot of the doomed 727 had to contend as he sought to land, many things could have gone wrong; and that fact was predictable in advance. It is easy to comprehend the psychological pressure on the pilot to try to land—after all, the airport was open and to refuse to land might be taken as confession of weakness or incompetence—but such pressures could hardly have applied to the officials who had the responsibility to close the airport when advisable.
>
> *The suspicion must arise that the phenomenal safety record of the commercial airlines operating in this country may be tending to create an aura of complacency, an atmosphere in which more gambles may be taken than the passengers would be willing to accept if they were aware of them.*

The italics are mine. For these were fighting words. "Complacency," "gambles." The *Times* was not blaming Eastern Airlines—not directly. No, it was those "officials." In much the same way, seventy-one years earlier, Herbert N. Casson had leveled his finger at the United States Inspection Service, which had approved the *General Slocum*'s life preservers and fire hose: "a helpless and perfunctory bureau, shackled by red tape and serving mainly as a refuge for aged office-holders."

The so-named officials, at the FAA and the Port Authority, were not about to take this lying down. The first thing they did was get into a fight with each other. The FAA claimed that the sole responsibility for shutting down an airport belonged to the operator—in this case, the Port. The PA, feeling that in essence it was being blamed for the crash, objected vigorously.

But this would never do. How could the airport, whose efficient operation rested on a delicate interdependency between the airlines, the FAA, and the Port Authority, get anything done if two of the three factions were warring camps? Accordingly, the two sides decided to shake hands and go on the defensive together.

On July 3, the two bodies issued a joint statement, a "clarification." "Any decision of an airport operator to halt flying at a field," it said, "would be dictated not by flight conditions in the air but only if something developed on the ground that affected the usability of runways." The two possibilities mentioned were a severe snowstorm or a crash such as the crash of Flight 66.

A crash, in other words, could close an airport.

But who was responsible for preventing the crash?

The clarification was followed by a July 7 letter to the *Times* from James L. Bispo, acting director, FAA Eastern Region, and Caesar B. Pattarini, director of aviation, Port Authority of New York and New Jersey. The letter decried

> the unfortunate implication that the issue of the airport being open or closed was paramount. This has been compounded by news reports questioning who has the responsibility for closing the airport in bad weather.
>
> This not only is incorrect but also conveys the thought that there is divided or uncertain responsibility on matters relating to the operation of aircraft. The Federal Aviation Administration has sole and complete authority for controlling air traffic, and it is under F.A.A. rules that pilots are granted final authority for the operation of aircraft. In adverse weather, a pilot makes his judgment on whether to land or to divert to another airport on the basis of information provided by the F.A.A. The facts that go into making such a decision are available only to the pilot, and the constantly changing conditions result in differing judgments by pilots as to continue an approach or divert. The times that an airport

operator on his own closes an airport are not related to conditions in the air. They are connected to ground conditions affecting the availability of runways, and such decisions are reached only after consulting with the F.A.A. and the airlines. Kennedy was, in fact, closed for nearly an hour after the accident to facilitate rescue operations. Another occasion when an airport may be closed by its management is for severe surface snow conditions.

The crash had tragic enough consequences without increasing the fears of the public through misinformation. The Port Authority and the F.A.A. are interested in maintaining the highest levels of safety at our airports.

Arm in arm, shoulder to shoulder—*shuck that blame.* In short—nobody was responsible. One could hardly be blamed for preferring the solid-brass Edwardian certitudes of *Munsey's Magazine,* the vaulting ad hominems against "the reckless, irresponsible director, who takes the rewards of his office without performing its duties, and the slipshod, negligent public official, whose aim in life is to get the highest possible salary for the least possible exertion. . . ." Against "Captain Van Schaick, the Charon of the East River"! There were no villains in public life in the late twentieth century: not Frank Borman; certainly not John W. Kleven. There were no Charons. People had forgotten who Charon was. Now there was only Business.

On October 15, Eastern Airlines filed a third-party action in Brooklyn federal court saying, according to the *Times,* "that any damages resulting from the crash had been caused by the carelessness and negligence of Federal employees who . . . failed to provide 'adequate and proper' air-traffic-control services and to give proper weather information pertaining to the flight." If Eastern was found to have been in any way negligent, the court papers asserted, this negligence would be secondary to that of the federal government. Thus any claims against the airline should be transferable in whole or in part to the government.

In the end, no one was responsible. Perhaps fault wasn't even the question. Maybe the only fault was the passengers', for having been born too soon. They died of insufficient modernity. Time has become so dense in our era that the whole idea of modernity, once a kind of glowing (or threatening) abstraction, has become diffused beyond recognition. Nineteen seventy-five would seem, in myriad ways, to be part of our era: The year still has the ring, at this quickly fleeting point at least, of contemporaneity. We still fly 727s. And yet if you could be magically transported for a few moments to the cabin of Flight 66 (a stranger to all aboard, but similar enough to them that no one would blink) just before it began its descent into the clouds that afternoon, while the clear sun still filled the cabin—if you could see plain the smiling, animated, still-alive faces of those doomed passengers (the force of the word doomed lying in the fact that you and I, too, are quite equally doomed, but that we know all the details of their doom, and they, poor fools, know nothing), you would feel, in the hairstyles and the clothing (polyester was in its heyday then, the most flammable of all fabrics), a palpable, almost racial variance from yourself. "The past is a foreign country," the British novelist L. P. Hartley wrote. "They do things differently there." The recent past, at the end of the twentieth century, is notable for its simultaneous difference and sameness. The 113 people killed by the crash that day at Kennedy Airport would never see or use a personal computer. A VCR. A home video camera. A compact disc player. No one on board wore a Walkman, because the Walkman hadn't been invented. No one had heard of AIDS. Or crack cocaine. In 1975, General Motors was just beginning to market the kind of rear-facing, molded-plastic infant car (and plane) seat that might have saved the life of the two-month-old—but the product hadn't yet caught on. And wind shear detectors, for cockpits as well as airfields, were in the works, but none was yet in use. The situation would shortly be remedied. It was too late, however, for the 113 dead of Flight 66, whose souls would lie unquiet in the northeast corner of the greatest airport in the world.

6

DIA

The People Mover!

"**I** got home at five o'clock the next morning," Ed O'Sullivan tells me, "and the phone rang, and it was the *National Enquirer.* And they wanted to know if it was true that the Port Authority police had smothered a hundred people to death with the foam they used to put out the fire."

❏

A while afterward I receive another shiny brochure, a progress report on the construction of the brand-new Denver International Airport, due to be completed in March 1994. Sad to report, it looks virtually as though someone had studied JFK as a negative example. The new DIA, which is being built on a virgin site (*seven times* the size of Kennedy's), and which will completely replace Denver's present hub, Stapleton (which has a notably poor safety record), truly looks (and, as we have found, we must take shiny brochures with a *little* bit of salt) to be some kind of super-mega-state-of-the-art airport:

> Denver International will have a four-quadrant runway design [the brochure reads]. This design will mean millions of dollars annually in aircraft delay savings to the airlines.
>
> More than 100 airfield configurations were considered. Planners received a great deal of direction from the FAA, airport management, the airlines, Airline Pilots Association (ALPA) and others before an airfield design was chosen. Only then was the terminal and the rest of the airport designed. . . .
>
> Denver International will have six full service runways organized into four quadrants, with simultaneous departures possible in two quadrants and simultaneous arrivals possible in the other two quadrants. . . .

71

The current airfield at Stapleton International Airport does not allow for simultaneous landings during instrument flight rule conditions [this is also true of JFK]. This has resulted in serious back-up and congestion problems throughout the national air transportation system. Denver International Airport has been designed to provide *three* [italics mine] simultaneous streams of arriving aircraft during instrument flight rules conditions. . . .

The advanced four-quadrant runway design, which prevents delays, was one technology developed with early FAA/airport cooperation. With this design, aircraft will not be required to cross another runway while taking off or taxiing directly to concourse gates [this was the cause of the USAir-SkyWest commuter crash on the ground at LAX in February 1991].

A new runway/taxiway surface control system at the airport that employs innovative lighting to guide pilots from runways to gates in limited visibility conditions is expected to be a model for the rest of the country. . . .

One could weep. And it gets worse. Much worse. There is a central terminal building of unparalleled magnificence, with a glorious multipeaked roof of translucent fiberglass fabric. The terminal's exterior communicates, rather than institutional oppressiveness, the windy elegance of a yacht race on a sparkling day, perhaps, or the tents of fabulous Samarkand. And how the cathedral builders of the Gothic era would have swooned at the daylit luminosity of the interior, which was everything they were trying for with their vaults and clerestories of sculptured stone! Not to mention

two major restaurants, 70,000 square feet of retail space, a children's play area, a chapel, office facilities, airport security . . . Once in the terminal, departing passengers can follow one of the pathways to security for clearance before taking an escalator down to the Automated Guideway Transit System (AGTS) station, which will take them to their chosen airside concourse.

The people mover! The final insult. DIA will have it, as Kennedy, as it were, bites its lip. The builders of the new airport have also included in their plans maximum concern for

1) the care of archaeological finds on the site
2) noise reduction

3) air and water quality

4) wetlands preservation

And—here is the real thumb in New York's eye—*all this appears to have been smoothly financed,* in the midst of a recession. Airport revenue bonds, federal grants, and revenues from Denver's existing airport system, the brochure says, have all kicked in to the total cost of $2.66 billion. AIRPORT PROJECT BELOW BUDGET, AHEAD OF SCHEDULE, reads one headline toward the pamphlet's end.✦

One could weep. What went wrong at Kennedy? There are crashes, and there are crashes.

✦ We must take shiny brochures with a *few* grains of salt. At the beginning of March 1994, due to lingering problems with DIA's $200-million baggage system, which has experienced power surges that engineers haven't been able to trace, the opening of the now $3.2-billion airport (its cost has been reported elsewhere as $4 billion) was postponed from March 9 to May 15, at a cost of $100 million, said cost to be borne by the new airport's tenants—primarily Continental and United. As a result, Continental may move out of the airport altogether, and United will certainly raise fares to offset its cash loss.

The root of the word *utopia* means "no place." Airport utopia, it would seem, is just that.

7

A Bright Burst in Dark Air

"Everybody would laugh—it really
wasn't gonna happen.
It happened. It happened quick."

Great businesses are like behemoths. Giant, complex organisms of neutral (or, sometimes, negative) moral value and limited life-span, they are begotten in heedless heat, they grow, they lumber forward a few paces, shaking the earth, and they come crashing down. The crash is remembered a little longer than the echoing footsteps. Pan American World Airways was such a business, the greatest airline the world has ever known, a seemingly immortal institution—until the day (Wednesday, December 21, 1988) when one of its thirty-eight 747s, registration number N739-PA, Clipper *Maid of the Seas,* lay in pieces, along with the remains of its 259 passengers, all over the dank earth near the small Scottish town of Lockerbie. The twenty-million-dollar plane had been blown to bits by ten to fourteen ounces of Czech-manufactured Semtex C-4 plastic explosive hidden in a bronze-colored Samsonite suitcase smuggled aboard from a Malta-to-Frankfurt flight while the 747 sat on the ramp at Frankfurt International Airport. The bomb was probably planted by Libyan intelligence operatives, most likely in retaliation for the 1986 bombing of Tripoli by U.S. warplanes, or for the accidental 1988 downing of an Iranian airliner over the Persian Gulf by the U.S.S. *Vincennes,* or both.

The triggering device was barometer controlled, and the low-altitude flight from Frankfurt to London was placid and—given the time of year—probably festive. At 7:03 P.M., thirty-eight minutes after Flight 103 to John F. Kennedy International Airport left Heathrow, Clipper *Maid of the Seas* climbed to thirty-five thousand feet—cruising altitude for the transatlantic leg—and exploded, a bright burst and awful noise in the dark air. One hopes all 259 souls aboard, students and pilots and flight attendants and soldiers and diplomats and business people in their outer lineaments, each containing a universe, perished instantly. One suspects not.

And that was the end of Pan Am. Plain and gruesomely simple. If advertising and public relations are the air in the soufflé of an airline's "image"— and the necessary underpinning for the kabuki of commercial air travel —commercial airplane crashes are the very worst public relations conceivable. Every crash deflates the fantasy—often a viable, solid-seeming fantasy—that commercial air travel is glamorous and fun and safe as socks. Crashes crack the composure of fearful and fearless fliers alike, delivering the final, irrefutable, truth: Metal is heavier than air.✦

Small wonder that one of an airline's first priorities, in the minutes and hours after a crash, is to paint out its logos on the hulk. News photographers arrive at crash sites with the same alacrity as rescue workers. One of Pan Am's worst pieces of luck after Lockerbie was the survival of a big piece of the nose of N739-PA, complete with the jaunty Pan Am–blue "Clipper *Maid of the Seas*" inscription. It was everything the terrorists—who, by striking at Pan Am, were attacking the corporation that was the quintessential symbol of America around the world—could have wanted. The relentless worldwide circulation of this image in the aftermath of Lockerbie delivered the insistent message: *Fly Pan Am and die.*

Pan Am's death, too, lacked the grace of instantaneity. The final moment came three Decembers later, when a hoped-for merger with Delta Air Lines fell through, and the world's greatest airline—and Kennedy Airport's biggest rent payer—simply locked its doors. If Pan Am's end was inglorious, so was its beginning, although the end was merely dead and squalid, while the beginning was imbued with the raffishness so dear to the spirit of American business.

Some men jumped from ledges after the stock market crash of 1929; Juan Terry Trippe—on whom the epithet *ruthless* has been hung by so many people that one almost suspects he coined it himself—leaped to prominence. Trippe, an old-line Wasp, was named in honor of the Venezuelan wife of his great-uncle: "His mother's ancestors," a biographical entry reads, unblushingly (and with leaden foreshadowing), "had taken part in the colonialization of South America." As a rich boy, Trippe built rubber-band-powered air-

---

✦ Much heavier. A fully loaded 747 weighs in the neighborhood of 800,000 pounds, an astounding 340,000 pounds of which is terrifyingly flammable aviation fuel.

planes and flew them in Central Park. After graduating from Yale, he became a bond salesman, with the intention of joining the family brokerage business. A banal enough story. But Trippe had immortal longings in him.

In 1923, at the age of twenty-four, he and a few friends bought seven surplus navy seaplanes for five hundred dollars each and started Long Island Airways, at Rockaway Beach, just across Jamaica Bay from the tract that would one day become Kennedy Airport. These were the sun-and-sand days of Long Island, and Trippe and his friends were young men. Long Island Airways was a fun outfit, dedicated mostly to sight-seeing hops and the odd motion-picture job. Imagine the heady olfactory cocktail of salt air and gasoline; the important sputter of prop engines in the clean, empty sky; waving reeds; cloche hats and grinning eyes.

The next year, Trippe buckled down. As other young men—Frank Lorenzo among them—would later do, he prestidigitated the air and spit of associations and ambition into a fully capitalized airline, convincing some Boston bankers to underwrite the Colonial Air Transport Company, which—Trippe family and Old Blue connections in Washington helping to grease the wheels—received the first U.S. airmail contract ever awarded, for a New York to Boston route. When Managing Director Trippe proposed expanding Colonial's route to Miami and Havana, his stodgy stockholders voted him down, but Trippe didn't miss a beat: he simply quit and opened a new airline.

One of Juan Trippe's greatest skills was a genius for useful friendships. The friends in this case were named Whitney (Cornelius Vanderbilt) and Hambleton (John T.). The new airline consisted of a single Fokker F-7 three-engine monoplane, yet a compliant Washington again awarded Trippe an important airmail contract: the first international route ever, between—hey, presto!—Key West and Havana. In 1928, Trippe-Whitney-Hambleton bought out a group of cash-poor military officers who ran a rival firm called Pan American Airways, Inc., and became Pan American Airways Corporation, with Whitney as chairman and Trippe as president and general manager.

In October 1929, New York City's first international passenger airline, the New York Rio and Buenos Aires Line, was only a year old, but it had made a glorious start. Its fleet of thirty-four aircraft—consisting of fourteen Commodores (converted Navy flying boats, the biggest and most luxurious passenger planes in the world), nine Sikorsky S-38 Flying Boats, six Consolidated Fleetsters, four Ford Tri-motors, and one Lockheed Air Express (the transcontinental speed-record holder, at a blazing 180 m.p.h.)—made up the largest commercial armada in existence. Then came the stock market crash. As NYRBA wobbled in the aftermath, Juan Trippe pounced. Once again he took advantage of his Washington friendships—chiefly with President Herbert Hoover and Postmaster General Walter Brown—to force a merger between Pan American and NYRBA. Trippe wanted NYRBA's planes, its pilots, and its South American routes, and he got them, he got them all, in one of the great tail-wagging-the-dog mergers of business history.

And Trippe had recolonialized South America.

Conquerors tend not to be sensitive by nature. A photograph of Trippe in his prime shows a head worthy of a Roman emperor: a cold-eyed, thin-lipped face, with a broad, ambitious nose and a Caesarean fringe of hair over the wide forehead. He spent the thirties opening up the world for commercial aviation—his own brand of commercial aviation. Operating out of the world's greatest marine-air terminal, in Dinner Key, near Miami, and with the aid of Colonel Charles Lindbergh, Pan Am explored possible routes over the Atlantic and over the Pole to Asia, and established bases on Pacific islands. World War II was a bonanza for Trippe: His well-established network of operations in South America and across the Pacific made Pan Am the natural contract carrier for the government.

In 1943, Trippe gave a speech before the National Institute of Social Sciences, a speech that would have visionary impact: Air transport, he said, "had a very clear choice—of becoming a luxury service to carry the well-to-do at high prices—or to carry the average man at what he can afford to pay."

It was Trippe's genius to choose both. In 1948—the year New York International Airport opened at Idlewild—he wrote a *Reader's Digest* article, called "Now You Can Take That Trip Abroad," that helped stoke America's giddy postwar enthusiasm for air travel. Not long afterward, Pan Am—now Pan American World Airways—instituted two-class service. In 1954, the company inaugurated the practice of selling round-the-world trips and other overseas flights on the installment plan. In 1958, Pan Am was the first airline to fly jets. By 1960, thirty years after Juan Trippe founded the company—through brilliant marketing, relentless cultivation of Washington power, and iron-fisted control of his company—he had turned Pan Am into the greatest airline, and one of the greatest corporations, in the world. In a government-regulated industry that limited competition between American carriers to the barest minimum, Pan Am enjoyed a virtual monopoly in its worldwide market. Around the planet, the company's globe logo was second only in recognizability to Coca-Cola's. By 1968, the year the sixty-nine-year-old Trippe retired as chairman and CEO, Pan Am's network was eighty thousand air miles, connecting the United States with eighty-five other countries. Its name and corporate symbol, on its building, towered high over Park Avenue, the preeminent commercial emblem in the greatest city of the most powerful country in the world.✦ Its Worldport at JFK International was America's prime terminus for travel into and out of the country.

And Pan Am had reached these heights not simply through aggressive marketing or brilliant business planning, but through superlative service. Many an airline has foundered through the simple blunder of taking its employees for granted—or worse, treating them as adversaries. Bad morale translates into lackluster service, which translates quickly into reduced revenue. At Pan Am, flight attendants were culled from thousands of applicants. Pilots had to take batteries of intelligence and psychological exams; they had to learn foreign languages. The company also paid better than the other airlines. "Our blood runs blue" was a company slogan, and it wasn't just a slogan. Corporate pride was fierce and monolithic.

"In 1969," reads a caption in Geoffrey Arend's picture history of Kennedy Airport, "Pan American World Airways again led the airline industry into another age of dramatic new equipment, placing an order with Boeing for 25 747's valued at $550 million." A year later, in January 1970, Pan Am took delivery of its first 747. Behind the Worldport, standing next to First Lady Pat Nixon, Juan Trippe's successor, Najeeb Halaby (father of Lisa Halaby, a.k.a. Queen Noor of Jordan) presided over the dedication, which was done in a new and interesting way. Instead of swinging the traditional bottle of Champagne, with the risk of messy froth and dangerous flying shards (or an embarrassing spectacle should the bottle refuse to smash), Pat Nixon pulled a handle on a Pan Am–logoed podium, triggering a neat, photogenic spray of some Champagne-like substance from an unseen source in the podium onto the nose of the plane.

An unbreaking bottle would have been a bad enough omen, but this sterile and mechanical apparatus—likely constructed at no small cost—carried its own bad symbolism. Pan Am had gone deep into debt to buy those twenty-five 747s, a move that displeased employees and stockholders alike. Every corporate giant carries debt, of course; the burden motivates some and staggers others. The age of dramatic new equipment was also an age of dramatic new decline for Pan American World Airways.

No matter what Juan Trippe had been, he had given his company a stamp and a sense of mission. After his departure, the air went out of his company. The seventies were especially unkind. Recession, inflation, and the Arab oil embargo hit all airlines hard, but Pan Am was in especially bad shape. In the fifties, the nation's seventeen domestic carriers had pooled their influence and

---

✦ Trippe originally wanted the company's name on the building in letters thirty feet high. He was talked down to fifteen.

convinced Congress to prohibit Pan American from flying within the United States. This wasn't such a big deal when the domestic carriers were flying only domestically and Pan Am owned the rest of the world. But once TWA et al. began to operate overseas, the game changed completely: Now anybody flying, say, from Paris to St. Louis (or vice versa) could take TWA the whole way, as opposed to flying Pan Am and changing carriers. Nobody likes to change airlines in midtrip—especially at Kennedy Airport, whose design has always punished such effrontery.

Pan Am also had to cope with the growing impact of the loss of three crucial routes: New York–Mexico City, Miami-London, and Dallas-Paris. Company loyalists claim that the Civil Aeronautics Board recommended Pan Am for all three routes, but that in each instance, the airline was beat out by nefarious intercession.

In the first case, then Eastern Airlines chairman Eddie Rickenbacker, who is said to have badly wanted the New York–Mexico City route, is said to have sent Thomas E. Dewey to the Eisenhower White House with a satchel containing $120,000 in cash—said to have been gratefully received for the Republican war chest. Eastern got New York–Mexico City. National Airlines is accused of having run the same gambit, with $200,000 for Nixon, to corral Miami-London, a route for which—Pan Am loyalists claim—it lacked both the equipment and expertise. And at the beginning of the Jimmy Carter administration, Pan American was aced out for Dallas-Paris by Delta, whose corporate headquarters—get it?—just happens to be in Atlanta, the capital of Carter's home state.

Were Juan Trippe's enemies finally getting their revenge? Whether or not the conspiracy scenarios are true, they seem—by the tough-guy gauge of corporate wheeling and dealing—a little whiny. Money and Washington influence had never hurt Juan Trippe one bit. Now that he was out of the picture, or his well-placed friends were no longer ascendant, or (just possibly) now that his enemies had gained the upper hand, the worm had turned. So what? Companies, even great ones, must evolve or die. Pan Am had lost its way.

In 1976, the company stripped down its Miami base, its flagship facility since the great Dinner Key days, to a line station, moving all maintenance operations to JFK. Then, in November 1978, Congress deregulated the airline industry, and what had been a staid, old-boy-dominated marketplace turned overnight into a Turkish bazaar. Suddenly any carrier could fly anywhere, Pan Am included. But Pan Am, which had no domestic network, *couldn't* fly anywhere. In a desperate move to catch up, the company began bidding for the primarily domestic, financially troubled National, against infamous upstart Frank Lorenzo (then at Texas Air) and Eastern. By the time the smoke had cleared, in January 1980, Pan Am had "won"—to the vastly inflated tune of almost a billion dollars.

The just post-deregulation eighties were a wild time for the airlines. One hundred fifty new carriers sprouted up, and 118 of them folded. Pan Am— saddled with huge debt, aging aircraft, and a new domestic system that it seemed to have no idea how to run—hemorrhaged money steadily throughout the decade.

Fortunately, Juan Trippe—who died in 1981—didn't have to witness the final result.

Thomas G. Plaskett became the sixth chairman of Pan Am in January 1988 and briefly braked the free fall. Under Plaskett, the company sold off real-estate assets, put the profits into refurbishing planes, and told the flying public about it. Pan Am stepped up consumer marketing to new heights. Then—eleven months later, to the day—came the worst marketing news in its history.

Lockerbie was a devastation, not only in terms of the loss of the aircraft and crew, and the lawsuits by the families of the passengers—unlimited once it was ascertained that Pan Am security in Frankfurt could not be cleared of having allowed the bomb aboard, and ultimately to rise to seven billion dollars—but also in the utter drying up of Pan Am's business. *Chilling effect* doesn't begin to describe the business aftermath of a terrorist bombing. The traveling public at large tends to be more forgetful and forgiving than the more sophisticated corporate-travel community, which vets every nickel spent and controls the most lucrative market: business and first classes. Dead executives cost money. In a single day, Big Blue-and-White lost its business business.

On January 18, 1990, Pan Am ran a full-page ad in Section A of *The New York Times*. It was entitled "Pan Am 1990 Progress Report No. 1," and under the headline

OUR ONE AND ONLY GOAL IS TO REBUILD
ONE OF AMERICA'S GREAT RESOURCES.
I'M PLEASED TO REPORT WE ARE RIGHT ON SCHEDULE.

it read:

On January 21, 1988, this management team took on the challenge of renewing Pan Am.

An airline monumental in its contributions. Vital in its importance. Historic in its significance.

For it was Pan Am, single-handedly and against enormous odds, that opened America, and the world, to international air travel.

Over sixty years ago, hacking airports out of the jungles of South America . . . building landing strips and refueling bases across the Pacific to the Far East . . . conquering weather and distance to cross the Atlantic to Europe, and on to the Near East and Africa.

Along the way developing weather forecasting and navigational systems that set standards for the entire industry.

Setting service standards by providing the first flight attendants, the first meals, the first First Class, the first movies, the first music.

And from the very beginning, assisting in the design and introduction of virtually every new aircraft from the early Sikorsky single engine flying boat to the world's first jumbo jet. The remarkable Boeing 747.

The aircraft that helped Pan Am open yet another world of air travel. The world of affordable air travel.

THEN CAME THE '70S.

Deregulation, increased competition, soaring fuel prices, recession and double digit inflation all hit at once.

Some airlines, because of the nature of their routes and competition, were hurt more than others. Pan Am was one of them.

And as often happens with companies reacting to financial adversity, Pan Am made mistakes in its turnaround efforts.

Unfortunately, it made *the* basic mistake.

Pan Am became so involved with its corporate problems that it lost sight of its customers' needs.

A RETURN TO BASICS.

Our first act as Pan Am's new management was to put into effect a plan for renewal, all revolving around our customers:

1. Invest the money required to return Pan Am to the service standards that once led the industry.

2. Rebuild employee commitment so that once again Pan Am people feel and act like the special people they are.

3. Provide financial resources by selling assets not fundamental to the operation of a strong airline.

To date, over $220,000,000 has been committed to this program, and the results are more than encouraging. They are measurable.

And in spite of some setbacks in 1989, we are on course . . . our customers' course.

A RETURN OF PASSENGERS.

We are now seeing record passenger growth system-wide.

In the hard-to-please First Class area, we're now carrying more passengers across the Atlantic than any other airline.

In Clipper Class, with service that is actually better than First Class on some airlines, we've shown consistent system-wide gains.

We now have one of the youngest fleets across the Atlantic, were first with the A310 Airbus, and operate the largest fleet of these big, roomy, technologically advanced aircraft.

In all, we continue to fly to more European cities than all other U.S. airlines combined.

We are the only U.S. airline serving the Soviet Union and the only U.S. carrier that serves every emerging country in Eastern Europe.

Our flights out of Miami are up 48% over 1989—now serving 68 international destinations and 27 domestic cities—from one of the fastest-growing areas of world travel.

The response to our quality of service on the Pan Am Shuttle has been so overwhelming that we now carry over 50% of the Boston–New York–Washington market.

Domestically, we now serve 43 U.S. cities, with a 13% gain in capacity, 1989 over 1988.

Internationally, Pan Am continues to be the number one U.S. airline to the world—flying to 85 cities in 53 countries on 4 continents.

SECURITY IN AN INSECURE WORLD.

The need for sophisticated aviation security is now being felt by travelers everywhere. On all airlines.

We'd like to emphasize that Pan Am security measures exceed the requirements of the Federal Aviation Administration and are among the highest of all U.S. airlines.

Pan Am today is not only continuing, but strengthening its historical leadership role.

We have now so enhanced our security systems, equipment, personnel and procedures that we more than ever exceed the security standards of foreign airlines.

Nothing is, or ever has been, as important to us as the safety and security of our customers—and of our own Pan Am people who serve them.

OPTIMISM OF A HIGH ORDER.

Pan Am is once again becoming the kind of airline that will deservedly attract more than its share of travelers.

Further, it is an airline in position to benefit from the tremendous growth that is coming in world air travel.

And while we have debt, it is the lowest long-term obligation of any major carrier.

We are most definitely beginning to see light at the end of the tunnel.

And we cordially invite you to discover, or rediscover, the Pan Am that is Pan Am again.

[signed]
Thomas G. Plaskett
Chairman and Chief Executive Officer
Pan American World Airways, Inc.

Well. *Hacking airports out of the jungles . . .* This was strong stuff. And not necessarily good stuff. It is all too predictable to note immediately that the light at the end of the tunnel—could the copywriter have borrowed a less felicitous cliché?—was in fact a headlight. Pan Am declared bankruptcy on January 8, 1991, almost exactly a year after the morning this ad appeared, then operated under Chapter 11 for eleven months before closing up shop for good. But—setting Schadenfreude aside for the moment—a moment of constructive deconstruction may not be out of order. What does this ad *mean?*

Whom was it aimed at, for one thing? Clearly not the average airline passenger—whoever, precisely, that might have been at the beginning of 1990. But take someone with, conceivably, limited funds and a pressing urge to visit Aunt Bertha in Kenosha—someone with a demographic not dissimilar to that group of first-time, discount fliers airline personnel have lately dubbed "The Clampetts." Would *that* flier have cared about Pan Am's glorious history of hacking airports out of the jungle? Clearly not.

No, given the ad's placement (not only in the *Times,* but in *Section A* of the *Times*), its language, and its important wordiness, it was obviously aimed at the movers and shakers who would be riding to work on commuter trains and in limos that morning, peering at the neatly folded paper over half-glasses and thinking, *Pan Am . . . hmm. Aren't they dead yet?* This was not so much an ad as an advertorial, a corporate *cri de coeur. We exist! We're important!! Help!!!*

The first and most salient point was that nobody except amnesiacs had forgotten Lockerbie—the advertisement's great untouched fact—for a second. And not only was the fact untouched, it was untouchable. It was an atrocity, a black hole. But it had to be . . . *acknowledged,* somehow. Somehow. Yet it couldn't be, quite. No, this ad was damage control of the first water. And damage control is, by definition, always a losing battle.

Some setbacks in 1989 . . . in fact, Pan Am had lost over *a million dollars a day* in 1989. And the rate was climbing steadily. In fact, it could be argued that as of January 18, 1990, the day of the ad, Pan American World Airways, Inc., was, among fellow corporations and consumers alike, a dead duck. It could be argued that what was for sale in the *Times* ad was not airline tickets, but—at distressed rates—an airline.

❐

It was four months after the ad, and seventeen months after Lockerbie, in the still almost funereal climate that followed the bombing, when I visited the Pan Am maintenance facility, including the famed Hangar 19, at Kennedy. The company was in a holding pattern then: there was hope that a merger partner could be found. But—to extend the metaphor—the ears of Pan Am's twenty-two thousand employees were popping. They had been making financial concessions for a decade, giving back raises, vacation days, and pension benefits, and the pressure was growing. The airline was coming down, fast.

Yet what I chiefly remember of that day is the *magnitude* of Pan Am's presence at the airport. It had, after all, been there since the beginning, and for forty years had been a mainstay of the facility: That doesn't go away till it goes away. The airline's hangars, offices, and maintenance buildings occupied a good chunk of real estate on Kennedy's western flank, more physical and psychic territory than that of any other tenant. The airport's other long-standing mainstay, TWA, also in grave fiscal peril, had its corporate headquarters and center of gravity at St. Louis's Lambert Field. The hearts of United, American, and Delta were elsewhere, too. But in a key way, Kennedy *was* Pan Am. You saw the buildings on your right as soon as you drove into the airport; you saw the big white-and-blue planes; whether you knew anything about it or not, you felt keenly the vast scope of Juan Trippe's vision.

I parked in the big employee lot of Building 208, the Pan Am jet center, and was processed in at the front door by security. The jet center was a gigantic, gloomy, fifties-modern building, with a sense of faded Ayn Rand–style corporate importance. The gloom was all the gloomier under the present circumstances, and security, which would have been thorough in the best of times at a jet repair facility, was meticulous. A guard escorted me through the engine repair building. It resembled a Brobdingnagian machine shop: I saw turbine engines in their pods, in various states of disassembly, on gigantic mounts; I saw tool and parts cost lists on the tiled wall. An item called a chamberscope, I noticed, went for $7,700; turbine blades—of which, I later found out, there are forty-three in the first-stage fan in the front of a Pratt and Whitney 747 engine—cost *$4,300* each. I was taken to meet the man I was supposed to meet, the managing director of engineering and quality control, a big, hearty fellow with an office whose window, two stories up, looked out over the entire jet-center floor.

The managing director said nothing of the airline's troubles: This wasn't the point of my visit. Business, like our lives themselves, consists importantly of busy-ness, the small strokes counting for as much as the large. Servicing aircraft and their engines, in a fleet consisting—as Pan Am's did at the time—of 160 planes, was an around-the-clock operation. Every airplane, the managing director explained, had to be serviced every time it landed: After every four to six hours in the air, a plane must be visually inspected, its logbook read for quirks, the oils checked. Then, the managing director said, in the case of the biggest and most complex plane, a 747 . . .

And my mind went directly to Clipper *Maid of the Seas,* the plane that never came home. And everything I heard and saw for the rest of my visit, I heard and saw in this context.

A 747, the managing director told me, was a machine so complicated that there was literally no one person who knew every piece of the plane. This apparently simple datum stopped me in my tracks; it seemed utterly emblematic of the modern world. The pyramids and the Gothic cathedrals of Europe had their drones and they had their master architects, men who knew every piece of the puzzle. Modern times have complexified out of all comprehensibility. Every one of us is, to a greater or lesser extent (no matter how much we protest our importance), a drone. A 747 went down in Scotland, and no one could begin to understand all the implications.

Every 250 flying hours (about once a month; these planes were in use more than 8 hours a day, every day) the director said, a 747 had to undergo a so-called A-check. The A-check was not unlike taking your car to the local service station. A mechanic walked around the plane, looked in the front and back of each engine, making sure, basically, that nothing was bent or perforated. The plane's nitrogen-filled tires (in case of accident, nitrogen is less flammable than air), engine oil, and hydraulic fluid were also inspected. In the B-check, done every 1,000 hours, two engines were examined thoroughly and two lightly; the procedure was reversed in the next B-check. The same alternating heavy/light inspection procedure applied to the wings, the two sides of the fuselage, and the tail, which would be looked at cursorily in one B-check and closely in the next.

In the C-check, done every 4,000 hours—approximately every fourteen months—both wings and their ailerons, as well as all four engines and their pylons, were opened up and combed for problems, and ultrasonic and X-ray pictures were taken of those areas where the sun didn't shine. And then, every three to four years (18,000 hours), a 747 underwent a D-check, in which it was completely overhauled—virtually rebuilt. While the plane sat in the "Erector set"—a great array of scaffolding in Bay 4 of Hangar 19—every part of it that could be opened up was opened up. The seats and floorboards were removed; the landing gears, engines, fuse pins, and flap tracks might all be changed. Every structural member of the aircraft was examined visually, ultrasonically, or radiologically. AD Notes—airworthiness directives from the Federal Aviation Administration—regarding parts that had given other planes trouble might call for modifications. Everything that had been finessed or allowed to slide for two or three previous B- or C-checks had to be taken care of. The entire plane was also repainted. A D-check took more than a month, or 44,000 man-hours, put in by three shifts working around the clock.

When the 747 was first manufactured, Boeing calculated its life expectancy at 50,000 flying hours—about twelve years. The day I visited Pan Am's maintenance facility, every one of the carrier's thirty-seven surviving 747s had been in service for seventeen years or more, thanks to the D-check, which was part of Pan Am's so-called Aging-Aircraft Program, a measure made necessary by the company's financial straits. Like many other airlines, Pan Am sold all its aircraft back to the banks in the early eighties; now every one of its 747s was leased back from various leasing companies, and virtually every part in those 747s bore a plaque attesting to the fact. These were planes with a history. Or, looking at it less charitably, Pan Am's 747s, part of Boeing's original 100 series—the company had since put out the 200, 300, and 400 series—were elderly planes. "Those planes were like a used car—an *old* used car," one aircraft inspector would later tell me. Pan Am was pushing the envelope on 747 life-span—pushing it carefully and methodically, but pushing it nonetheless.

The managing director introduced me to the director of inspection, a buoyant, plucky fellow who had played baseball in the navy. The director of inspection introduced me to the manager of quality control, who conveyed further aggressive assurance. When I asked the manager if working on airplanes made him a nervous flier or a confident one, he said, "I think if you don't believe in what you're doing, you got no business doing it. I can fall asleep while the aircraft is taxiing for takeoff." Each man gave me his business card, with his name and title in black and the little globe logo, along with the Pan Am name in trademark windswept letters, in Pan Am blue. Then I met Les Radley.

He had no business card, or if he did, he never offered it to me. He was just an aircraft inspector—albeit a senior one—not a director or a manager: a slight, self-effacing, gray-haired man in dark-blue work pants and a light-blue work shirt, with rings under his large blue eyes, a shy smile, and a quiet voice. It occurred to me, when the manager of quality control, walking me through an employee lunchroom, introduced me in passing to Radley, that his was the first soft voice I'd heard all morning. I asked if I might sit down and chat. The manager shrugged, and Radley said sure. The manager evaporated.

The inspector was sitting at a green picnic table in the windowless room, eating a meatball sandwich he'd taken from a brown paper bag. In the background, another inspector was changing out of his work clothes, whistling—past the graveyard?—the old *Dick Van Dyke Show* theme song. Quiet Les Radley told me he'd been working for Pan Am for thirty-five years. He was from farm country, outside Buffalo. This explained the voice. He'd gone to work in the Miami station in 1955, and had moved his family to New York when the maintenance facility down there closed in '76. He liked his job pretty well: it was just about the only job he'd ever had. His work, he said, made him a fairly calm flier. "You hear the different noises, and you know what they are," he said, quietly. His wife, however, was of the white-knuckle school. Radley drove a Buick, he told me, and serviced it himself.

When he finished his sandwich, I asked hesitantly if he could show me Hangar 19. He said he didn't see why not. We walked over. It was—is—a quite incomparably gigantic building, the biggest indoor space I'd ever seen, five or six stories high, and long and wide enough to work on four 747s at a time. Four were in there that day. It's easy to forget just how big a 747 is. We see them miles above, or across a runway; or we walk directly inside and search impatiently for our seat and an empty overhead compartment. To stand directly beneath a 747, especially when it's sitting quietly within the size-enhancing confines of a garage—even a humongous garage—is a goose-bump-inducing experience. The word *mighty* comes easily to mind. I thought of Juan Trippe's presumption, and his optimism, in buying twenty-five of the planes at a clip, brand new and untried, and monumentally expensive. He must have stood next to one of them before he wrote the check, and thought—forty-year airline veteran and aviation pioneer notwithstanding—*Holy shit.*

Radley took me aboard Clipper *Crest of the Wave* (I thought, again unavoidably, of *Maid of the Seas*), which sat in the Erector set. We had to climb up three levels of metal scaffolding to get to the doorway. The plane was in the process of being prepared for the Civil Reserve Air Fleet (CRAF) Program, in which the air force borrows commercial 747s, and their crews, during times of national emergency. The preparation involved stripping the plane's interior, then flying it to Wichita, where Boeing installed a big cargo door in the side of the fuselage and strengthened the floor to accommodate military vehicles.

Clipper *Crest of the Wave*'s interior was down to framework and floorboards. To see a naked plane is to realize how much of the cabin of a commercial jet is ingratiation. This was an aircraft without illusions, and somehow it bore sharp metaphorical witness to Pan Am's present financial state. No gay colors, no peppy graphics (cheery red-and-blue seat covers had lain all over the cold, wet earth at Lockerbie). Just a couple of guys with blowtorches and power drills, and some hanging utility lights. The ribs of the aircraft—its studs and joists, if you will—were aluminum frame members every twenty inches throughout the fuselage. Unsheathed wires hung everywhere. Virtually the entire body of the plane, Radley told me, was aluminum, except for the engine cowlings—titanium—and the landing gear, made of chrome steel. We walked up the plane's spiral staircase and into the cockpit, which was stripped of seats and controls—bare of everything but, weirdly enough, an old-fashioned Boston pencil sharpener, exactly like the one from fifth grade, mounted on a bulkhead. So much for high tech.

I noticed two things I had never known existed in a 747 cockpit: a separate crew entry door, on the right, and, on the left, an escape hatch. Underneath the hatch was an inertial cable-reel apparatus, marked CREW EGRESS SYSTEM. This brought up all kinds of interesting possibilities. Under what conditions, exactly, might the crew egress separately? Pan Am, which had pioneered in many areas, was the first airline to introduce the practice of crews' wearing naval uniforms, in the 1930s. Was this just window dressing? Had the custom of going down with the ship, or at least leaving last, stayed in the navy?

I leaned into the upstairs lavatory, and leaned right out again: The smell inside the tiny enclosure was hootingly, doing-a-jiggingly, overpoweringly foul. Airplane toilets have always fascinated me. (If not inspired me. Something about the excessive dryness of the plane's ambient air, combined with fear of flying, the unbanishable sense of dozens of strangers seated (not to mention *standing,* waiting impatiently for the same all-too-common space) just outside the door—something about all this has always made high-altitude evacuation a—as they say—nonstarter.) I assumed for years—without asking anyone about it—that the powerful sucking swoosh of flushing represented a momentary interchange between the pressurized cabin and the barometrically hostile outer air; that the waste was simply shot out into the troposphere, seven miles up, and magically scattered and purified in the cold ether. Not so. Of *course.* (Roll eyes here.) How could this theory account for the fact that you could go, and get that same follow-up swoosh, while the plane still sat on the ramp? Not to mention the untoward possibility of frozen coproliths hailing on Wichita.✦

Of course the fact of the matter is that the—how shall we say—waste products are simply flushed, with that ineffectively smell-killing blue disinfectant, into holding tanks aboard the plane, said tanks to be unloaded upon landing by people whose thankless job it is to work for waste disposal companies that siphon the stuff off into tank trucks and take it away . . . somewhere. (I don't know where. I don't want to know. Should I have interviewed one of those people for this book? Maybe. Maybe you could find one of them and interview him or her yourself.) Why had this one lavatory on Clipper *Crest of the Wave* been insufficiently purged? It was a question I was too embarrassed to ask quiet Les Radley.

We went back to the lower deck and rewalked the 231-foot length of the jet, as though it would tell us something further about the difference between airplanes, with their soar and lift, and airlines, with their supermarket squalor. Four brand-new, olfactorily virginal lavatory units had already been installed down here: It seemed a hopeful sign. Amid the cozy, busy, men-at-work atmosphere, as the mechanics hammered and drilled in the big, big plane, I felt lulled enough to ask Radley if business had picked up at all in the year and a half since Lockerbie. He smiled slightly. He had a sad smile.

❐

One afternoon two and a half years later—four years after Lockerbie, and one after the death of Pan Am—I drove out to West Babylon, Long Island, to see Les Radley again. We hadn't kept in touch. In fact, I had to remind him we'd met in the first place. A lot had happened to him in the interim. He'd worked for the rest of the year we first met, while his pay got lower and lower. Then

---

✦ Stop the presses! Since writing the above, I have read reports—eerily enough—of *this very thing happening* in Georgia, Illinois, and Washington State. Just what you'd expect: Airplane toilets leak the blue flush stuff—and associated matter—at altitude; the conglomerate freezes in the upper air and drops on populous areas below. A two-foot-wide chunk of the so-called "blue ice" left a crater in a backyard near Atlanta; another chunk tore through someone's roof near Seattle. *Life*—as Sinatra sang—*gets more exciting with each passing day.*

in January 1991, Pan Am declared bankruptcy. This didn't mean an end to business; in fact a number of airlines have operated nearly normally under Chapter 11, while attempting to reorganize.✦

Pan Am, however, had a lot more to lose than other airlines. As 1991 proceeded, it sold off its proud heritage bit by bit: the Pan Am Building, the Pacific routes, the Atlantic routes, the shuttle. It was as though a film were being run backward—Juan Trippe coming back to life, getting younger and younger; Lindbergh, growing slim and handsome, returning, in reverse, from his flights of exploration; the airline getting smaller and smaller. Finally, at the end of the year, the South American routes, the seed of the enterprise, were all that remained. Delta hovered in the wings—whether as partner or scavenger, it was impossible to tell. There was talk of creating a vastly reduced Pan Am 2, which, at least, would keep the name alive, with a hint of the good old flying-down-to-Rio days. Delta would own 45 percent, and Pan Am's creditors—Boeing, the IRS, the pension fund—would own the rest. Delta made vaguely agreeable noises, then changed its mind. And then one day—December 4, 1991, to be precise—Pan Am was gone. Just like that.

Two days before, Les Radley had driven the twenty-four miles west to Hangar 19 he'd driven every working day for fifteen years. "I worked afternoon shift, and I worked overtime that night. That was a Monday," he told me. Radley looked the same as last time we'd met, only the big rings under his eyes were even deeper. We were sitting in the kitchen of his small, white-vinyl-sided tract house in the flatlands of West Babylon, drinking coffee as his wife, Rose, put away the groceries we'd just brought in from the car. It was a modest fifties house, dark and smelling vaguely of cat food. In the hall beyond the kitchen door a white crucifix hung on the wall. Outside the kitchen windows, as the light faded, a strong west wind blew through the bare branches.

"I went in to work at two forty-five," Radley said, in his soft country voice. "I was there till three-fifteen the next morning, 'cause I worked overtime. And then I had Tuesday and Wednesday off, which was the third and the fourth. On December third was when the bankruptcy judge, [Cornelius] Blackshear, met with Delta and the unions and Pan Am, and they were gonna come out of bankruptcy. And that was the day that Delta said they weren't gonna come through with any more of the money they had more or less promised.

✦ Eastern flew bankrupt from March 1989 until its demise in January 1991. As of this writing, America West, Continental, and TWA have all operated under Chapter 11, in seeming defiance of the laws of gravity, then lived to tell the tale. Yet while bankruptcy per se may not seem an inducement to passengers— broke airlines tend to be especially tatty where amenities are concerned—the flying public might keep in mind that not only do insolvent carriers often offer bargain-basement fares, but the FAA is super-vigilant about overseeing their maintenance procedures.

"I heard about it on the radio—the all-news station—on Wednesday. They said Pan Am had ceased operations. Then I turned on the TV, and they were showing people at the terminal, all upset because their tickets weren't being honored."

"December twelfth," Les Radley said, "I went back in, to turn in my Port Authority badge and pick up my last check. And at Building Two-oh-eight, the Jet Center, there was a line out the door and around the building."

I asked him how many employees Pan Am had when it ended.

"I guess maybe nineteen thousand," he said.

"How many at Kennedy?"

"I would say maybe six, seven thousand." He sipped his coffee. "There were a couple of guys behind me on line—well, their checks weren't there. I guess it was a foul-up, you know. And they were devastated—'We got no money, where's our check? You promised us our check today.' I guess they got the check eventually, but they were *hurting*. They were practically in tears—kids at home, got no money, got no food. Was bad, you know.

"Everyplace you went," he said, "you were followed by a security guard, 'cause they were afraid we were gonna do something—steal something, or maybe do some damage. Things like that. I felt bad. You go out there and you're followed around by a guard like—you're a criminal. I had to go upstairs and clean out my locker, and a guard followed me. Everything I took from my locker, my clothes and my personal stuff—he watched." Radley shook his head, still incredulous.

"Do you have any idea who gave that order, that everybody be followed by a guard?" I asked.

His voice was even quieter than usual. "Had to be Pan Am, you know." And quieter still. "Had to be, you know."

Every Tuesday night for a year or so afterward, former Pan Am employees, Les Radley among them, would meet with Congressman Thomas Downey in Downey's Amityville office, not with any special agenda in mind but just for solidarity's sake. "Just to get together," Radley said. "And to find out about any benefits we might have coming to us—if you have trouble paying your electric bills, you can get help; if you can't afford heating oil, you can get assistance paying for that. And if you have trouble with health insurance, you can go to Congressman Downey's office, and they try to help you with that."

The meetings were crowded and vociferous to begin with, but attendance slowly diminished as people found jobs or moved. Or lost hope. Many of Pan Am's casualties landed on their feet, but perhaps just as many did not, and

among the latter were numerous instances of desperation: There were sui-
cides; there was homelessness. Perhaps hardest hit were men in their middle
fifties—too young for Social Security, too old to find jobs easily. Also, the
stress of the last plummeting years left untold numbers with chronic health
problems. And one of the airline's points of pride had always been that it took
care of its own. "That's one thing about Pan Am," Radley told me. "If you
were sickly, they would give you a job that you could do. You know, they kept
people on for years. There were guys that were crippled, had to walk with a
crutch. Pan Am took care of people like that—they would get a sitting-down
job, something to keep 'em employed, with their health benefits. There were
a number of people they took care of. I don't know what happened to those
people once Pan Am folded."

Les Radley was, in his own way, extremely lucky. He was sixty-one
when the company died; his son and daughter had grown up and moved away.
His wife had always worked—most recently as a housecleaner and home
health-care aide for an elderly woman. The Radleys rented the upstairs of
their house to a boarder, which took care of their mortgage payment. And
Les's full pension kicked in seven months after December 4. (One of Pan
Am's major creditors had been its own pension fund—the total debt, in dis-
pute, was somewhere between $400 million and $900 million. But all pen-
sions were guaranteed by the Pension Benefit Guaranty Corporation, a federal
agency: good news for Pan Am pensioners as pensioners, bad news for them
as taxpayers.) He also drew unemployment benefits for a year after the close-
down, and, though he owned a lot of worthless Pan Am shares, he'd paid his
taxes for thirty-five years. In February of 1993, his Social Security benefits
kicked in. There were also other ways—respectable enough, but let's leave it
at that—of augmenting the family till.

"'Course I'm payin' my own medical now, which is gonna be over three
thousand dollars a year," Les said. "Still, if we put everything together, I'm
making just about as much as I made at Pan Am. I mean, I hate to be sixty-
two years old, but if I had to rely on just my pension, I'd be lookin' for a job."

"You started with the company in '55?" I asked, after a while.

Radley nodded. "September twenty-sixth," he said. We were on our second cup of coffee. "I'd just come out of Embry Riddle Aviation School. Originally Rose and I are both from Buffalo—out in the country near Buffalo. I'd
been in the air force, for almost four years. And I wanted to continue with aviation in some form. So I went to Florida and worked around—I worked for
Florida Power and Light for about a year, and I could see no future there. And
I worked in some factories and things down there. Finally decided that I could

go to aviation school under the GI Bill. Which I did."

"With the intention of becoming a mechanic?"

"Mm-hm. Or flight engineer, or something. I got out of Embry Riddle in September of '55, and Eastern and Pan Am were both hiring. So I had a choice." He laughed a little. "As it turned out, it wouldn't have made any difference."

I asked what planes he'd worked on at the beginning of his career.

"Well, they had the DC-6s," he said. "And there were some DC-4s still kickin' around. One of the vice-presidents of the Latin American division—they had divisions back then: Latin American, Pacific, and Atlantic—the vice-president of the Latin American division, he had his own personal DC-3. It was a plush airplane. We worked on that occasionally. Whenever it needed something."

"What part of the plane was your specialty?"

"Engines, and the airframe, whatever. They kinda moved you around to keep the job more interesting. Then the navigational electronics—specialties."

"But then planes became much more complicated."

"When the 707 came, right. We went to Pan Am School. They had what they called a training department, where they had half a dozen instructors. The instructors would go to Boeing or Douglas, and they would get the information back and teach us."

"And then you came north to Kennedy."

He nodded. "I came up here in February of 1976, as the 707 was being phased out, and they were bringing in the 747s. The bankers that Pan Am owed money to, they decided that Pan Am couldn't afford two main overhaul bases, so they phased out Miami—made it a line station. They told us if you didn't have at least thirty-five years with the company, if you stayed in Miami, you were gonna get laid off. So you either get laid off or come to New York."

Was that, I asked, the first inkling he'd had of Pan Am's financial peril?

"Well, they say that the money problems started when Juan Trippe bought all the 747s."

"When did you see the handwriting on the wall?"

He gave a quick, mirthless laugh. "I guess probably—well, after they bought National, I think. Cost them a bunch of money—Pan Am put out almost *a billion dollars* to buy these routes. And then, maybe it was a year later, they could have started flying those routes without paying *anything* for 'em. 'Cept for the start-up costs, you know. You wonder what some of 'em were thinking about; you'd think that they must have had people, maybe in

Washington, that might have had a hint of what was happening. But they pushed ahead. Seemed like we never had a friend in Washington," Les said.

Mrs. Radley, in the midst of preparing dinner, perked up. "Never," she said. "Fact, there's a video out, *Last Days of Pan Am*? Have you seen it? It's put out by some video people in Boca Raton—my son sent me a copy of it. It tells about all the politics that was involved in—"

"It goes back to Dinner Key, in Miami, with the flying boats," Les said. "And it goes right down to—they meet the last flight that Pan Am ever made. It was Barbados to Miami. And they interview the pilot, and the stewardesses; shows the airplane comin' into Miami, and the fire trucks are out there, and they're shootin' these water cannons. The airplane goes under the arch of water." He laughed a little. "It's a tearjerker at the end, you know."

"Did you feel devoted to the company?" I asked him.

He made a small sound, its tone quite unconveyable in print. "Yeah."

"Did you feel that way to the end?"

"Yeah, I think so. Even though they"—he laughed again—"even though they took a lot of money away from us, you know—give-backs, concessions. We gave up a lot. They increased something like fifteen dollars a week for medical; we gave back vacation days; we gave up Good Friday as a holiday. And Washington's Birthday. Got stuck with a lot of stock; that's useless. They gave it to us in lieu of raises. That's where I messed up—I should've gotten rid of that stock."

"But how would you know?" I said.

He shook his head. "Well—that's the handwriting on the wall you're talking about—I should've seen it. Now it's useless."

"It was like losin' a part of our family," Rose Radley said, from the shadows at the end of the kitchen. She laughed bitterly. "Because he had been with them so long, it was like, more than half our lives Les devoted to the company."

"Right." Les nodded.

What, I asked, had been the first tangible effects on Pan Am employees of the National purchase?

"I think it was about in 1981—'81? Eighty-two?"

"What happened?"

"Well—we stopped gettin' raises." He laughed. "What was it, 1981 we had our last raise, hon?"

"I can't remember that," his wife said. "Seems to *me* they started goin' downhill ever since we moved up to New York in '76. *We* started goin' downhill, because we had to move up—we had to start with a whole lifestyle, a home, and whatever. Michael was out of high school, and our daughter had two years to finish in high school. *She* was devastated."

"Did you ever consider changing jobs?" I asked Les.

"You mean—"

"To another airline," I said.

"Well, with all the time I had with Pan Am—to go start out with one week's vacation, or no vacation, and probably a lot less money—"

"Besides," Rose Radley chimed in, as she chopped vegetables, "we never thought they would go under." She laughed.

Les nodded. "It was always a possibility," he said. "Everybody, you know, would say, 'Someday you're gonna come and find a big lock on the door.' And everybody would laugh, but"—he laughed a little—"it really wasn't gonna happen. Well, it happened. It happened *quick.*" He shook his head. "It happened quick."

The kitchen was quiet for a while. "The company kept saying, 'Things are gonna get better,'" Les finally said. "'We're gonna come back to where we were in the sixties and seventies.' Things like that."

"Did they tell you what their plan was?" I asked.

He shrugged. "Then there was all this tension between the National employees and the Pan Am employees," he said. "Pan Am didn't know how to run National's system, and National did. But Pan Am wouldn't listen to the National people. They were like 'We bought it; we're gonna run it. You work for us, so you keep your mouth shut.' So it didn't work from the start. Because Pan Am—they could run an overseas operation, but they couldn't run a system that flew inside of the United States, the short hops. They had no idea what to do. National was a popular airline. But then after Pan Am took over, it didn't amount to a whole lot."

I asked him if he could list for me the last few CEOs of Pan Am.

"I was thinking about this one guy just before you came," Radley said. "What was that Pan Am president at the end?" he asked his wife.

"Plaskett."

"Plaskett," Les said. "Thomas Plaskett. He was at the end. He was in when Lockerbie happened. I guess he had four years, then before him it was Ed Acker. He came from Braniff and Air Florida. He was—not very popular. He was in maybe five years. Then there was a guy that was a general in the army—Bill, uh . . . first name was Bill. Remember his name, dear?"

"No. Before Acker, you mean?"

"He was an air force general," Radley said. "I can't think of his name.

First name was Bill. Then there was a Captain Gray.✦ These were all—well, I guess they just didn't seem to know how to run an airline. When Acker came over, he had been with Braniff, and I think he was there when Braniff went belly up the first time. And there was questions about missing pension money at Braniff.✦✦ I don't know why Pan Am ever picked him up.

"But then he left—he left with a million dollars and a nice home down in the Caribbean. And the last I heard, he's involved with two or three other people, runnin' some kind of shuttle up in the New England states—some rinky-dink airline up there."

"And these guys didn't say anything to you about their plans for restoring Pan Am to its former greatness?"

Radley thought for a second. "Well, they were gonna shrink," he said. "They were gonna get rid of the routes that were not making any money. This Pan Am Two would've been a lot smaller. Their timetable was about that thick"—he held his thumb and forefinger a half-inch apart. "Would've been a lot of people would've lost their jobs on that."

"Was Delta the first suitor that came along?"

"No, there was a couple—I think they even talked to Trans World Airlines. But that would've been a disaster." He laughed.

"I had a chance to go to Delta," he said. "I was interviewed at the Travelodge at JFK. By an inspector foreman from Delta. And at that time I was close to bein' sixty-one. So right from the beginning I really didn't want to go with Delta, 'cause I figured, my son is living in Miami; I always wanted to retire in Florida. So, you know, why should I go with Delta, because the new Pan Am Two is gonna be based in Miami. They said they would move you, and pay you relocation money, so I said, I'll stick with Pan Am. I really didn't want to go to Atlanta, or any other place. Might've been a mistake, but I just didn't feel like pickin' up and movin' again, at sixty-one. At that time it looked like Pan Am was gonna reorganize and come out of bankruptcy, and there'd be no problem. Didn't turn out that way."

✦ The six chairmen of Pan Am were Juan Trippe (served 1927–1968); former pilot Captain Harold Gray (1968–1970); Najeeb Halaby (1970–1972); former air force brigadier general William Seawell, who bought National and greased the skids (1972–1981); Edward Acker (1981–1988); and Thomas Plaskett, on whose head Lockerbie landed (1988–1991).

✦✦ Braniff was still solvent when Acker left its presidency in 1975, "not long after that airline owned up to unaccounted ticket sales and use of funds for payoffs in Latin America and contributions to Richard Nixon's 1972 re-election campaign," according to a 1982 article in *Business Week.* Acker went from Braniff to the chairmanship of Air Florida, where he engineered a spectacular turnaround.

*

It was black outside the kitchen windows. "Hopefully," Les continued, "when all of Pan Am's finances are melted down, like they said, we'll get our vacation money that they owe me, plus my severance pay. Fifteen thousand dollars. Sick pay, severance, and seven weeks' vacation."

"And when is that supposed to get resolved?" I asked.

"We won't get that," Rose Radley shot, from the end of the kitchen.

"Maybe we'll get a piece of it," said Les, softly. "There was a Teamsters bankruptcy lawyer at one of our meetings with Congressman Downey. He said, 'You'll get something, someday; but you may not get a hundred percent. You may get fifty percent; you may get twenty-five cents on a dollar.'"

"We won't get it," his wife said, firmly. "If we get ten cents on the dollar, we're gonna be lucky. What bothers me the most out of this whole thing is that the people who went with Delta, they have gotten their vacation pay, their sick pay—"

"They got everything," Les said.

"They started to work with Delta, Pan Am paid them all their money," his wife said. "The ones who were out on a limb"—she laughed bitterly—"got nothing."

"Well," Les said. "They say when they get all the parts and equipment sold, Pan Am will be just a lump of money, and then they'll distribute maybe something to us, some to the creditors."

"That one's just wishful thinking," said Rose.

"Some to Boeing, some to the IRS, some to the pension fund, I hope."

"Very trusting," Rose Radley said. She laughed harshly. "I've been thinkin' I'm gonna have to keep my job scrubbin' floors." And laughed again. "Can't wait for that."

I took out a newspaper clipping I'd brought along—it was an article in the *Times* about Delta's recently receiving a two-million-dollar fine for lax maintenance—and asked Radley about it.

He laughed. "Oh yeah, we saw that in the *Daily News,*" he said. "Think it was mostly for faulty logbook entries, and things like that. Mostly it was paperwork."

"It says," I said, "That Eastern, in '86, was fined nine point five million dollars for *seventy-eight thousand* safety infractions."

Radley smiled and shook his head.

"Pan Am never had any problems like that?" I asked.

"Oh, there were fines, sure," Les said. "The FAA is great for pickin' up— you know, you're sittin' there looking at the little tray table that folds down;

that little sign that says 'Life Vest Under Your Seat'? They'd get on a Pan Am plane, and maybe out of five hundred seats, there'd be a couple of those little decals missing—maybe some kid would have peeled it off. They'd look at that, and they'd come back a week later—if those two decals were still missing, they'd fine Pan Am a thousand dollars for each flight the plane had made. Things like that—they jump on that.

"I mean, you could put a new decal on, and get a kid come on the plane and pull it right off. Then the FAA inspectors would walk on the airplane and a drop of fuel would hit 'em, and they'd say, 'Oh, it's raining.'" He laughed. "You know, they'd let something like that go, that really amounted to something, but they'd pick on the little things."

"Did any airlines have bad reputations for maintenance while you were in the business?" I asked.

"Oh yeah," Les said.

"Were there any you wouldn't fly as a passenger?"

"Not really, but some—just seemed like Eastern had a lot of landing-gear problems over the years," Les said. "I don't know why—I mean, it wasn't too complicated. They were always having problems in their landing-gear shops. They were always having the fire trucks come out when they landed, 'cause they would come in with faulty landing-gear indications, you know."

"What were the problems due to, do you think? Pressure from higher up to hurry things through?"

"I would say that's probably the biggest thing, yeah."

"Were you under time pressure when you worked?" I asked.

There was a long silence. "Oh yeah," he said. And then, "You know, they'd give you a reasonable amount of time to do something. But the inspection department was a job where a lot of people didn't want the responsibility, because the money wasn't all that much more. So they had trouble gettin' inspectors. So they brought a lot of people into the department that really shouldn't have been there. You know. They needed bodies, so they went out and they got bodies. The bodies didn't know what they were doing in a lot of cases. Those were the people that were pressured. It was bad—there was a core of good people there, but then there was a bunch of people who really didn't know much about what they were doing."

"Did that ever result in any safety problems?"

"I don't think so, 'cause somebody always covered for 'em. Or they would come and say, 'Can you help me here? I don't know what to do.' Or they would take 'em off the job and put somebody else on."

"I saw a story on TV saying that some of the airlines subcontract maintenance work out to cheap shops," I said.

"They also want to do a lot of their work overseas," Les said. "They can do it cheaper. The airlines have been wanting to do that for a long time. I mean, if Pan Am could have subcontracted out their work on the 747s, they wouldn't have needed all these expensive facilities in New York.

"But I don't think Pan Am really ever cut corners. I mean, even when they were in bankruptcy—the FAA was around much more after Pan Am went through bankruptcy than they ever were before. They walked through, and they'd look at the logbooks.

"I never worried too much about it," Les said. " 'Cause in a lot of cases, I figured I knew more about the airplane than they did. They're schooled in paperwork. That's their big thing. If the paperwork is good, everything else has to be good. Even though it may not be good.

"After January of '91, when Pan Am went into bankruptcy, you had to pay cash for everything. If you got a planeload of fuel, you had to have the cash, 'cause Ogden Allied, the fueling people, they wouldn't put fuel on the airplane unless they got their money."

"Did Pan Am price itself out of existence by not cutting corners?" I asked.

"No, they just never seemed to get caught up with the times," he said.

"But Hangar Nineteen seemed so modern."

"Well, to look at it, it might have been. But we often joked—if it wasn't for two-by-fours and a rope, Pan Am would never get anything done. Like when they changed landing gears—instead of having nice equipment to do it with, you had to do it with a rope and a two-by-four. The motorized equipment—like the trucks and the cherry pickers and the vans—at the end, it was gettin' in atrocious shape."

He thought for a moment. "The other thing," he said. "They were hiring what they call B-scale people at Pan Am—they'd hire 'em at a lesser amount of money. For the maintenance department. The union agreed to let a certain percentage of mechanics be B-scale mechanics."

So they did cut corners. "When did that start happening?" I asked.

"I guess in the late eighties, maybe. You know the Aviation High School up in Long Island City? Pan Am would go up there and hire mechanics. They'd graduate, and that night they'd be workin' the midnight shift. Where a regular mechanic was makin' sixteen dollars an hour, they'd start these guys out at half that, with the understanding that every six months they'd get raised up until they'd make what the regular mechanic was makin'. They had B-scale inspectors, too." He shook his head. "Those guys were unbelievable."

"Did other airlines do this?"

"I think American had hired some B-scale people. Then they realized it wasn't working, and they did away with it after a few years. I think Pan Am never gave up the B-scale people. They picked up people from Eastern when Eastern closed."

"Theoretically," I said, "some of the same people who weren't so good at landing-gear repair?"

Les laughed. "Maybe," he said.

"All of the airlines have been fined," Les said after a while. "But Pan Am really, as far as loss of life through crashes, was good. Except for Lockerbie—you couldn't blame that on maintenance. There are very few crashes that Pan Am ever had that I can remember that were maintenance related—they're either weather related, or something else."

"What was the effect on the Pan Am rank and file of Lockerbie?" I asked. "Did it really seem at that point as though a curtain was coming down?"

"Yeah," he said. "I think Pan Am was beginning to come up. Seemed like they were refurbishing the airplanes, and more people were flying Pan Am. And everything was looking brighter."

"The employees felt better," Rose Radley said.

"The employee morale was pickin' up. Plaskett had just come on board. And then after Lockerbie, people just didn't *fly* it. Before, companies would send their executives to Europe on first class or Clipper Class, you know. Then they just stopped puttin' 'em on it. They'd go on Lufthansa or British Airways, or some other airline. They kept showin' that picture on the TV— the crane pickin' up the nose of the airplane, you know." He laughed sadly.

"They had a Lockerbie memorial out here at Hofstra," Les said. "Plaskett spoke. And I went to it."

"How was it handled?"

"I thought it was very nice," he said. "Plaskett seemed like a decent enough fellow. I think if it hadn't been for Lockerbie, he might've really done something."

The kitchen was silent for a minute. "I guess morale just never came back up," I said.

"Not after Lockerbie, I don't think," Les said.

"The event itself was so awful, and then there was the business fallout."

"And there was the lawsuits," he said. "I guess the big thing was, they really lambasted the Pan Am security. You know, on the local news—some TV commentator went out to Pan Am at JFK, and he walked all over the field, got on airplanes, got off airplanes, went into the baggage area, where you could easily put something—I won't say the word. Nobody stopped him, and he didn't have a badge or nothin'.

"I had some experiences with the security at JFK," Les said. "You know, some of the people couldn't even speak English—like they just got off the boat, they give 'em a uniform, and that's it. That was another thing, I guess—when you're on hard times, maybe you don't spend as much on security as you would've when times were good, you know? Some of the people I ran into, at the Worldport—when you drove down from Hangar Nineteen, you didn't run into security until you actually got to the Worldport. When I was working, we were sent down to the terminal to maybe check on something on an airplane. On the hardstand. A lot of people would wander around down there without badges, and they were never challenged. We were never challenged."

"If you were taking your dream trip these days," I asked the Radleys, "would you think about all this stuff? Would you try to pick the right airline, the right airplane? Or would you just say the hell with it?"

"Well," Les said, "if you pick a 747, you got four engines, right? If you go on an Airbus, you got two. So, you want to go four engines or two engines? Old airplane or new airplane? I would think about it before gettin' on an Airbus, maybe. Or a 747. Well, there are some new ones."

"Would you think about it?" I asked Rose. I suddenly remembered Les had told me, two years before in the jet center, that his wife was not a happy flier. "That's right," I said. "When the plane bumps, you grab the armrest."

"She grabs *me*," Les said. "Leaves her fingerprints on me."

"I don't know what I would think," Rose said. "I'd just go. I'd feel like you're in God's hands, whatever happens."

"That Aloha flight out in Hawaii—" Les was talking about the Aloha Airlines 727 whose skin literally blew off while the plane was flying at altitude; one passenger was sucked out of the aircraft, but miraculously, the pilots were able to land. "When you think about old airplanes," he said, "with old skins, you know. Pan Am had some skins that looked—*whew*—pretty rough."

"We flew Aloha," his wife said.

"You did?"

"We went to Maui a couple of years ago," Les said.

"And I didn't even think about it," Rose said.

"We flew from here to Honolulu in one of the old, old Pan Am 747s," said Les. "Pan Am had the oldest. A lot of hours. I think Boeing, when they built the airplane, it was designed for fifty thousand hours. Pan Am had some that were *ninety* thousand. This was one of them.

"Anyway, I was on my thirty-fifth-anniversary trip. Thirty-five years with Pan Am. You'd make a reservation in Clipper Class, with an automatic upgrade to first if it was available. Every five years you could get get that. We flew Clipper from here to L.A., and first class from L.A. to Hawaii. Then we flew first class all the way back."

He shook his head. "Even so, though—you could see Pan Am was gettin' shabbier and shabbier. The planes lookin' shabbier, stewardesses' uniforms were gettin' shabbier. And they'd run out of juice, and food—I know they ran out of food for employees a lot of times. There were times we'd be getting on a flight, and they'd say, 'Look, you have to be served last, and if there's anything—'"

"That didn't happen on your anniversary trip, I hope," I said.

"No, no."

"We were celebrating our wedding anniversary, too," Rose said.

"Thirty-seven years," Les said. "Thirty-five with Pan Am. When we told the steward that, he snuck us a nice bottle of Champagne. And we had it when we got to Maui."

"So you have your fortieth wedding anniversary coming up next year," I said.

"Next year. Right," Les said.

"But not Pan Am," said his wife.

8

Terror

Bombs and Dollars

W e're going to see where they shoot the hijackers. Sammy Chevalier and I are in a Port Authority pickup, moving along a service road somewhere on the airport.

"The scenario is," Sammy says, as he drives, "a hijacker waves a pistol at a pilot and says, 'I want to go to Cuba.' The pilot says, 'OK. But we'll have to go refuel first.' Then he taxis over here, and the police sharpshooters try to get a bead on him."

He stops the truck. I'd like to tell you just where we are, and how, exactly, the police sharpshooters get their bead, but as much as I trust you *personally* not to go out and hijack a jet, you'll probably agree that there are those we'd just as soon leave in the dark. Hijackings are a grim—if somewhat out-moded—business. Their peak period was during the late sixties and early seventies, and because the FAA and the FBI have made it somewhat harder for people to take airplanes hostage (and because several hijackers were dispatched, at various airports, through means similar to those Sammy is showing me now), the crime largely seems to have gone out of fashion—which suggests the ever-present possibility that it may come back in again. Kennedy has played host to several such incidents, most recently the February 1993 landing of a Lufthansa Airbus hijacked over Belgium by a twenty-year-old Ethiopian student with a starter's pistol. In a scene reminiscent of (and no doubt nearly as costly to mount as) the penultimate moments of *Bonnie and Clyde* and *Butch Cassidy and the Sundance Kid,* when the slightly built lone gunman (having already given up) emerged, cowering, from the plane, he found himself facing a sea of FBI agents wearing helmets and flak jackets and carrying assault weapons. Helicopters whirred overhead. The hijacker surrendered for a second time.

Suddenly Sammy grabs his binoculars. There's a big bird sitting out on the end of a fence—"a rough-legged hawk," Sammy says. "He's got feathers down his tarsus, unlike the red-tailed hawk or the marsh hawk." The hawk's tail rises and falls. "He just muted," Sammy says.

"Pardon?"

"He took a crap. They have to lift their tail to do it."

❐

I was in a second-floor conference room in the Port Authority Building at Kennedy, at a late-November meeting to determine the various plans of action to be taken at the airport in the event of a snowstorm. Riveting enough stuff for some people; less so for others. I noticed a man sitting in a chair against the window wall, looking monumentally bored. He wore an indescribably ugly blue-brown-gold tie, a white shirt, a brown sports jacket, black polyester pants, and black buckle loafers. He kept leaning back and sitting up in his chair, looking around. *Cop,* I thought, involuntarily. He was a smallish man, not good-looking, with short, Vitalised gray hair. He had deeply pockmarked skin, dead-cold slitty eyes, and almost no lips. His eyes kept moving around the room; he kept shifting in his chair as contingency plans and various types of plows were discussed. *He looks too much like a cop to* be *a cop,* I thought. Finally he crossed his legs, and I saw the pistol strapped to his ankle.

Now Captain Frank Fox is talking to me in his office upstairs in Building 269. "I grew up in Astoria," he tells me. Today he's wearing a nice red tie with his white shirt; behind his desk, free from having to scan the room for miscreants, he exudes a benign—well, a more benign—aura. "We never came out here. That was out in the country." He joined the force thirty years ago, he tells me, just out of the marines, and he began, like everyone else, as a pool patrolman, working the Lincoln Tunnel, working La Guardia and Idlewild.

"When I was a patrolman here, it was mostly traffic enforcement," he says. "That was back in '62. It was like a farm out here then. None of these buildings were around; it was wide open. You didn't have nearly the volume that you do today. Terrorism was unknown. There wasn't even any pickpocketing."

He eventually became a detective sergeant at La Guardia, and it was there, at the end of the aviation-event-intensive year of 1975 (Flight 66; Overseas National), that a big bomb exploded in the TWA arrival area, killing eleven people and injuring fifty-six. Fox was assigned to a task force that studied the bombing, which was never established as a terrorist incident, though it was believed to be the work of Croatian nationalists.

He came back to Kennedy as a captain, and joined the Office for Special Planning as assistant manager to Ed O'Sullivan. "The purpose of the OSP was to assess the state of security at all PA facilities, especially the airports.

We would attempt to breach security, wearing civilian clothes," Fox tells me. "Often we were successful." In particular, Fox and his operatives were able to gain access to Kennedy's fuel farm. "And we checked the pillars supporting the end of Twenty-two Right to see what the impact of bombing them would be," he says.

If Fox's incursions resulted in any beefed-up measures, he isn't talking. But he isn't exactly pushing a picture of Fortress Kennedy. The chief result of the office's incursions seems to have been . . . recommendations.✝ "The OSP still exists, but it's kind of watered down," the captain says. "But it was put together with the idea that it would just be a two- to three-year project. We did a very comprehensive study. We took a lot of photographs.

"The problem with security at Kennedy is not so different from the problem with everything else at Kennedy," Fox says. "When it comes to security at this airport, many, many people have a piece of the action, so to speak. You have any number of government agencies—the FBI, the DEA, Customs, Immigration. And each airline has its own exclusive area, and it's the airline's sole responsibility to secure it. I regretted that the central terminal fell through, but to us it would've been just one more building to police.

"The airports weren't built with security in mind. They have to be retrofitted. We have a cyclone fence around Kennedy—could it be breached? Sure it could be breached.

"But the threat of terrorism in this country is very low," he insists. "Is it likely that the IRA would put a bomb on a British Airways plane taking off from Kennedy? It is unlikely. Why? It's a question of money. The IRA is smart. They know that if the battlefield came here, their contributions from the States would dry up."

And what of the possibility of Mideast terror's coming to JFK? Airport employees are not unanimous on the subject. The police sergeant who drives the armored vehicle the PA cops would use in the event of a terrorist attack told me, "Between you and me and the four walls, it's an accident waitin' to

---

✝ In 1985, the OSP, under Ed O'Sullivan, made a study of the vulnerability of the World Trade Center's underground parking garages to terrorist bombings, and presented a detailed list of proposed security measures to then Port Authority executive director Stephen Berger, who adopted about a third of the measures and rejected the rest. (As a quasi-governmental agency, the PA is also not subject to New York City fire codes.) When asked the reason, after the February 1993 World Trade Center bombing, O'Sullivan said, "Expense."

In November 1990, the Port Authority sponsored a $16,970 dinner at the World Trade Center's Windows on the World restaurant, for an Urban Summit of American mayors. In March 1992, the PA threw a luncheon for three hundred port-industry agents and guests, featuring an open bar and buffet tables full of iced shrimp, clams, oysters, and ethnic dishes. The tab was $27,425. A 1991 annual outing for bond underwriters and investment advisers, featuring lunch and a yacht tour of the harbor, cost $37,042. A 1988 luncheon for Port Authority employees and retirees cost $94,000. The list goes on.

happen." "But you know something?" a Department of Agriculture inspector responded. "It hasn't happened yet. Why not?"

Kennedy was on Level 4 alert—the highest state—during the Persian Gulf War, a very nervous place indeed. Nothing happened. In fact, despite several Mideast wars and considerable national tension; despite the fact that every key political and religious figure in the world, controversial and other- wise, passes through on a regular basis—there has never been a serious ter- rorist incident in the airport's history. This is, of course, largely due to the careful ministrations of people such as Frank Fox: the PA Police, the FBI, and the State Department. But might it be that another factor is also at work?

"It's just impractical for Mideast organizations to import terrorism here," Fox says. "It's too far away.✦ It's easier for them to get attention closer to home, for a lot less money. It's all economics," Fox says. "It's the same thing that drives security measures. El Al only has two flights out of Kennedy a day. They can afford to do what they do. TWA has forty to fifty flights a day. If they did the kind of checking El Al does, people would be lined up out in the street. It's all economics."✦✦

✦ As of this writing, the jury is still out on how far away the World Trade Center—the headquarters of the Port Authority itself!—was from whatever group delivered, on February 26, 1993, a two-thousand-pound wake-up call.

✦✦ And public relations. In October 1993, Captain Fox was relieved of his command and transferred to the Public Safety Department headquarters in Jersey City when he approved overtime payment for two airport patrolmen who drove to Manhattan to check on the condition of airport manager Richard Rowe, who had been involved in an auto mishap.

9

Infrastructure

$

The greatest airport in the world is rising from the meadows at Idlewild in New York City. It will cost $71 million. Filling, grading, planting, drainage, field lighting utilities, runways, taxiways and aprons will cost about $35 million. The administration building, together with loading docks, apron and parking spaces will cover well over three hundred acres and cost about $10 million.

The airport will bring millions of dollars monthly in commerce, business and traffic to the City of New York. When in full operation, thirty thousand passengers will go through its gates daily. Many tons of mail, express and freight will be handled. Forty thousand men and women will be permanently employed in airport activities. The airport is a costly undertaking, yet it will be one of the best investments the City ever made. It will pay its way.
    —MAYOR FIORELLO LA GUARDIA, 1945

Where did Kennedy go wrong? Or did it, really, go wrong? On a white-hot July Monday a month before the end of World War II, Fiorello La Guardia brought seventeen of his fellow mayors from around the country to a rickety enclosed wooden observation tower in the middle of a desolate sand flat by Jamaica Bay in Queens, for an official presentation. A photograph of the occasion survives: It shows the Little Flower, looking sickly but decisive, holding a long pointer over a big map-table. Flanking him are the other mayors, most of them, like La Guardia, in their shirtsleeves, the neckties short, the trousers high. The faces around the table are heavy, masculine, and almost grim with concentration.

The map is a plan for the great new airport to be built on the site—the greatest airport in the world, for the greatest city in the world.

Ten miles to the north, the mayor's old grand dream, the airport that bears his name, only six years old at the time of the photograph, is, in the end-of-war travel boom, bursting at the seams. And—hemmed in on the south by Robert Moses' Grand Central Parkway and on the north by Flushing Bay—La Guardia is virtually unexpandable. Moreover, its runways, built on sand, are in the process of sinking into the bay. The money to shore them up will have to come from a city deep in a hole of its own: a budget hole greatly deepened by the $200 million in annual service fees on the huge debts amassed in the construction of the highways and bridges and parks planned and executed—in a unique pas de deux of mutual manipulation and visionary improvidence—by Robert Moses and Fiorello La Guardia.

So here, on a map-table in a tower in the middle of Idlewild Marsh, one month before Hiroshima, four months before the dying La Guardia will be swept out of office, is a plan for a glorious future: a sunlit, technically burgeoning future of the sort the twentieth century had been promising since its outset. A map of the proposed airport in a 1943 issue of *Popular Science* shows eight runways, a factory site, a great axial promenade in the terminal area, extensive parking, a heliport, a seaplane basin. All on a huge plot—five thousand acres, ten times the size of La Guardia. The plan on the map-table that day in July 1945—modified, for a large fee, by one of Moses' pet engineering firms—was similar, and no less grand.

Why, then, are the mayors frowning? Any old photograph, studied hungrily enough, both admits us to and bars us from the past. The occasion apparently was a solemn one. No doubt this was a project that La Guardia—the dreamer, romantic, fanatical civic improver, and former aviator (he commanded U.S. Army air forces on the Austro-Italian front in World War I)—was dead serious about. Perhaps the mayor, given his health—he had only two years to live—was simply not his old boisterous self.

And it was hot up there in the wooden tower, despite the open windows and the onshore breeze: The light in the picture is the glaring, hazy, northeast-maritime light of July. Yet even heat and solemnity don't seem fully to account for the scowls on these men's faces. Perhaps, instead, their frowns can be attributed to overconcentration. The future is hard to imagine. Even for visionaries. La Guardia—who had romantic visions of a great city, who loved charts and maps but left the exact planning to others—is attempting to show his fellow mayors a future he doesn't fully comprehend himself. Robert Moses, after all, had planned the airport. And while Moses' plans were always very exact, and tended to get built, even they usually turned out in ways the Power Broker himself hadn't anticipated.

Concrete was being poured for the new main runway at New York International even as Mayor La Guardia gave his presentation. (Thirty years later— not long after Eastern 66, which crashed onto concrete—concrete runways would go the way of concrete highways.) Construction of the airport had begun three years earlier, in April of 1942. One of the first projects was the laying of seventy miles of storm drains, to control the tidal flow of Grassy Bay (the inlet of Jamaica Bay on which the airport was to be located). Now the bay itself was being dredged, to a depth of thirty feet. The sand dredged up from the bay floor was being spread over the marshy areas of the vast Idlewild site.

Idlewild—that beautiful name, name from the dreamtime. Dream was quickly becoming reality. The site—which consisted of two types of terrain, swampy grass and grassy sand—recalled the old country-lane, butter-and-egg days of Long Island, the days before an expanding population required every square foot to be filled in and fiscally justified. Over the sandy flats still lay the decaying links of the Idlewild Golf Club (the last remnant of the beer baron's pleasure dome recalled by Len Klasmeier) and the decaying runways of Jamaica Sea Airport, where Klasmeier took his first flying lessons, at $8.50 per twenty minutes. Along Cornell Basin, the arm of Bergen Basin that hooked in from the bay, were strung squatters' beach shacks, peeling in the salt air, air suffused with the hazy, timeless oceanside miasma of sexual salt, fated fun. In this case fate's term was precise. Squatters pay no rent. The shacks were bulldozed, and Cornell Basin filled with sand. Playtime, the old gay time of frolicking flappers and knickered golfers and leather-helmeted flyboys, was officially over. The present was money. Big money. MONEY.

❑

The $71 million Fiorello La Guardia spoke of in his address—more than half a billion in today's dollars—had not gone as far as he'd thought it would. (Money never did with La Guardia. He left a debt-ridden city when he yielded the mayoralty; when he died he had only a heavily mortgaged house in Riverdale and eight thousand dollars in war bonds to his name.) The $71 million covered only the base preparation of the site: dredging, bulldozing, sewer digging. To construct the glorious airport of the plan on the map-table would take another $100 million to $200 million. Maybe—could it be?—more.✦

✦ By the end of 1955, an additional $76 million had been sunk into Idlewild. Five years later, the total had risen to $288 million. By the end of 1965, the airport had cost more than $381 million.

111

Wartime had kept a check on municipal construction; now new construction was needed. But there was no money to do it with. New York City, which ran La Guardia Airport and which would run Idlewild, was swimming in debt. The situation came to a head exactly at the moment the war ended and William O'Dwyer took over the mayoralty from La Guardia. O'Dwyer was a Democrat, and the state government in Albany, under Thomas E. Dewey, was Republican. To get the city out of debt, O'Dwyer needed to raise taxes, and Albany had to give permission. Albany was unlikely to oblige. Moreover, O'Dwyer—a big, brawling, hardheaded realist of a politician—entirely lacked Fiorello La Guardia's visionary fervor. About building great airports and everything else. He looked into more immediately practical uses for the Idlewild site: an industrial park, a low-cost housing project. Into the grandeur gap stepped Robert Moses.

Leave it all to me, Moses told O'Dwyer. Through ultra-Byzantine maneuverings—nothing out of the ordinary for him—the Power Broker sold Governor Dewey on a tax-raise package that would get New York City out of debt, at the same time vastly increasing the power of Moses' Triborough Bridge Authority and also creating a New York City Airport Authority, which, like the TBA, would be a public/private authority with the ability to issue its own bonds.

O'Dwyer realized only after the dust had settled that his savior was a dubious one. The unique stamp of Robert Moses' TBA (as a result of his 1946 wheeling and dealing, it would subsume the former Tunnel Authority and become the TBTA) was the fact that its financial dealings were private, while the public paid its debts. Hence, in 1945, the city's $200 million in service fees on various old TBA bond issues. And now, with the new Airport Authority, there would be new bonds—big ones—and new debt. In addition, Moses was proposing to guarantee a high rate of return on the bonds, and sweeten the deal for potential Airport Authority investors, by raising hangar and terminal rentals at La Guardia and Idlewild by as much as 600 percent. The airlines, most of which were just getting into the business, howled. Eddie Rickenbacker, the World War I flying ace and founder of Eastern Airlines, walked out of a lunch meeting with Moses and said, "I'm going to Newark."

He meant the airport. Founded in 1928, Newark was tatty and outmoded. But now the Port of New York Authority—Moses' nemesis, and a symbol, for many old New York pols, of "Jersey politics"—was proposing to spend $75 million to enlarge the airfield, making it the world's greatest hub. So, rather than lose face to New Jersey—or yield even more power to Robert Moses—Mayor O'Dwyer turned La Guardia and Idlewild over to the PA.

*

112

THE AIRPORT

The Port of New York Authority—or Port Authority, or PA, for short—stands as a living symbol of uneasy compromise in the interests of fiduciary gain. "The Port of New York Authority is a public corporation, an agency of State Government; it is, in fact, an agency of both the States of New York and New Jersey," reads an idiosyncratically capitalized 1970 public-relations pamphlet.✝

> The reasons for its creation can be traced back several hundred years. At that, it was an accident of political history, occurring over 300 years ago, which divided a common Port area between what ultimately became the States of New York and New Jersey. Far less accidental, however, were the disputes resulting from that division which developed between the two States throughout the Nineteenth Century.
>
> First, a quarrel arose over which State should be able to license steamboats on the Hudson River. Then, the States disagreed over the location of the boundary line itself. This they settled, politically, at least, through the Treaty of 1834. Other arguments, such as waste disposal in New York Bay and rate wars between shipping companies, usually were decided in the courts. On some occasions the rivalry—fanned by newspapers and civic groups—erupted with small arms warfare between police units.

Small-arms warfare may be the most honest expression of the political subconscious, but after the mustering of troops and equipment for World War I's Allied Expeditionary Forces through the Port's antediluvian facilities proved to be something of a mess, the two states decided to calm down. At the end of 1918, the Joint Commission on Port and Harbor Development [the pamphlet continues] "recommended the formation of a permanent interstate agency, corporate in form (like The Port of London Authority), to carry out a unified program of port development. It was to be created by compact between the two sovereign States under the 'compact clause' of the United States Constitution."

The deal was finally done on April 30, 1921, when, at a ceremony in the Great Hall of the Chamber of Commerce of the State of New York, the compact between New York and New Jersey that created the Port of New York Authority was signed. "Through the Port Compact . . . [the pamphlet continues] New York and New Jersey established a public corporation, responsible for its services to the people through their elected representatives. *This gov-*

✈ *The Story of the Port Authority,* revised edition, published by the Port Authority.

ernmental enterprise was required, like a private corporation, to be self-supporting or fail. . . ."

The italics are mine. Public corporation? Private corporation? The distinctions begin to boggle the mind. In America, to the best of my understanding, a public corporation is one that is publicly held: Stock is owned and traded; the company's books are open. A private corporation offers no stock, and the books are closed. An authority is something else again. The institution is ancient. "The first of these entities that resembled private corporations but were given powers hitherto reserved for governments—powers to construct public improvements and, in order to pay off the bonds they sold to finance the construction, to charge the public for the use of the improvements—had been created in England during the reign of Queen Elizabeth," writes Robert Caro in *The Power Broker.*

Yet despite the popularity of authorities, including the Port of London Authority, in England, the idea never really caught on in America until the Depression, when taxation was no longer sufficient to underwrite public works projects.

> With the lone exception of the Port Authority [Caro writes], every public authority created in the United States had been created in a single pattern: each had been established to construct and operate one, and only one, public improvement, a single isolated bridge or tunnel or sewer system, to issue only enough bonds to pay for the construction of that improvement, and only bonds with a fixed expiration date, and, when that date arrived—or sooner, if revenue was collected faster than expected—to pay off the bonds, eliminate all tolls or fees, turn the improvement over to the city and go out of existence. The Port Authority, empowered to operate several improvements, had become America's first "multi-purpose" public authority, but each of its projects fit the traditional pattern since each was financed by a separate bond issue and both Authority members and public officials expected that as soon as each issue was paid off, *the tolls on the facility financed by that issue would be eliminated* [italics mine].

The Port Authority was a special case. It didn't get to be that way through sharp planning, however, but through fiscal disaster. Its first bond issue, in 1926 for the Arthur Kill bridges, wasn't worth the paper it was printed on, and the new authority went into a fiduciary tailspin it came out of only when it somehow inveigled New York and New Jersey to let it take over the Holland Tunnel, an endless bonanza of tollbooth change. Yet while a filling of the coffers was pleasant, it didn't solve the problem of financing those projects that wouldn't generate Scrooge McDucklike mountains of nickels, dimes, and quarters. The PA's mandate, after all, was to raise money for new construction through project-specific bonds. Three years later, in 1934, the body's general counsel, a kind of visionary genius named Julius Henry Cohen, came up with the solution. What about a new kind of bond, secured not by a single project but by the authority's general revenues? It sounds so simple, but it was revolutionary. The consolidated bond was born, and with its birth, the Port Authority's books—its *real* books, since the PA *isn't* really a "public corporation" at all, but a unique blend of self-importance and public-spiritedness, sanctum-sanctorum self-interest and window-dressing accountability—closed forever. The Port Authority could collect Himalayas of silver and use the money for anything it damn well pleased. The till could rise in blessed privacy, as the authority's directors and commissioners, and the bondholders, and the underwriters, all smiled, and the public paid the toll.✦

When the Port Authority took over New York International Airport from New York City on June 1, 1947, it was officially assuming a huge burden. Not only did the city expect its annual lease payment of $350,000, there was also the matter of that pesky $71 million it had already sunk into the marshy sands of Idlewild. New York wanted its money back. No problem for the PA: It had that and plenty more. It had been in the black for years; moreover, there was a postwar traffic boom on. Millions of people were sitting, cursing, in their fuming cars on the inadequate roads in the tunnels and on the bridges that crossed the city's rivers, and paying for the privilege of doing so.

And the airport looked to be another cash cow. Photograph after photograph shows the big-jawed men, in their important gray suits and heartrendingly ugly ties, sitting and signing the leases that would make their airlines—Peruvian International, Seaboard and Western, National, TWA, American, and many others—the Port Authority's tenants at Idlewild. All these carriers flew cargo, to varying degrees, but cargo flying (and storage, forwarding, and theft) wouldn't become an important part of the airport until the mid- to late fifties. Passengers were the ticket after the war. Thousands of

---

✦ Have I ridden this hobbyhorse far enough yet? Never believe for a second that your tollbooth quarters—or dollars—are doing anything else than paying for some commissioner or foreign trade representative's shrimp-and-lobster lunch. The bridge, or tunnel, was amortized years ago; paint and maintenance costs chicken feed; and the toll collectors earn *bubkes*. The origin of the word *turnpike* is quite literal: A seventeenth-century English device containing wooden pikes would not let a wagon pass until Ye Toll was paid. The British have always had an admirable directness about their bloody-mindedness; we Americans are oilier. Tolls are smiling, legalized highway robbery.

Americans, eager to get out and see the world the war had kept them from, were beginning to fly commercially for the first time. My grandparents had flown before, but the splendid luxury trains and passenger liners of the twenties and thirties—lost worlds!—had always been their conveyances of choice. Suddenly they were flying Pan Am to Havana, TWA to Palm Springs. And the rich weren't the only ones taking to the skies. Juan Trippe's sparklingly altruistic 1948 article, "Now You Can Take That Trip Abroad," ran not in *The New Yorker* or *Town and Country* but in *Reader's Digest*. The point was clear: Mr. and Mrs. America were being sought after.

And were showing up. And as the airlines burgeoned, so did the PA, with airline lease payments and passenger landing fees now added to its surging cash flow. The Port Authority that Sammy Chevalier joined as a young helicopter pilot in 1948 did not have to pinch pennies, especially where the comfort and convenience of its top echelons were concerned. Helicopter flight was exotic in 1948, and as expensive then as it is now. But then, PA officials needed (and still need) a way to avoid all those . . . *inconvenient* traffic jams down below.

The great plush years for the Port Authority lasted a quarter of a century: while the traffic-toll and landing-fee revenues piled up, while the consolidated bonds added to the real and the stated surplus. But unlike Robert Moses' Triborough, the PA never had (with the narrow exception of Julius Henry Cohen) any great visionary; no single genius ever guided its development. It was an arranged marriage between New York and New Jersey, rather than— as the Triborough had been—a kind of urban-development religion. The PA was merely a massive precinct, a congeries of bridges and tunnels and docks and airports, growing and falling apart in fits and starts, getting patched and added to when necessary, generating capital that went to further patch and add, and to remunerate (handsomely) its leaders and (reasonably well) its workers.

The rise of Kennedy coincided, more than coincidentally, with the Port Authority's halcyon days. The fifties were a boom time at Idlewild, as a number of historical factors cooperated. A growing world economy and cheap oil led to the 1952 introduction of the transatlantic coach fare. Then came the end of the Korean War, and the airline industry[*] went wild. The beginning of the jet age (the Boeing 707 was introduced in 1954, was ordered in quantity by

---

[*] To a great extent in those palmy days, the American airline industry *was* the airline industry: around the world, the vast preponderance of air miles were flown by U.S. carriers (almost all of them, overseas, by Pan Am), with very minor competition from nationalized airlines such as BOAC (later to become privatized as British Airways), Air France, Lufthansa, Iberia, KLM, and the like.

Pan Am the following year, and first flew out of Idlewild in 1958) made what had come before look pallid. And as the airlines grew, so did the airport.

There wasn't much planning at first. The very concept of an airline terminal, after all, was brand new. Unlike rail and bus terminals, which had operated at capacity for decades, airports simply hadn't had enough traffic until recently to justify giving terminals much thought. The 1943 *Popular Science* plan for New York International didn't seem to show any kind of terminal at all—the most prominent buildings were hangars, arrayed around the central promenade and "parking field" (for cars).

Indeed, until a few years ago, flying—like ocean liner travel, which it was replacing—had a lot of outdoors to it. My own first flight, in 1958, on an Allegheny DC-3 between Hazleton, Pennsylvania, and Newark, fit squarely in the old mode of airline travel: The airfield was small, sunny, and very windy, with lots of private planes tied down on the apron. We got out of the wind in a tiny brick building, which contained a couple of rest rooms, a few vending machines, some molded-plastic chairs, and plenty of cigarette smoke. After too long a wait, the heart-stoppingly beautiful plane, with its blindingly bright nude aluminum skin, taxied up roaringly. Outside, the noise as the wind blew and my heart pounded and the propellers crescendoed down, was terrific. The sun sparkled off the DC-3. We walked across the tarmac and up the rolling ramp.

This simple experience, so deathlessly vivid and exotic to me—I was seven—was repeated millions of times for millions of passengers in the early and middle days of airplane travel. It made sense; it was of a piece with the medium. Planes rose on the wind, cut through the wind. Why not face the wind, smell it, before you stepped aboard?

Not that there was any choice. Before the invention of the Plane Mate (that jackknife-mounted waiting room on wheels), before the advent of modern airport design, with radial passageways, gate-side plane parking, and telescoping, bellows-sealed entry corridors—before commercial flight became a hermetically sealed, sociologically alienating, environmentally toxic, high-positive-ion, pneumatic-tube type of experience, which spat you out on the other end of your voyage feeling weak, woozy, dehydrated, and disoriented, there were the grand days when you were buffeted by wind (on the apron) and noise (on the apron and in the plane), and when you arrived at your destination weak, woozy, deaf, and exhausted from hour upon three-hundred-mile-per-hour hour in the air. You knew you were flying then!

In the early and middle days, Idlewild was just as much of the tarmac, wind, and rolling-ramp school as any other airport. In the old days the central terminal—the *only* terminal—was the old one-story cinder-block administra-

117

tion building constructed in the early forties by the WPA. In the center of the building stood a dinky three-story control tower, with anemometer, weather vane, and antennas on top, and a big electric Bulova airport clock facing the driveway. Quarters were cramped inside: The desks of the various airlines sat cheek by jowl, and airport employees willy-nilly knew each other by first name. There were a few tiny shops, a bank branch. Passengers, male and female, wore hats. The women wore gloves. Flying was still an elite experience. Mr. and Mrs. America may have been beginning to participate, but hoi polloi, the masses, were at home watching their Philcos.

Quonset wings were added to the terminal to accommodate the increase in traffic. But soon the steady influx of money to the airlines (and from the airlines to the Port Authority) created new imperatives:

> On March 10, 1955, a "Master Plan" was unveiled and construction began. A "Terminal City" would be built at Idlewild with a magnificence beyond compare. On a tract of land, 655 acres in total, would rise a mile long oval of passenger terminals, one for each major U.S. Airline.
>
> Like jewels on a necklace these terminals would surround a landscaped area of parks and fountains. As centerpiece a magnificent structure with a sweeping arch called the International Arrivals Building would sit next to the eleven story control tower with its white Radome ball up top and form the theme of this great new air gateway. "The IAB" as it is called was designed by Skidmore Owings and Merrill who also designed the Air Force Academy in Colorado. Adjoining the IAB, the East and West Airline Wing buildings allowed for each of the foreign air carriers to design and create their own separate interior passenger service facilities.
>
> —GEOFFREY AREND, *Great Airports: Kennedy International*

Airport technology was still sufficiently primitive in 1955 that Thomas Sullivan, the chief architect of Idlewild's unique unit-terminal design, could begin with a clean slate. The idea, originally, was to keep the terminals far enough apart to minimize airplane cross-traffic on the taxiways. And the financial strength of the airlines was great enough, and the volume of car traffic to Idlewild low enough, that the idea of building these individual terminals[*] and stringing them around a central roadway system seemed to make a

---

[*] Some of which were financed with Port Authority funds, which the airlines then paid back through higher-than-normal rent. In other cases, the airlines found third-part financing.

118

kind of brilliant sense. It had a Robert Moses visionariness to it. According to Arend:

> Now along the outer oval of "Terminal City" arose the major airline buildings. United and Eastern Airlines opened theirs in October 1959, American's opened in 1960, next came Northwest Airlines. All were considered bellwethers of modern design and passenger convenience with airlines outdoing each other for impact and image. Ramps of Eastern's terminal were suspended by a series of stainless steel cables. Creating imaginative visual forms, American Airlines' 317 feet of stained glass across the facade of the terminal (some 8000 individual pieces) was the largest expanse ever created. For the 655 acre Terminal City with parking room for 6000 cars, a system of underground cables and pipes was laid out to rival the ancient Roman system of viaducts. A central heating and air conditioning plant connecting all the buildings of Terminal City was put into operation and a 500 room hotel was built at the airport's entrance. An entire telephone system complete with a telephone building geared to handle more calls than the city of Denver was built.
>
> Editorial writers reaching for superlatives were overwhelmed. One typical report in 1959 stated, "The eye receives but cannot entirely take in Idlewild's vastness, shapes and colors, all dedicated to the proclivities and esthetics of flight: 4,900 acres (all the land from the Battery to Forty-second Street); buildings rhomboidal, curvilinear, parabolic, rectangular, shafted of glass, steel and concrete. Idlewild is a staggering proposition."

The proclivities and esthetics of flight. Where is the purple editorial writing of yesteryear? And the swooping optimism? The sixties brought further innovative architecture to the airport. Pan Am's elliptical terminal, with its dramatic, four-acre concrete roof, arose in 1962, as did Eero Saarinen's soaring poem in concrete, the TWA Flight Center. New wings for the IAB followed in 1969, as did the new National terminal and the Pan Am Worldport. The British terminal—the first, and still the only, freestanding terminal of a foreign airline at Kennedy—went up in 1970.

And then the building stopped.

The seventies were a bad decade for commercial aviation, a bad decade for Kennedy Airport, a bad ten years all around—aesthetically, politically, economically. The Calley trial. The George Wallace shooting. The Nixon reelection. The ascent of Lon Nol. Terror at the Munich Olympics. The death of Harry Truman. Watergate. The rise of disco, polyester, and the very large collar. The Arab oil embargo, and the world energy crisis.

In 1973, the embargo raised the price of jet fuel from thirteen to forty cents a gallon, putting a whammy on the airlines from which they still haven't recovered. And there was plenty of whammy to go around. In 1974, world-wide inflation slowed economic growth to near zero in most industrialized nations. Air travel slumped, and the airlines cut back their payrolls drastically. Well-paid airline cargo workers were let go, and cheap subcontract laborers—known as "ramp rats"—were brought in.

The 1959 Idlewild had been a gem, the international airport state of the art. *It worked.* And it looked beautiful. In the central plaza of Terminal City, amid broad lawns and vast beds of tulips, ducks paddled in the great Fountain of Liberty. By 1975, lawns, tulips, ducks, and fountain were all gone, paved over to make more room for cars. Organized crime, under the direction of the Lucchese crime family of the famous Five Families of New York, was in complete control of all cargo operations at Kennedy—a thirty-billion-dollar-a-year grab bag. The Kennedy Airport of 1975—the world spins mercilessly fast—was a dirty, physically deteriorating, automobile- and crime-ridden anachronism in the making. And worse, it seemed, was to come.

In 1977, it was discovered, according to a *New York Times* account, that Port Authority "commissioners and managers were authorizing themselves to fly around the world first-class, or trading in first-class tickets for economy tickets for themselves and their spouses, taking Port Authority helicopters on shopping expeditions, and getting reimbursed for fictitious guests on expense accounts." *Deluded enthusiasm in a high place: How could this last?* says the *I Ching.*

In December 1978, $5 million in cash and $850,000 in jewelry were stolen from the Lufthansa cargo terminal at Kennedy. This, too, was an inside job.

The month before, Congress had deregulated the airline industry. The idea was to diversify the marketplace—raising the number of carriers and increasing competition, thus building the nation's business and lowering fares, and, in the process, allowing the masses to fly as never before.

Only the last goal has been fulfilled, with asterisks. As the big carriers used their size to push the little carriers out of business, single airlines—such as TWA in St. Louis, USAir in Pittsburgh, Delta in Atlanta—began to domi-nate major airports and their geographic sectors. The result was the rise of a network of airports commonly referred to as hub-and-spoke. The hub-and-spoke system has allowed many flyers to travel without the nuisance of switching carriers, but has meant routing nightmares for those who, for example, wish to fly from one small city to another small city that is close by as the crow flies but in another airline's sector. It has also contributed to a number of only-store-in-town-type abuses: aggravated flight delays due to cluster scheduling in peak periods (a convenience for airlines, an inconvenience to the rest of us), inflated fares, reduced amenity (eagerness to please, in commerce, rarely being a result of altruism).

What's more, the increased debt load that the major carriers optimistically took on in the 1980s, as well as unexpectedly high fuel costs in the early nineties, have put every large U.S. airline in jeopardy.

With the result that the hub-and-spoke system itself has begun to decline.

With the result that the old-fashioned multicarrier airports—like Dallas–Fort Worth, LAX, O'Hare, Miami, and, yes, JFK—suddenly look a little more flush. Yes, Pan Am and Eastern fell. Yes, the Gulf War cut sharply into passenger and cargo revenues. Yes, JFK 2000 collapsed. Yet Kennedy, curiously, prevails. Says *Moody's Municipal Credit Report* for the Port Authority of New York and New Jersey, dated March 2, 1993:

> Notwithstanding the cessations and financial and operating difficulties of several major carriers, all aircraft gate positions . . . are being utilized and it is presently expected that substantially all of such gate positions will continue to be used. . . . All measures of airport traffic were up markedly from 1991. Thus far, total passengers are up 5.4%, aircraft movements are up 8.4%, and air cargo is up 11.2%

Unlike the Port Authority's Forty-second Street bus terminal, to which cynics have been known to compare it, Kennedy consistently operates in the black. In fact, if the seventies and eighties could be compared to a patch of severe turbulence, the airport itself might be thought of as a jumbo jet that has shaken and flexed in the chop, yet emerged in oddly sound working order.

10

Infrastructure 2

Lights. Power. Fuel. A Capable Woman

Y ou're floating in, say, from Chicago—or London or L.A. or Warsaw—at the end of a long travel day, wafting in on prevailing westerlies and the lingering haze of bad airplane Chardonnay, and you look down there into the spangled blackness, and—you can't help yourself, decline of civilization or no—it all seems so dear, so ordered, so *beautiful,* the terrestrial world: the orange crime lights and those white strobes flashing down toward the foot of the runway at a thousand miles an hour (you're coming down fast now, whispering, somewhere inside you, the traveler's prayer: *Just let me land in one piece and get home fast—please please please*)—and there are those reds, greens, and ambers set so neatly right into the pavement, not to mention those mysterious deep-blue lights alongside (*big* bump, smaller bump, buckle, settle, then that unspeakable roar—why does it have to be so loud, so urgent? oh well, as long as it stops the plane). And then the terrible speed diminishes, and you're safe, you know it; the smugness and slight boredom of completion settles in, and the world is no longer miniature and dear but large and encroaching, and airport lights are the very last thing on your mind (as those blue lights, almost as dark as the darkness, and slightly misty from the Chardonnay, roll by), edged far to the back by the all-important question: *Where's my stuff?*

There are seven thousand aeronautical lights and lighted signs on Kennedy Airport's runways and taxiways, and Joe DeVito knows every one of them. Intimately. DeVito, who has a long, kindly, World-War-II-infantryman sort of face, began his career with the Port Authority at the very bottom, mopping floors at the Forty-second Street bus terminal in 1953. From there he advanced through the ranks, from helper to electrician, to foreman, to his present position, Kennedy's chief maintenance supervisor for electrical systems.

One sunny afternoon he takes me out in a PA pickup to show me around.

123

Airport people like to do this. They love the place. They're proud of their jobs. And why not? Kennedy may be outmoded, coming apart at the seams, misconceived, unwelcoming, and ill planned, but in the most fundamental sense, *it works. Eppur si muove.* The planes come and go. The people come and go (and stop, frequently). The cargo moves (often to unexpected destinations). The fuel and water and sewage flow, usually the right way, and so do the heat and cool air, adequate or not.

And the electricity. "We have four main substations here, and we buy our power from Con Ed," Joe DeVito says, glowing with pride as we drive over his turf. "It comes in at twenty-seven kilovolts, then we step it down to forty-one sixty, and distribute it throughout the airport—to every building, to the fifteen hundred streetlight poles, to all the traffic lights, to all sixty-five hundred aeronautical lights, right down to the low-voltage fire alarms. We have a staff of fifty working on it night and day. It's a city here, Jim."

Joe DeVito loves lights. He loves electricity. His office is full of glossy airport-light catalogs from the Crouse-Hinds division (Windsor, Connecticut) of Cooper Industries, which manufactures virtually every fixture at John F. Kennedy International. "The lighting on the field is a high-voltage system, a series system," DeVito says. "Every light is connected to the transformer. If the primary circuit goes out, we go crazy." Bulbs are easier, though no less crucial. DeVito's men (and women) cruise Kennedy night and day, scouting, hawk-eyed, for burned-out bulbs, which are replaced immediately. This is not fussiness but necessity. Airport runways and taxiways have a deceptively simple look to them: What are they, after all, but big roads for planes? And yet the bigger the airport, the greater the traffic, and the higher the stakes. The 1977 Pan Am–KLM jumbo-jet disaster at Tenerife in the Canary Islands (593 killed) happened on the ground, in the fog, and could have been prevented by a stop-bar lighting system in the taxiway pavement—a system like the one Kennedy is testing, and which DeVito is now stopping to show me.

We're out on taxiway Papa—the corner of Papa and Papa Alfa, to be precise. Flat marine light, milky-blue sky. What we're looking at doesn't seem very dramatic: just three little green lamps set flush into the pavement at the intersection. When a radio signal from the tower changes the lights to red, a pilot has to stop: Traffic is coming the other way. Only with a combination of green lights and an oral "Go" from the tower can the pilot proceed again.

Yet the stop-bar system, DeVito emphasizes, is still in the experimental stages: Kennedy is the guinea pig. "Most of the centerline lighting around the world has been tested here," he says. But all is not proceeding smoothly. "If the lights get stuck on red, electricians have to go out and turn them off. We're gonna stick with the hold bar"—banks of unchanging amber lights, cautioning rather than ordering—"until the kinks are out of the stop-bar system."✦

Kennedy's taxiway and runway lights are on all day, every day. The principle is safety. (Likewise, planes keep their landing lights on during takeoff and landing, whether it's a sunny noon or a socked-in midnight. "See and be seen," as Sammy Chevalier has told me.) The brightness of the centerline lights can be adjusted on a mimic panel in the control tower. "We use the highest brilliancy in fog and other low-visibility conditions," Joe DeVito says. "The top brilliancy is so bright, pilots can't look straight at it. It makes the lamps burn out more frequently. We replace the centerline lights three times a year or more, but aircraft impact, snowplows, and bad weather all take down longevity."

Next time you're landing at Kennedy after dark, blink off the Chardonnay as soon as your pilot announces the descent, and watch. If you're lucky enough to be approaching from the west on a clear night (the good-weather wind behind you), you'll get a glorious view of New York Bay and the canyons and towers of lower Manhattan—a view that thoroughly elides the misery, folly, and brutish contention below, and that fails to pall, even after the hundredth time, even for the most case-hardened New Yorker (this one was born at Lexington and Seventy-seventh). Then as you come in over Brooklyn—you're on what's known as the Canarsie approach—and over the invisible border into Queens (fair Queens!), if you're on the left side of the plane, you'll see an amazing sight: lines of white strobes, shooting toward your destination at a thousand miles an hour, strung alongside the bridge struts of the Brooklyn-Queens Expressway. John Cardinal Newman *may* come to mind:

> Lead, kindly Light, amid the encircling gloom;
> Lead thou me on!
> The night is dark, and I am far from home;
> Lead thou me on!

This array has an awesome, secret look to it, not unlike the great navigational marker in the frozen north that Superman used as the key to his Fortress of Solitude.✦✦ The strobes are, of course, the beginning of Kennedy's lead-in system.✦✦✦ Your plane descends over the good citizens of Ozone Park and

---

✦ It hasn't happened. As of this writing, the stop-bar system is on permanent hold.

✦✦ Need it be said here? No, it needn't; but I'll say it anyway: The great dream of every man, super or otherwise, is to have his very own Fortress of Solitude.

✦✦✦ Every light that guides the plane while it's in the air is under the jurisdiction of the FAA; every light that guides the plane on the ground is the responsibility of the Port Authority. Likewise the plane itself.

Howard Beach—a disproportionate number of whom are allied with, or sympathetic to, New York's five crime families, and none of whom, probably, are entirely inured to the sound of jet engines.

There are further lead-in lights mounted on various buildings in Queens (even on top of the packed-with-illegal-aliens-in-transition Travelodge at the entrance to the airport!).

A mile or so from Kennedy, you may have sighted what your pilot has already become aware of: three sets of red and white lights on either side of the runway threshold. This is the approach-light system, also known as VASI (visual approach slope indicator). Unlike the electronic glide path used on instrument runway 4 Right, this visual system is meant for clear weather, and tells the pilot at a glance whether the plane is descending at the proper angle—about 3 degrees, or seven hundred feet per minute. What the pilot and you want to see is (for a wide-body aircraft) two sets of all-white lights followed by one set of all-red lights on both sides of the threshold, or (for a standard jet) one set of all-white, then two sets of all-red. If the plane is too high, you'll see nothing but white lights. If you see only red lights, check your flight insurance.

Next, you'll see a fourteen-foot-wide stripe of light leading to the center of runway 13 Left: Condenser discharge lights in the centers of the bars flash in precisely timed sequence, giving the effect of tracer bullets shooting down the center of the stripe toward the landing surface. Then (as you watch the traffic on the Nassau Expressway grow larger, and wonder, in some small corner of your soul, *Are we going to make it?*) come the touchdown lights, elevated (and easily breakable, upon accidental impact) bars of three white lights on either side of the centerline. Next are the threshold lights, four by four, and green (red on the other side, for takeoff). Then, touchdown.

The in-pavement centerline lights begin. Again—sorry—you can't see these, but in case you wanted to know, they're white. (These, too, look different from the other side: For takeoff, they're red for the first thousand feet, alternating red and white for the next thousand feet, and all white the rest of the way. What you *can* see are the elevated edge lights on either side of the runway. White. (White, too, for takeoff, but amber for the last thousand feet.)

Next, depending upon how quickly the plane decelerates, there are several alternatives for exiting the runway. These are called high-speed turnoffs, and they are indicated by green in-pavement centerline lights. After leaving the runway, the plane proceeds onto a taxiway and rolls in toward the terminal; the pilot continues to see green in-pavement centerline lights. As you roll along, leaving or arriving, you may notice rectangular fluorescent signs with white numbers and letters on a red background. These are runway markers:

THE AIRPORT

13L, 22R, and so on. Similar signs with black letters on a yellow background⁺ indicate the taxiways, from Alfa to Zulu.

And here are the elevated edge lights, colored that deep dreamy blue that may somehow manage to convince you, despite massive evidence to the contrary, that flying to far-off places remains, at heart, a romantic and glorious, and even a poetic, thing.

❑

Rudy Hohenfeld, Kennedy's top gun in heating and air conditioning, is a large man, with a broad forehead, pale eyes, and a football physique: he somewhat resembles a cross between Carroll O'Connor as Archie Bunker and Rudolph Wanderone, a.k.a. Minnesota Fats, and his voice is remarkably similar to the actor Sheldon Leonard's. A gruff character, in other words. But it's all facade: Hohenfeld and his wife, he admits to me after we've spent some time together, have a longstanding and irrepressible habit of taking in stray dogs and cats, and ten years ago, after years of marriage, did roughly the same thing with an infant boy, much to their own amazement.

Ten years ago Rudy Hohenfeld was commuting from his house in the Sunnyside section of Queens to the Port Authority's World Trade Center, in downtown Manhattan, and not enjoying it very much. It wasn't the work he disliked—he was a first-line maintenance supervisor, in charge of the WTC's titanic air-conditioning and refrigeration plant (with an installed capacity of fifty thousand tons, or *six hundred million* BTUs—take that, Fedders window unit!), on the fifth sublevel beneath the street between the Twin Towers. It wasn't the work, it was the drive. The subtle charms of Robert Moses' Brooklyn-Queens Expressway and Brooklyn-Battery Tunnel were lost on him. Hohenfeld had started his career as an apprentice at Kennedy Airport's Central Heating and Refrigeration Plant (CH&RP) back in 1964; he had taken the World Trade Center job, a plum, when it came up; but by 1988, he'd had it with sitting in traffic twice a day. He came home to Kennedy.

He just wasn't a Manhattan kind of guy. "I was born in Bushwick, Queens," he tells me, as we drive over to take a look at the CH&RP. "I grew up in Forest Hills. My first memory of the airport? I remember in 1958, when I was getting out of the Navy, I flew in here on TWA. I got out at the TTB— the Temporary Terminal Building. It was still up then, just a big Quonset structure. And I walked out and saw cattails."

Hohenfeld shows his ID to a guard at the plant's front gate, and we pull into a small unpaved parking lot. There are muddy holes and earth-moving

⁺ Soon to be—soon *scheduled* to be—yellow on black. All lighted signs at Kennedy are due to be replaced in 1994, to the tune of some ten million Port Authority dollars. The new taxiway signs will give more information, telling not only the plane's present location, but also the nearest intersection.

127

equipment all around, for unlike most facilities that desperately need renovation at Kennedy, the CH&RP is *actually being renovated,* from top to bottom, to the aforementioned tune of $150 million, by KIAC Partners, a consortium composed of a couple of gas companies and some private entrepreneurs. The change will be epochal—for the first time ever, the airport will generate its own electricity on a full-time basis. Gigantic natural-gas-powered turbines will do the job, and more: A by-product of the generation is heat, which will be used to heat water and run air-conditioning compressors (the process is called *cogeneration*). KIAC will sell hot water, chilled water, and electricity both to the Port Authority and to the terminal tenants. It will even sell electricity to Con Ed.

Why couldn't the Port Authority have thought of this? The question hangs in the air. In any case, the new arrangement is a vast relief. For the fabled 1957 "system of underground cables and pipes . . . laid out to rival the ancient Roman system of viaducts" achieved its own antiquity quite a while ago. "In the present system there are four zones of underground pipes," Hohenfeld says, as we sit for a moment in the pickup truck's cab. He takes up a lot of space in a pickup truck cab. "Each zone has three pipes—one to send the water out, one to bring the water back in. And one is a standby, which we can use for either purpose. It's like a spare tire.

"We can shut down the system zone by zone, and reroute the water, when we have to," he says. They often have to. "The pipe is eight-inch-diameter black steel. Schedule-eighty pipe—that means it's a half-inch thick. You have welded joints, twenty- or forty-foot sections. In all the years that I've been here, this whole distribution system has been ... what's the term?" He searches a moment, then finds it. *"Fraught with problems."*

"What problems?" I ask.

"Ground water," Hohenfeld says. "Corrosion. It's wetlands here. Nothing out there is original. We do a lot of digging."

That's putting it mildly. In 1989 and 1990, the Port Authority spent $21 million to build a portion of a concrete tunnel under the extremely frequently dug-up central terminal area. Had it been completed, the tunnel would have conveyed luggage between the planned new central terminal building and the terminals of the various airlines. The central terminal building, of course, wasn't built, and now the tunnel segment sits unused. *New York Newsday,* in one of the recent investigative pieces, dubbed the passageway "The Tunnel to Nowhere." The name stuck like spit.

"Newsday's Tunnel to Nowhere," Hohenfeld says, "would've taken care of our problem. The pipes could've run through it, and they would've been impervious to water. It didn't happen.

"KIAC and the Port Authority are going to replace the pipe system with a Swedish product," he says. "They will downgrade the plant—lower the temperatures and pressures—and install bigger-diameter pipes. The new pipes will run in a loop underneath the central terminal area. There won't be any zones, but there will be isolating valves—you'll be able to shut off a particular terminal to work on it."

After years of stagnation and decay, it's an almost dizzying transformation for Kennedy. "Between when I began here in '64 and when I left in '73, there were no changes here," Hohenfeld says. "Then in '88 I came back just in time for the roller-coaster ride. I figured I would come out here and be part of rebuilding the airport. It would be akin to the phoenix rising out of the ashes. We would meet the competition of other airports taking traffic away from Kennedy.

"But it was a tired place when I came back here. The JFK redevelopment took off and died. The Gulf War, the economy, the threat of terrorism—all of it contributed to lowering traffic at the airport, which hurt JFK 2000."

"Is the redevelopment dead?" I ask.

"I don't think so," he says, quickly. "You have your roadway system, which is being renovated right now. You have your new tower. You have a possible new hotel in the central terminal area. Delta will rebuild the Pan Am facilities, and American is rebuilding Terminal Three. You have the TOGA consortium—Lufthansa, Japan Airlines, Korean Air, and Iberia—totally rebuilding the old Eastern terminal, Terminal One.

"All right, take that Tunnel to Nowhere that they singled out. It was started when things were good. Then things changed. Why single it out? There are those of us at the lower rungs who are out here breaking our asses every day—why make me ashamed to say I work at Kennedy, when it's my bosses' fault and not mine?"

We get out of the pickup. Hohenfeld goes inside a trailer and emerges a few seconds later with hard hats for both of us. His last words are still ringing in my ears, and he seems to realize it. "A lot of foreign countries come over here to see how the Port Authority works," he says, correctively, in a subdued voice. "It's gratifying to work for a company that's well respected."

We head into the Central Heating and Refrigeration Plant, a rectangular, Golden Section–proportioned, glass-faced building that would have done Mies van der Rohe proud. The plant is divided into two halves, cooling on the right, heating on the left. The color-coded compressors and pipes of the cooling area are visible through the facade—a nice, lilting visual touch for the single utility building in the central terminal area. OK, it looks like 1964—but *good* 1964. Some things hold up.

Inside it feels the same way. Who would've guessed the place was out-moded? You could've fooled me. In the Tim Burton (director, *Batman* and *Batman Returns*) view of declining infrastructure, the Gothic gloom of public works matches the ever-increasing corruptibility of human nature. In real life things are more complicated. Yes, the undercapacitied pipes may be rusting away underground; sure, the Port Authority may be taking a big fall on Kennedy Airport. But inside the CH&RP, in the cooling area, you wouldn't mind throwing down a checkered cloth and having a picnic lunch. This is the good face of old-fashioned low technology: clean, neat, efficient-looking. No grease; no sweaty guys in undershirts; no visible flames; no rivets about to shake apart. Swept tile floors; plenty of space and light. The green pipes are for chilled water, the blue for condenser water, the red for hot water. Someone has written CALL JOE NOW in chalk on a bulkhead, just so the place shouldn't look sterile. And the noise level is tolerable: The big green refrigeration machines (seven of them: one with a 6,000-ton, or 72-million-BTU, installed capacity; two at 5,500 tons; and four little guys, 1,000 tons apiece) roar away gently.

"The new steam turbine will be in commercial operation in the second quarter of '94," Hohenfeld says. "It'll produce all the hot water for the terminals, and the present system will serve as a backup. Here on the cold-water side, the present refrigeration machines will work together with four new machines."

We walk toward the heating side of the building. "And what about you?" I ask. "Where do you go?"

"The Port Authority privatized this operation with a net loss of twenty-five jobs," he says, Sheldon Leonardishly. "These people will not become unemployed; they will either relocate or work for the cogenerating plant. Four people will stay here. I am not one of them. I will continue to be responsible for the Port Authority's heating and air-conditioning operations for the IAB and assorted perimeter buildings."

He pauses a second, then looks me straight in the eye. "You gotta bear in mind," he says, "that walking around here, having spent so many years here, and to no longer be directly involved—*it tears your heart out.*"

I nod. The moment—an intensely emotional admission by a male to another male, a stranger—hovers, undeniable, unpursuable. We walk on. "Some of the guys who were working here were the sons of the guys who used to supervise me," Hohenfeld says. He shakes his head. "It's not sour grapes, but having spent all these years out here, and having expected all these changes at the airport, and having expected to retire as head of heating and air conditioning—" He pauses, and shakes his head again. "It's a change."

THE AIRPORT

We walk under the portal to another huge room, a room dominated by six black, gigantic two-story boilers. This is more like what I was expecting, more Industrial-Revolution, more demonic. Appropriately, we go down a few steps into the room. I inspect one of the boilers, which has a small window in front, through which a hellish flame is visible. Mounted above the window is a metal sign, which reads:

LAMONT

FORCED RECIRCULATION

GENERATORS

THE INTERNATIONAL BOILER WORKS CO.

SINCE 1886

E. STROUDSBURG, PA. USA

Lamont Forced Recirculation Generators! International Boiler Works Co.! Writers—relentless, feckless, often hopeless pushers of the abstract—are ever in search of *the real thing,* the more concrete (and therefore the less feckless and abstract) the better. Here, in front of me, is a *real* real thing. Or is it?

My whole quest through the airport, it suddenly occurs to me, has been a continual process of seeing the concrete—the huge, the weighty, the solid, the technological—getting shoved around by the abstract—the emotional, the economic, the unpredictable, the irrational. Four planes make it through a wind shear; one doesn't. The best intentions, the most advanced electronics, and the most efficient means fail to have much of an effect on cargo theft at Kennedy. A giant, powerful airline, steeped in history, packed with person-nel, and built around beautiful, mighty machines, simply vanishes one day, for reasons people pretend to understand but fail to comprehend fully.

Here are boilers—Lamont Forced Recirculation Generators!—large, black, serious, very heavy machines, highly efficient and in good repair—yet being nudged aside by Progress, an abstraction. As is their steward, looming beside me. Likewise, we ourselves, despite our modern insistence on the tan-gible and technological, are in the grips of abstract forces we barely compre-hend.

It is just at this moment that something very strange happens.

Having taken in the forced recirculation generator to the limit of my com-prehension, I'm staring around the boiler room—in particular, at some big green-gray sheet-metal conduits mounted up near the ceiling. This part of the CH&RP has windows up near the roof line rather than the floor-to-ceiling dis-play glass of the cooling side; and in the pallid afternoon light, on the face of one of the conduits, I see a chalk inscription—not unlike the CALL JOE NOW

131

graffito in the other room, only in different handwriting and, for some reason, upside down. It reads: HONG KONG BANK.

This strikes me as very slightly odd: Why is this written there? Is there a Hong Kong Bank I haven't heard about somewhere on the airport, which this conduit is somehow responsible for? Or—you never know—did the section of sheet metal get written on before it was installed as part of the conduit?

I turn to Rudy. "What's 'Hong Kong Bank'?" I ask.

"Pardon?"

"Up there," I say. "Written on the ventilator, or whatever it is." But even as I point toward the conduit I'd just looked at a moment ago, I realize that the inscription is no longer there.

"I don't see anything written up there," Hohenfeld says.

And he's right. There's nothing there. At all. I blush. I search; I cock my head; I peer at nearby conduits to make sure I'm looking in the right place. *Nada.* Was it a reflection? A trick of the light? A hallucination of some sort? On the contrary—what I saw had the tangible, slightly grainy quality of an actual chalk inscription: the most banal, Thursday-morning sort of physical fact. And the most banal sort of inscription. It didn't say MENE, MENE, TEKEL, UPHARSIN or PREPARE TO MEET THY GOD or KNEEL TO XANTOR.

Mind you, I am of the most skeptical, empirical turn of mind when it comes to anything like . . . whatever this was. I have never seen a ghost or a UFO; I have never had anything like a hallucination. There must, I think, be a physical reason for the appearance, and the disappearance, of this peculiar message. Yet I can think of none.

A random visit from the spirit world in the boiler room at Kennedy? *Hong Kong Bank???*

❐

Jet fuel just happens to be one of a great many things that Jerry Biscardi, Kennedy's general supervisor for aviation fueling, knows about. He is a peculiar sort of polymath, a Long Island guy through and through (Elmont). Potbellied, built low to the ground, he walks fast, talks fast, lives on candy bars and potato chips. "I love junk food," he tells me, cheerfully, as he plunks some change into the candy machine in the airport maintenance department's headquarters in Building 141. A chocolate-covered granola bar thunks down into the hopper. Biscardi takes it out and peels it. With his unreconstructed Long Island accent, salt-and-pepper beard, swept-back head of dark hair, animated features, and big brown-rimmed glasses, he might be the bassist in a weekend oldies band. Mainly, though, he's just a working stiff and enthusiastic sports dad—he happens to have three extremely large football-playing sons nicknamed Lunch, Luncheonette, and Sandwich.

THE AIRPORT

"You wanna know about fuel? What do you want to know?" he asks me. He's sitting behind his extremely messy desk in the small enclosure he occupies in the maintenance supervisor's office upstairs in the Administration Building. His sons' photographs—*big* boys—line the walls.

I ask him to fill me in from the top.

"OK," he says, giving the desk a quick bongo tap. "OK. We here at Kennedy Airport are the largest users of aviation fuel in the world. We've used as much as one point four billion gallons a year—these days it's more like one point two billion.

"We use an average of five thousand barrels an hour here—that's two hundred ten thousand gallons. That's an average. Fuel consumption varies widely throughout the year—it spikes in the summer, around Labor Day. There's a smaller spike at Christmas. It's tourism, plain and simple. Funnily enough, the curve is exactly the opposite of home heating-oil use."

"How much does it cost?"

"Depends how much you're buying," Biscardi says. "If you're pulling it for a private plane, it can be a dollar ninety, two dollars a gallon. Three dollars a gallon at Kennedy, with all the local, state, and federal taxes. See, if you just buy a couple hundred gallons, you're not buying enough to support a discount. These days, the airlines pay about seventy-one cents a gallon. But they buy by the millions of gallons."

"Seventy-one cents a gallon?" I say.

He nods. "Today."

He gives a little smile. "Anyhow. We—when I say *we,* I mean the Port Authority—we don't own the fuel; we just store it. The airlines have fuel-purchase agents who spend all their time trying to get the lowest price. It's a big business, as you would imagine. They usually buy their oil—that's what they call it, oil—off-spec, then they blend it themselves. Sometimes they're buying some pretty funky stuff.

"The Port Authority's fuel agent at Kennedy—that's me—is responsible for the receipt, storage, and distribution of aviation fuels. What I do, essentially, is manage Ogden Allied, which actually handles the fuel.

"So we have to provide safe and adequate storage for the fuel. In return, the permittees—the airlines—pay us a fifty-five-hundredths-of-a-cent-per-gallon storage charge. That adds up to about six million dollars a year. Now, you'd think that once you'd amortized the initial capital outlay to build the place, that'd be gravy, right? Well, we have to keep the harbor dredged thirty feet deep as part of our responsibility to the federal government. We have to maintain the barge docks. And in 1977, the Clean Water Act and RECRA—the Resource Conservation and Recovery Act—came into our lives.

"Years ago," Biscardi says, "when aviation fuel was very cheap, once we'd filtered out water, we'd just throw out the waste fuel—the sump. The product was so cheap, and the volume so large, that it just didn't pay to save it. Do you save paper clips in your office?"

I do, actually, but I'm ashamed to admit it.

"That's what it was like. It was like paper clips."

"Where'd you put it?" I ask.

He looks as if I'd asked a ridiculous question. "We put it in the ground."

I'm momentarily stunned by the patent political-incorrectness of this response. "In the ground," I repeat.

"Yeah. But then, after the Arab oil embargo of 1973, jet fuel went from thirteen cents a gallon to forty cents. So we started recovering oil and selling it. Then came RECRA. Now we're really into that environmental stuff. But it costs money. This year we spent fifteen million dollars on environmental upgrades. We had to spend six million just to rewire the tank farm—the wires had been underground, but the jet fuel in the soil corroded them.

"We have three to four million gallons of jet fuel in the ground under the tank farm. In 1978, the Coast Guard cited the Port Authority for polluting Bergen Basin—the fuel was leaching through the seawall on the tidal change. So we built a wall. A twenty-four-foot subterranean wall on the seaward side of the farm. Made out of bentonite clay—completely impervious to both oil and water. Five million dollars. The wall also holds back the water from the sea.

"Grassy Bay was dredged thirty feet deep when they built the airport," Biscardi says. "And they laid the sand they dredged up on top of the grassy meadow that was here in the old days. Now that grass is eight to thirteen feet underground. I've dug down there; you can still see green. We call it the meadow mat. It's just as impervious as bentonite clay—when organic material decays, it becomes colloidal. So what you have these days under the airport is two completely independent aquifers, separated by the meadow mat. On top of the mat is what's called a perched aquifer. And what you have under there, right now, is three to four million gallons of oil floating on this perched aquifer. Like a big contact lens. In fact, the oil lens is what it's called.

"We're getting it out. Slowly but surely. Jet fuel has a very low specific gravity, so it floats just great—we always know exactly where it is. We build leaching wells that separate the fuel from the water. Then we have to clean the water to DWS—that's drinking-water standards—and pump it back into the bay."

"How does the fuel get to Kennedy?" I ask.

"Through the pipeline, mostly from the Gulf of Mexico, down in Louisiana," he says. "Some of it comes from the North Slope of Alaska. But

The old tower *(left)* and the new, more problematic one. At 321 feet, the new tower is quite an impressive erection, yet—given that it was built to rise over the never-built central terminal building—its height is unnecessary.

Smarte Cartes. Note the parking structure in the background: its levels are so close together that car antennas scrape the ceilings; snow-clearing trucks are too tall to drive up to the roof.

The coronary is the leading cause of death at Kennedy.
The airport averages one a day.

IAB carousel. "This is New York at the end of the twentieth century, the American century: the greatest city in the greatest country in the world. Where are sunlight, grandeur, beauty, mystery, philanthropy, welcome, awe?"

One of Kennedy's finest as the night watch begins.

A collar. Teams of skilled pickpockets work the IAB.

The IAB. Travelers and resident. The airport has a homeless population
of about 150.

Ramp rat on the hardstand.

Jet-A aviation fuel—clear kerosene—travels through underground pipes to the hardstand, where trucks like the above pump it into the planes. A 747 like the one in the background holds more than forty thousand gallons fully loaded.

Jerry Biscardi and his domain, the fuel farm. Each tank can hold 510,000 gallons of Jet-A. Kennedy uses 210,000 gallons every hour, every day, all year.

Biscardi rising.

British Airways Concorde—the rocket. The coolest commercial airliner on earth and, at almost twenty years of age, wearing out fast.

Unwanted immigrant.

The Beagle Brigade detects dangerous contraband.

Part of Kennedy's bird population takes a rest.

the vast majority is from Louisiana. Through the pipe, underground. Up along the Mississippi River, then the pipeline branches east, through Pennsylvania, into New Jersey. We take title of the fuel in Linden, New Jersey, from the Colonial Buckeye Pipeline Company. The line comes from Linden over Staten Island, through the Verrazano Narrows, into Brooklyn. At New Lots Avenue it splits—one line goes to La Guardia; one goes under Aqueduct Race Track, then comes out here.

"We used to be a one hundred percent barge facility here. In, say, 1979, we had five barges full of aviation fuel coming into our Bergen Basin dock every week. But in the eighties, barge traffic diminished as we became more dependent on the pipeline. For one thing, the pipe just carries so much more fuel. Also you have to pay a fee if the barge sits at your dock for a while. The big barges don't exist anymore.

"But we maintain the dock—just in case. Fuel is the lifeblood of the airport. If you don't have the fuel, the planes don't fly—it's as simple as that. And you could not bring fuel to this airport in trucks—the line would be endless."

"How do you heat your house, Jerry?" I ask.

"Oil."

"How much do you pay a gallon?"

Biscardi shrugs. "I don't know."

We take a left out of Building 141's parking lot and head down to the airport's western edge. On our right is a blue finger of Jamaica Bay, surrounded by cattails. "That's Bergen Basin," Biscardi says. "It's really not bad-lookin' water."

"How'd you get here, Jerry?" I ask.

"Me? My father was a maintenance supervisor at La Guardia," he says. "I'm trying to get my sons into the Port Authority, too. Anyway—I tried a semester of college at Farmingdale after high school, but I wasn't ready for it. So I worked for the PA for a couple of years. I did everything—mopped floors at the bus terminal, picked up paper at the airport. Then I got drafted. In '68.

"I went to Vietnam. Got a Bronze Star, Purple Heart—did the whole thing. I was in the artillery. First Army Corps—Eye Corps. Westmoreland was our commanding officer. I met him once. Up where I spent most of my tour, right near a Michelin rubber plant on the Cambodian border. I was in the country from Tet of '69 to right before Tet of '70. I had a good time. I mean, I had fun doing my job, being at war. When I got hit it wasn't very glamorous. We were dug in, in Minh Tongh. They'd been hittin' us with mortars. And a round came in and hit a timber in the dugout, and a splinter hit me in the lip. They took me to a dentist's office to patch me up. I couldn't believe it—a complete dentist's office right in the middle of the jungle in Minh Tongh.

"I had a good time in the army, but that didn't mean I wasn't eager to get out. I heard if you went back to college you could get out early, so I did it. I went back to Farmingdale to get out forty-five days early. I studied electrical engineering.

"I went back to school in the spring of '70, but it didn't really sit right with me. So I went back to work for the PA. I worked in Buildings and Grounds at La Guardia—more maintenance. And I fell in love with aviation. I wanted to be a pilot, but I couldn't because of my eyes. Then somebody said to me, 'You ought to become an aircraft dispatcher.' More school. Airline Operations Training, Inc. Charles Lindbergh was on the board of directors— I met him, too. And I learned to be an airport operations agent. I ended up working in the La Guardia tower, as a sound monitor.

"Still, working indoors—it wasn't right for me. It wasn't physical. So I took the gardening test. And I got on the gardening crew at Kennedy. Picking papers at first. Now, there are guys I knew then who are still picking papers. But I didn't want to do that forever. So I got a degree in horticulture and ento- mology. I learned everything about plants and bugs. Rose through the ranks. Went from a trades-helper gardener to a journeyman gardener. Met a lot of characters along the way. Everybody in maintenance is a character. I also landscaped the Jewish and Protestant chapels at Kennedy. They were beauti- ful buildings. It was really a shame they had to be demolished.

"But then, with my kids growing up and everything, I had to start making more money. So I took this big, all-day test with all these parts, that the PA gave to people who wanted to go into management. Like a bar exam. And the good thing was, I have this, like, total recall. And because I had studied all this different stuff—electrical engineering and horticulture and entomology and aviation—I did pretty good. On the science section, I scored in the top two percent in the country. I ended up working in the environmental control unit, under Joe Gallagher. And because we were doing all these things with fuel, this is where I naturally ended up."

As we round a curve, a huge gray-white Ogden Allied tank truck passes in the other direction. "That's my baby!" Biscardi yells.

In the near distance looms, eerily, a white specter of a building: the for- mer Pan Am Hangar 19. I point it out. "Yeah," Jerry says, in a life-goes-on voice. "United is probably gonna go in there."

We pull up at the entrance to the tank farm. "Jet fuel is the *plasma* that makes the big birds work," Biscardi says. "Look at those tanks—aren't they beautiful?"

I allow that they are, and they are, sort of. There are, he says, sixty-two of

136

them here at the bulk farm—there's a smaller satellite farm, for daily storage, closer to the terminals—and the big, broad two-story-high cylinders gleam a slightly surrealistic silver in the midday light.

We drive onto the lot. "Do you have security people on the farm?" I ask.

Biscardi turns to me with a small smile. "Oh yeah, we have security," he says. We drive down an alley and turn right. "They told me they were going to get a minority firm in here to watch the place," he says. "I said, 'Oh, great.' I mean, I could imagine somebody really fucking up, and then me not able to do anything about it. But then Brenda came."

"Brenda?"

"There she is," Biscardi says, indicating a wiry, very tough-looking black woman in jeans, strolling along with Walkman headphones clamped to her ears. "She's amazing. She's"—he searches for a word—*"paramilitary."*

"What's her company?"

"I forget. Brenda!" he calls out the window. She walks along, dead to the world. Paramilitary or no, this is an oddly limited kind of security—or at least, so it seems to me. We pull up right next to her. "Brenda!" She catches sight of us, pulls one earpiece aside.

"Brenda, what's the name of your security company?" Jerry asks.

"Finest Escort and Protection," Brenda says, with a brief gleam of smile. She pops the earphone back on, and the tough face returns.

We drive on. "The tank farm was built around 1948, when the city ran the airport," Jerry tells me. "The Port Authority took it over when it was partially built. Back then, the fuel was trucked to the gates and put into the planes with overwing nozzles. In those days, aviation fuel was very cheap. They used a mixture of gas and kerosene—what they called Jet-B. Now they just use Jet-A, which is pure kerosene. A modern turbine engine will burn anything, but kerosene is cheaper and cleaner, and it's also a lubricant. You know what they say—'Crystal-Clear Kerosene.'"

Each tank, Biscardi tells me, has a capacity of 510,000 gallons of Jet-A kerosene. Each tank has a low alarm, a high alarm, and a high-high alarm. "And every one has its own personality," he adds.

We tool around the big tanks. "I'm a *skootch*. A nudge," Jerry says. "I want things around the farm done yesterday. New wires, new roads, new curbs on the roads. And I'm very against low-bidders. I'm always giving my boss a hard time about it. I say, 'If it was your house, and you were building a six-thousand-dollar kitchen, and some guy came in and said he could do the job for four hundred dollars, would you give him the job?'"

"You said before you had the farm rewired?"

"Yeah. It's all above the ground now."

We turn a corner. "On the busiest day of the summer out here," Biscardi says, "I'll say to some Ogden Allied guy, 'What do you hear?' And he'll say, 'Nothing.' And I say, 'That's right.' You got three million gallons coming in here and going out every day, the roof of each tank moving up and down, up and down on the fuel, and it's all dead silent.

"We have seven days' worth of fuel here at the bulk farm—twenty-eight million gallons. It gets transferred from here to the satellite farm, where we have forty one-hundred-thousand-gallon tanks—four million gallons. That's one day's worth. The satellite farm is strictly for day storage—from there we select the fuel and send it up to the airline."

"Through the pipes?"

"On through the pipes, to the apron, into the hydrant cart. The hydrant cart pumps it into the plane."

He grins. "So I study horticulture and entomology, and I wind up here," he says. "Hey, at least I ended up on a farm."

We're back at the gate. "My kids have gotten so sophisticated," Jerry says, "that when they call my office asking for their dad and somebody says, 'He's at the farm,' they say, 'Bulk or satellite?'"

The all-facility radio in the pickup squawks: "Seventy-nine—gimme a sweep of Thirty-one Left." Bird patrol.

"We have over fifty miles of pipes under the airport," Biscardi says, as we drive out. "There are two and a half million gallons of fuel underground at any given time."

"Do you ever spill any?"

"Oh, sure. We spilled sixty thousand gallons last year—any number of ways. It can spill out of the wing tips when you're filling up a plane; a pipe can break. These big ten-thousand-gallon baloneys—that's what we call the tank trucks—they can jackknife. But when I go to a spill, I don't say, 'How'd you fuck up?' I say, 'How can we clean this up?' I like close-knit groups—I don't like adversarial relationships."

Biscardi slows down the truck and smiles. "We're right over pipes," he says. "I feel them."

"You feel them?"

He's grinning mystically. "See that over there?" He points to a small metal door in the pavement. "Acoustic listening post," he says. "You lower a microphone with a magnet on it, it clamps onto the pipe. You can hear if the fuel's flowing or not. Me, I don't need the mike."

On toward the ramp. "Our biggest enemy is water," Biscardi says, as he drives. "We're constantly in the process of filtering out water—constantly, constantly. The funny thing is, with the environmental stuff we do, we're

138

doing exactly the opposite. In the process of removing water, we waste fuel. That fuel goes to other uses—heating oil, industrial oil—"

The all-facilities radio crackles. I can only make out key words: *"American DC-10 . . . bird strike at forty-five hundred feet . . . at the gate."*

"He's all right?" I ask.

"Yeah. He's at the gate. You wanna go look?"

Down taxiway India, over toward the American terminal. "So, speaking of bird strikes, were you here for ONA?" I ask, meaning the 1975 Overseas National crash.

He shakes his head. "Man, *that* was a fire. *Thirty thousand* gallons. That sucker burned and burned and burned. Yeah, I was there. I got hurt. The fire was so ferocious that we had to go get extra foam—I was pulling down a can of it and the top came off in my hands, and the can landed on my head."

We drive around in back of American, but can't find anything that looks like a bird-struck DC-10. I wonder where, in the vicinity, is the DC-10-struck bird. Laughing-gull heaven, probably.

Now we head back to the IAB, and pull up next to a blue-and-yellow-liveried Lufthansa DC-10 sitting on its hardstand. A dirty-yellow Ogden Allied hydrant cart—a truck, actually, with pumping and filtering equipment aboard (there are one hundred of them at Kennedy)—is sitting under the plane's wing, one hose attached to the pipe head, flush with the tarmac, another hose clamped to the DC-10's wing tank. The young Ogden Allied driver gives a wary nod to the Big Kahuna as the cart's motors drone.

Biscardi nods back. "See, his coalescer is removing water from the fuel right now," Jerry says. "It's a tremendous responsibility. It's not like your car driving along the highway—if you get some bad gas in the line, you stall and pull over. If jet engines get bad fuel at thirty-five thousand feet, there's nowhere to pull over. Every time I hear about a midair crash, that's what I think about."

"Lufthansa owns this fuel?" I ask.

"Lufthansa already owns the fuel that's going into this aircraft. Like I said, they pay us a half a cent a gallon to store it for them. But then, beyond that, Ogden Allied spends thirty-five million dollars a year here for fuel movement. So every time an airline fills up, they pay thirty dollars for the hookup, and two-and-a-half-cents-a-gallon handling fee for whatever they put in."

"Lufthansa can afford it."

"Lufty's in pretty good shape. Tee-Way worries me," Biscardi says.

"Tee-Way?"

"TWA. Right now, it represents thirty-five to fifty percent of the fuel used on the airport. If Tee-Way goes out of business, the price of fuel doubles.

When Pan Am left, we took a tremendous hit, but at least TWA picked up some of the slack. When Eastern left, nobody picked up its routes. That was rough."

A JAL 747-400 touches down, tires screeching, on 22 Right.

"Every day is the same at Kennedy," Jerry says. "Dead quiet until two-thirty in the afternoon, then the shit hits the fan."

❐

Maintenance Group Supervisor Diane Zalewski and I are standing in a cold and empty hangar—the shell of what used to be a Pan Am training and repair center, Building 17—watching a backhoe dig up the concrete floor. The building will soon be refurbished for Tower Air, a charter company that keeps a small fleet of 747s at Kennedy, but in the meantime it's still gutted, stripped of all sellable equipment. The dishonored ghost of Big Blue-and-White howls through the rafters. The backhoe chops and rears.

"What happened?" I yell.

"A water main ruptured," Zalewski shouts, over the machine noise. "A lead joint blew out, so now he's gotta break through seven to eight inches of concrete to get at it." A square-jawed, blue-eyed young woman with short brown hair and a complexion permanently reddened by outdoor work, she majored in phys ed at Queens College, playing softball and basketball during the school year and cutting grass at Kennedy during the summers. When she tore ankle ligaments going for a rebound, she left school and came to the airport for good. Starting out as a general maintainer, she found herself drawn to structural mechanics. "My father's a master carpenter," she says. "I always wanted to do that, but it wasn't so easy to get into for a woman."

Gentle-voiced and slightly shy, Zalewski smiles and blushes easily, but from warmth rather than any lack of confidence. She is utterly direct about what she does, and how she gets it done. She fixes the airport. Rather, she and her twenty-person group fix it. All of it: pipes, bridges, roofs, runway signs, taxiway delineators, buildings.

"We do a lot of rigging—floor-to-roof bracing," she says. "Painting. Line striping on the runways and taxiways. A lot of catch basin work. Scuppers— you have these troughs on the sides of the Van Wyck that catch everything that comes down from the highway. You can imagine what comes down from the Van Wyck."

A man in coveralls, carrying a shovel, walks by and smiles. "Hey, Tony," Zalewski says. "Tony Reyes," she says to me. "Up there on the backhoe is one of my best payload operators, Robby Biscardi."

The driver waves. "Related to Jerry?" I ask.

THE AIRPORT

"His brother," Zalewski says. "I have some of the good guys working for me."

We go back outside and get into her pickup. Zalewski loves her work, she tells me—even when, as is guaranteed to happen at Kennedy, it drives her crazy. It could be a lot worse. She could be sitting at a desk someplace. She could still be a cop.

After starting out on maintenance at Kennedy, she transferred to the Port Authority force. She served from 1985 to 1987. "That was the longest two years of my life," she says. "I gotta be busy. I just got bored."

"Did you work at the airports?" I ask.

"I was at Kennedy for the first year," she says. We're driving south, toward the airfield. "The second year was a little better. A little. The interesting work comes down at the bus terminal. It's wild over there. But the airport—oh, the airport is awful. I call it, you become brain-dead. I was on foot patrol at Delta, standing in a fixed spot for six hours at a time. Nine times out of ten you just go into a state where you're not prepared for anything that happens.

"So I had to leave. All the cops said, 'Why are you leaving? It's a great job—twenty years and out.' I said, 'If you can't do two, you can't do twenty.' I mean, twenty years of that, and you're gonna kill somebody. And you got all the means to do it with, right there."

In '87 Zalewski came back to maintenance. ("And I woulda got a big pay jump—five, six thousand dollars—if I woulda stayed on the police force for another month," she says. "I *had* to leave.") She went into the environmental unit, becoming its first woman supervisor.

"Did you get any flak?" I ask.

"Not so much flak," she says. "But there are some guys—you know what they say. You can't teach an old dog new tricks. There was rough language, stuff like that. I can use that language, too, but only when I get mad. And it was never anything personal. They always seemed to respect me. I always got along."

We pause on taxiway Quebec. "See, we repair the taxiway signs," she says, pointing to one of the black-on-yellow fluorescent boxes.

"What do they cost?" I ask.

"The four-by-four-footers, eight hundred to a thousand dollars," Zalewski says. "The big eight-footers, the runway signs, they're fifteen hundred."

"Each?"

She nods. We hang a left on the outer perimeter road. Now we're cruising down along 31 Right, parallel to Rockaway Boulevard. "There's the new satellite garage," Zalewski says, pointing to the low, spiffy-looking, pale-green building, near the foot of 22 Right, that was constructed last year to house the Port Authority Police crash-and-fire-rescue equipment. "That's been a horror," she says. "The first contractor built the floors out of level, so the rainwater would gather. They used to have a sign in there—'Lifeguard on Duty.'"

We head off through the marshy area near the northern perimeter where Flight 66 came down. "That's Sammy's bird thing," she says, pointing toward the pigeon shack. A big bird is floating over the cattails. "That's a hawk."

We turn south onto the Major Bill Carter Highway. "After environmental I went into gardening," she says. "It was pretty good. I mean, landscaping is OK in the summer, but what do you do in the winter? When this group opened up, I came back. I like the diversity—I like doing something different every day. Also I wanted to learn more about structural work. I wanted to work with metal." She stops the truck at the end of 22 Left, by the mouth of Thurston Basin. The water sparkles blindingly in the midday light. "This is the best spot in the airport," she says. "In the fall the colors are amazing."

We sit silently for a minute, watching it. Then Zalewski shifts into drive, and we head back in.

Along 31 Right, through the space between TWA International and TWA Domestic, I can see the new, six-story parking garage that was to have been connected to the never-built central terminal complex. "Are they using that garage yet?" I ask.

"Yeah, they're usin' it," she says sardonically.

"Why? What's wrong with it?"

"That was another great contractor," Zalewski says, shaking her head. "The ceilings are so low that the car antennas scrape. And because the ceilings are so low, that means they can't drive trucks in. Which means they can't remove snow on the roof. Which also means they can't change the lights up there, either—or at least they can't use trucks to do it."

"So," I say, after a minute. "Do you think you'll stick with the job?"

"I've got no choice," she says. "Five years ago, I was ready to pack it in and go to Maine. I mean, I grew up in Bayside. I was sick of the city. I love Maine—the people, the countryside. Everything. But the economy didn't help me out. There would've been nothin' for me to do up there—I would've starved. So I stayed here. The five-year plan became the thirty-year plan. I bought a house out on Lake Ronkonkoma."

"How far is that from the airport?" I ask.

"Sixty miles."

"Sixty *miles*?"

"I know, I know," she says. "People say, 'You're crazy to live that far out.' But I'm the one that's gotta pay the mortgage."

"Is it pretty out there?"

Zalewski shrugs. "It's Long Island," she says. "I never wanted to live in Long Island."

11

The Doctor

Fatal Asparagus Trucks,
Sundry Infarctions, Apprehended Mules.
The Golden Hour

D r. Louis Abelson happens to love the Island, thank you. And why not? He has lived in its most beautiful regions all his life—by the sea at Rockaway, for almost seventy years; ditto at Montauk, since 1974. He's a tough old coot who has done quite well. Compact but big-chested, white-mustached, slit-eyed, fiery-skinned, he bears a striking resemblance to the bluff cartoon tycoon on the Chance and Community Chest cards in the game of Monopoly. The resemblance is not inappropriate. Abelson and his childhood friend and partner, Dr. Leon Star (they met on Rockaway Beach in 1928, in a boy's book scenario: Abelson, a seventeen-year-old lifeguard, tweeted the fifteen-year-old Star out of the surf), founded Kennedy Airport's Medical Facility as a privately held business in 1951, originally sharing a Quonset hut with the Port Authority crash-and-fire-rescue unit; over four decades they turned it into a money machine.

"Both Star and I had just gotten out of the service," Abelson says, in his hoarse growl, as he shows me around the Facility one afternoon. A former championship swimmer (City College, 1933; gold, silver, and bronze medalist at the first Maccabiah Games in Palestine, 1932) and Army Air Corps medic in the China-Burma-India theater during World War II (he has a Bronze Star pin on his lapel), he walks with a chesty, swashbuckling gait, as though he'd just emerged from a big surf on a sparkling day. He's wearing a British tweed jacket, crisp (but not too crisp) white oxford broadcloth button-down shirt, striped Lands' End rep tie, pressed khakis, and Bass walking shoes: Dress British, Think Yiddish. Abelson, though, is not a de-hebraized

Jew (he was brought up in an Orthodox household in Flatbush) but something else again—*Amerikanisch.* He emanates a palpable air of Second World War, the kind of verbal swing/swagger that flourished during our last great Era of Self-assurance. "We tried to set up shop in Rockaway, but it was pretty tough going," he tells me. "All the doctors who hadn't gone to war had a lock on the trade. So whatever you could do—and still stay legal—you did.

"This TWA guy I knew said they could throw us some business from time to time—you know, the occasional ill passenger or hurt employee. Strictly nickel-and-dime stuff at first. But the airport grew, and so did we."

Over the next three decades Abelson and Star built the Facility from a bare-bones practice into a beehive, with a staff of seventy-five surgeons, internists, nurses, and technicians treating forty thousand patients per year. Star died in 1989, and Abelson continued on his own for a few months until the beginning of 1990, when he sold the business to a consortium headed by Anthony P. Parrinello, M.D., for a pretty profit. We stick our heads into Parrinello's office for a moment. The new boss is a tall, preternaturally vigorous looking man with a head that resembles a Roman bust—albeit a Roman bust with a deep olive tan, big, glowing teeth, and remorselessly self-confident dark eyes. Lucrative franchises are, apparently, good for morale.

In the meantime Abelson, no slouch in the entrepreneurship department, remains as a consultant. *Consultant:* that magical, or less than magical, word. Magical, in Abelson's case. He is polymorphously consultative. His four-page résumé contains an eye-widening roll of gigs: "Senior Aviation Medical Examiner, FAA. Senior Aviation Medical Examiner, CAA (United Kingdom). Designated Consultant, U.S. Public Health Service. Consultant, U.S. Department of Justice, Immigration and Naturalization. Consultant, Drug Enforcement Agency (Contraband Enforcement Team). Consultant, British Airways. Consultant, Trans World Airlines. Consultant . . . Consultant . . . Consultant . . ."

Life has given him much; at eighty, he wants more. He has the air of an operator, an eye for the main chance. The airline consultancies mean he flies those airlines for free. He uses the privilege often. He drives a gray cellular-equipped BMW 325i convertible around the airport as if he owned the place; he parks wherever he pleases. Cruising along Kennedy's roadways in the taut tan *Gemütlichkeit* of Lou Abelson's Beemer, you see the airport differently: The sky opens out; the pace slows down; the history seeps forth. When Abelson and Star first hung up their shingle here, the site was all sand and reeds and tidal marsh—the bedrock (such as it was) of *Ur*–Long Island, the landscape of Idlewild, where cigar-chomping beer barons in wool tank-top Jantzens once lolled with their fleshy pinafored honeys.

THE AIRPORT

The Medical Facility shared quarters only for a short time. Soon it moved from the ignominious Quonset into its own building, a small one-story structure, surrounded by a white picket fence, out among the waving cattails, a half mile northwest of the central terminal area. It might as well have been the Bronx. "It was the desert," Abelson says. "The outside edge of the airport. Nobody thought there'd ever be anything here—now we're smack in the middle of the place." *Mutatis mutandis,* Building 198 stands just where it has stood for nearly forty years—which, today, is hard by the JFK Expressway, taxiway Victor Alfa, and the foot of runway 13 Left. It is an utterly functional looking, white, squared-off two-story edifice, unimpressive until you realize that it has very few counterparts at other airports anywhere. If your heart attacks you at Schiphol or Dallas–Fort Worth or O'Hare, you will probably die waiting for an ambulance or on your way to the hospital. If your heart attacks you at Kennedy (and somebody's does, on an average of once a day, every day of the year), the ambulance crew need only negotiate the airport's roadway system to reach you and apply CPR, then buck the roads again to get you back to the Facility— no mean trick, it's true. But odds are you'll make it.

Coronaries are big business at JFK, Abelson tells me. And that's just the beginning. With all that cargo moving around, there are plenty of industrial accidents. A ramp worker was once crushed to death by a container of frozen asparagus. Unwary stevedores are often knocked over by jet blasts. Escalator mishaps, you will recall, are frequent at Kennedy, especially among newly arrived Third World types who have never seen such a device before.

But first aid is only part of the picture. "The emergency room—that's our bread and butter," Abelson says. In the late fifties he and Star began to discover more substantial dishes. That was when they started doing Class 1 pilot physicals for some of the airlines that flew into Idlewild. "It's a tremendous responsibility," says the doctor. "If you put a man up there and something happens, it comes back to haunt you." It's also a big business: As Star and Abelson's reputation spread, their profits increased. These days, the physicals are a financial mainstay for the Facility. The FAA mandates that pilots have an EKG at age thirty-five, then another at forty, and once a year thereafter, with a physical once every six months. Pilots pay for the physical themselves; the exam for U.S. pilots costs ninety dollars at the Facility, a comparatively low going rate. The medical center's doctors perform about four thousand pilot physicals a year.

The Japanese physical is something else again. "The most thorough in the world," Abelson tells me. "It all started after that JAL pilot crashed his DC-8 on purpose into Tokyo Bay a few years ago. It turned out he had a his-

147

tory of mental problems. That was a huge deal in Japan, a national tragedy. Ever since, the JCAB—that's the Japanese Civil Aeronautics Board—has required a complete work-up once a year for all pilots. A cardiac stress test; an EEG, to detect any possible brain tumors; all kinds of blood tests." The exams cost thirteen hundred dollars a pop, and the Facility does quite a few of them. "The JCAB and Nippon Air came over a couple of years ago to check out the Facility and eat steaks at Peter Luger," Abelson says, smiling. "They liked the trip."

There is also the wide world of drug testing. Wider than ever, these days. In December 1989, the FAA began mandating random drug testing for airline pilots. "Before pilots are hired, they can be tested for twelve different drugs," Abelson says. "Once they're on the job, they can only be tested for five. We use the acronym CAMPO—that's cocaine, amphetamines, marijuana, PCP, and opium derivatives. We have one TWA crew, and one from North American Airways, being tested this afternoon." Is anything likely to be found? "As far as I'm concerned, drugs are not a problem with airline crews," Abelson says, flatly—although there are those that disagree with him.✦

Alcohol, however, is a different story. Truck drivers, train engineers, and airline pilots—what, Herr Doktor, are the common threads? Loneliness, monotony, underpayment. Truck drivers and train engineers are more likely to come from a lower socioeconomic stratum than pilots, one where uppers and pot tend to be the drugs of choice. Pilots—generally male, generally middle class or above, and generally approaching middle age—drink. "It's a problem," Abelson admits. Blame the sorrows of the profession: the shakiness of the business (a number of U.S. pilots are going to work in Japan these days, either following airline closedowns or in anticipation of them), not to mention the maximum difficulty of maintaining any sort of family life with a five-day-a-week travel schedule.

"Now, sitting around in a bar getting loaded one hour before flying— that's very rare," he says, referring to the 1990 incident in which a tipster in a Fargo, North Dakota, bar blew the whistle on a three-man Northwest Airlines crew that spent a whole winter night drinking a prodigious amount of alcohol, then flew ninety-one people—without incident!—from Fargo to Minneapolis.

✦ According to Joel Ehrenkranz, M.D., a drug-testing specialist, the CAMPO test may not be enough. "Pilots have very few positive drug tests," Ehrenkranz says, "but pilots do abuse drugs. They're very savvy about not getting caught." The substances Ehrenkranz refers to are palliative rather than recreational, and the physical complaint they address—jet lag—is universal and severe among pilots. Benzodiazepines such as Valium can ease jet-lag symptoms and not show up on the FAA's random tests.

Yet while Valium can smooth the rough edges, it does nothing to aid alertness. It has been suggested in some quarters that the navigational error that led Korean Air Lines Flight 007 to wander into forbidden airspace and get shot down by Soviet fighters in September 1983 may have been caused by a combination of fatigue and drug use in the cockpit.

THE AIRPORT

The crew was cashiered. But doubtless there are hundreds of crews that ought to have been, and ought to be, and are not. "My daughter was a flight attendant for Saturn Air—they flew out of Shannon [Ireland]," Abelson says. "Well, you can imagine what went on in Shannon. But the way they handled it at Saturn was, if a pilot got drunk, all ten attendants would just call in sick. So the airline would get the message, and change the crew for that day."

Employee solidarity; boy's club high jinks . . . many people, strangely enough, still consider alcohol a genteel sort of drug and, in a kind of hangover from the twenties and thirties, regard drink-related incidents short of tragedy with a tut-tut. Hard drugs are something else again. When I bring up the subject, Abelson promptly leads me out the front door of the Facility and heads toward a big white windowless trailer parked in the lot. He has a fast, important-looking stride: the Doctor's Walk. "They catch hundreds of these mules a year here," he says, over his shoulder. "It doesn't matter. They keep coming anyway. It's a margin business. Some are bound to get through, and that's all they need." He is referring, of course, not to four-legged mules but the two-legged variety: the kind that play a major role in carrying millions of pounds of illegal drugs into the country every year. "They're mostly Nigerian, for some reason," Abelson says. "But it depends where Customs is concentrating that week. They come from all over the place—Europe, North Africa, South America. Of course Customs can arrest on suspicion. It's the only way you're going to get most of these people."

"Why's that?" I ask, easily falling into the role of straight man.

" 'Cause they have the drugs inside them," Abelson says.

Inside the trailer is a row of metal beds, all unoccupied save one. On it lies a thin black-skinned man in a hospital gown. His right wrist is handcuffed to the bed. A burly Port Authority cop nods at us.

"The dealers pack the heroin in condoms," Abelson says, as though the man on the bed weren't there. "Then the mules swallow them. I don't know how they get them down. All for an airline ticket and a little pocket money—maybe a couple of hundred dollars. And the almost certain chance of getting caught."

The man on the bed reclines passively, staring into a nonexistent vista. The whites of his eyes are very yellow. It's the mule stare: long-suffering, at once all-knowing, resigned, and stupid. He's in another world, almost drugged-looking himself. Distance is the best defense—especially when you're being used as a pack animal, then talked about as an object.

"Customs brings 'em right over, and we X-ray 'em," Abelson says. "The packets of heroin show up as egg-shaped blurs on the X ray. They swallow the most amazing amounts."

James Kaplan

I ask the man his name. He tells me and says he's from Tyler, Texas—
although, from his accent, it sounds as though he's spent more time in Lagos
or Port-au-Prince than in Tyler. He spells out his name for me, answers my
questions in a monotone, staring at some spot out over my shoulder as I write
in my notebook. Where is he really from? It doesn't matter. Who am I to be
asking all these questions—cop, reporter, curious bystander? It doesn't matter. Nothing matters. He'll be free again soon, to rent his most intimate ori-
fices to the drug trade.

"How many packets did you swallow?" I ask.

"Sixty-eight," he says, in the flat voice.

Abelson puffs air through his nostrils and shakes his head. "How many
has he passed?" he asks the cop.

"Forty-nine," the cop says, shaking *his* head. Some duty.

"The stuff has to be wrapped in seven layers of condom," Abelson tells
me, as we leave the trailer-jail. "Of course, a lot of the time, it isn't. So if it
breaks in the middle of their gut, they're in big trouble. If it's cocaine, they
die. Period. End of story. If it's heroin, *and* if we get to them quick enough, we
can reverse the effect with Narcan. We've had three die on us.

"I've never had a boring day in all the years I've worked here," he says,
as we walk back into the building. "You're seeing so many diverse facets of
medicine—you're not sitting here doing deviated septums.

"There are two big things you have to worry about here—crashes and terrorism," Abelson says. "With terrorism, there's just not much that can be
done. How do you keep from having another Lockerbie at Kennedy? If you
instituted totally adequate security measures, you'd have to take twenty-four
to forty-eight hours to board an aircraft. And then any macho terrorist who
doesn't mind dying can take a plane out with some plastique strapped to his
body."

"Can't that be detected?" I ask.

"TWA has a machine that can detect Semtex," Abelson says, referring to
the widely used Czech-manufactured plastic explosive. "But it cost a million
dollars. If every airline has to have a million-dollar machine at every gate, in
this economy, you're going to have a lot of broke airlines. A lot *more* broke
airlines.

"As far as crashes are concerned, things are definitely getting better—
supervision and maintenance are improving all around," he says. "And *planes*
are getting better. Any pilot would tell you a 747 is better than a DC-6 or 7."

Statistics or no statistics, however, the possibility of plane crashes—*pace*
apprehended mules, sundry infractions, and fatal asparagus trucks—is the
most pressing reason (if only psychically) for the existence of an airport med-

ical facility. The concept is abstract to most of us: a newspaper event, a piece on the evening news. It's anything but abstract to Lou Abelson. Military planes crashed all the time during World War II; as an Air Corps medic, he saw crashes, and their aftermaths, on a regular basis. "The one that stuck in my mind was a C-47 that flew into China from India, over the Hump," he reminisces, using the old nickname for the Himalayas. "It had currency on board—payroll for the Chinese troops. I was stationed at K'un-ming at the time, at the eastern end of the Burma Road. I saw the plane crash. Maybe someone hit it with a bazooka or something—I don't know. It was a clear morning. The C-47 just went *boom* at a couple thousand feet, big puff of black smoke came out, and then it dove straight down. It made a hole about twenty feet deep. There was Chinese money all over the countryside. The guys on board? They were buried."

He shakes his head. "I once saw three B-29s crash within a single hour in a sandstorm, in Masirah, near Oman," he says. "And then at the end of the war, you had one out of *every* three planes going down—it was unbelievable. Bad maintenance, it really was. The whole attitude was, everybody just wanted to go home."

The maintenance improved in postwar commercial aviation, but in the old, low-tech days of flying, New York International, soon to be known as Idlewild, saw more than enough accidents. Flying was just plain dicey in the Truman and Eisenhower years, before the advent of instrument runways and sophisticated avionics. A little snow, a little fog, a sleepy pilot—*boom.* "There's the Seaboard and Western Airlines crash," Abelson says, pointing to a black-and-white photo on the wall. "That was in '58."

We're walking down a hallway that reeks of that sweet-scary doctor's office bouquet: rubbing alcohol and examining-table vinyl? "The first bad crash here was '54," he says. "Alitalia. Twenty-six died. Pilot fatigue. It was a December morning, close to noon—kind of overcast, with a light drizzle. A rotten day. The guy made two or three approaches, then hit an approach-light stanchion as he came in, and went right in the water. Leon Star was having lunch at the old Brass Rail in the Temporary Terminal Building with George McSherry, the director of the Port Authority. Star ran out in water up to his chest and began pulling people out. There was no fire. Just wreckage and bodies. It was a Sunday, and I was at home. As soon as I got the call, I raced to the hospital to meet the incoming ambulances.

"Then there was the Aeronaves de Mexico crash, in January of '61. I missed that one—I was on vacation in the Caribbean. They took off in a snowstorm and hit a car on Rockaway Boulevard. Miraculously, only a couple of people died."

"Were you here for Flight Sixty-six?" I ask.

"Yup."

"Was that the worst you've seen?"

Abelson shakes his head. "No," he says. "The worst one I saw was an American Airlines DC-6 or 7, around 1959. It was a noise abatement take-off—low power, sharp turn—and suddenly the plane just dove into Jamaica Bay. I was working at Peninsula General Hospital, and through the operating-room window I saw a big billow of smoke over Broad Channel. I got there just ahead of the fire engines.

"The plane had crashed into shallow water. There were no flames—just wreckage all over, and parts of bodies. The seagulls were diving on guts and brains. The firemen were coming out of the bay bending over and vomiting."

The first sixty minutes after an airplane crash are known as the Golden Hour: the period in which lifesaving measures—control of shock and hemorrhage, the performance of tracheostomies or thoracotomies or the like—must be instituted if victims are to survive. But who will institute them?

We walk out a back door of the Facility. Directly in front of us stands a remarkable vehicle, boxlike and some thirty feet long, all windows and white corrugated metal: It looks like a particularly aggressive mobile home. "This is our C-H-E-M," Abelson says, beaming.

"Your CHEM?"

"That's Containerized Hospital Emergency Mobile," he says. "This was a brainstorm on the part of Leon Star and me. It's essentially a seagoing container with a Sherman tank engine and four-wheel drive. It's got a top speed of fifty-five miles per hour. The whole idea was that you could put thirty to forty accident victims into it, take care of their immediate needs, then load the whole thing into a C-130 transport plane. If you deflate the tires and use hydraulic lifts, it just clears the entrance of a C-130 by two and a half inches."

He opens the front door and we step on board. It's cozy yet spacious inside: Behind the cockpit are a stainless-steel operating table and, in an aft compartment, twenty cots. More cots can be added, Abelson tells me. "The generator can run for three days, so we can wait out most situations," he says. "Here's the refrigerator. Star and I designed the whole thing. The ironwork was done by some people we know here at the airport, so we saved a little money there. The rest was rigged up by Medical Coaches in Oneonta."

"What did it cost?"

"Half a million, out of pocket," Abelson says, in a clipped voice, like the canny old poker player he is. Then one side of his mouth rises into a thin smile as he shows his hand. "But we now lease it for fifty thousand dollars a year to the Port Authority."

12

IAB 2

Checking It

"How has *my* airport changed since I've been here?" Ernest Davis, the chief of passenger processing for the U.S. Customs Service at Kennedy—a large, direct, big-bellied black man with a small revolver on one hip and a beeper on the other—has been with Customs since 1950, in inspection since '58, at Kennedy since '72. "The number of flights, definitely," he says. "And the size of the aircraft. A 747 in the 400 series can carry five hundred people. Now, if you have three of those coming in in an hour, the system begins to flatten out."

We're in Davis's office on the second floor of the IAB. On the wall in back of him is a large chart listing, on a month-by-month basis, the number of passengers traveling through Kennedy's five major terminals, including the IAB, and the number of total Customs seizures, broken down into categories: soft narcotics, hard narcotics, merchandise, and currency. There aren't, I must admit, quite as many seizures as I would have expected in a great airport receiving something on the order of twenty thousand international passengers a day: the totals for each month tend to be in the high double digits—86, 91, 93.

"From time to time we keep trying different methods of passenger processing," Davis says. "But we can't inspect the way we did in the fifties. There are eight million people coming through here a year today—if you stopped every one of them, they'd all still be here."

"So do you work by profiles?" I ask, repeating what I've heard about Customs methods.

Davis presses his lips and shakes his head. "You can't say profiles," he says. "You'd get taken into court."

"But then what are you looking for?"

"I can't talk to you about that," he says, impatiently. "Listen. We're playing catch-up ninety percent of the time anyway, so we don't want them to know what we're thinking."

"So you miss stuff?"

"Oh yeah. It's a calculated risk. One thing in our favor, though—the largest percent of people are honest. You can't process people with the thought that everybody's dishonest. I've had people get home from the airport and call me up with pangs of conscience about items they should've declared."

Muriel Key's reputation as one of the toughest Customs inspectors on earth—or at least at Kennedy Airport—has preceded her. "The softest thing about her is her teeth," one man told me, grinning and shivering deliciously as he told me about the time Key strode onto a plane full of Iranian diplomats and pulled a gun on a noncompliant emissary. Not usually hypersensitive to such issues, I nonetheless wondered, as I listened to this story and grinned back, to what extent male terrors are involved: those teeth! That gun!

I wonder even more when I meet Key, who, in person, merely seems like a pleasant—albeit quite direct—petite blond middle-aged lady with a passing facial and vocal resemblance to the late actress Selma Diamond and an unquenchable passion for the New York Giants (she buys season passes at Giants Stadium, and flies to as many away games as possible). Key, who's been in the business for twenty years, is in charge of a roving squad of inspectors whose job it is to facilitate the flow of passengers through Customs by quickly assessing who presents a low risk for smuggling and who does not. Like her boss, Key evades the touchy subject of passenger profiles, but she does admit that the most intense attention is given to travelers from what are called the high-risk source countries: Nigeria, Mexico, Colombia.

"Do I enjoy the work?" she says, nasally. "I love it. I love the interaction with the passengers. You meet a lot of nice people here. The celebrities are great. Nixon and Kissinger are two of the nicest people in the world. Joan Collins. I feel so bad for this woman—people were banging on the *windows* as she went past. They come in and they're treated like pieces of meat.

"The nicest people are the sports figures," she says. "Frank Gifford—what a sweetheart. And the baseball guys like crowds. Who else? I met Bon Jovi—he's a doll. Julio Yglesias—a doll. Walter Cronkite—also a doll. That actor Robert Culp, though—" She shakes her head.

"You meet a lot of jerks," Key says. "Some of the traveling public is really rude. And Saturday is always a bad day. And all in all, you're here a lot of hours. It's tedious, but it's great. The big excitement is when you find narcotics."

And what, I ask her, of the fabled Iranian plane incident?

She shakes her head dismissively. "It wasn't that big a deal," she says. "It was back in '88—this planeload of Iranian diplomats had come in for the fortieth anniversary of the UN. A male Customs inspector and I went on board, along with a female Immigration inspector, and this one Iranian guy started freaking out—'No women! No weapons!' he kept shouting."

"You were carrying a weapon?" I ask.

"My regulation sidearm, holstered," she says.

"Why would a Customs person carry a gun?"

"Sometimes when you get someone carrying narcotics, they get rambunctious," she says. "It's really just for deterrence. We never draw."

"Do you practice?"

"Four times a year, at the Nassau Firing Range."

"So anyway—the guy on the plane?"

"So he's shouting—'No women! No weapons!'—and then he starts *pushing* me. Well, I'm sorry—I have a thing with Iranians in the first place. All this sexist nonsense. And I finally just got a little impatient with the whole situation. So I put my hand on the pistol. Just *put* it there. It never came out of the holster. He backed off."

Key shrugs. "People complain about having to wait in line—a lot of times it's not our fault. Anyway, what's the alternative? I've gone to Greece and Brazil—the airports there are ridiculous. They don't even *look* at what's going through. No wonder they have terrorism."

"What's changed since you first got here?"

"In the seventies the big seizures used to be all marijuana and hash," she says. "Now it's heroin and cocaine. And security has gotten much stricter. We used to have access to everything; now we can't get to the gates—you need a special ID.

"The other thing is, diplomats used to be *diplomats*. Now they're coming in from all these nothing countries, and you don't know what the hell they're bringing with them."

"So—Muriel. Is Kennedy better than other airports? Worse than other airports?"

"Every one is different," Key says. "But this is a unique airport. It's the melting pot. They always knock JFK, but what they forget is that it's really five little airports. Or not so little. I mean, we get a bad rap because we're New York. A small town is a small town—they say, 'Hi, how are ya?' In New York, it's 'How are ya—good-bye.'"

❐

James Kaplan

Officer Hal Fingerman of the Department of Agriculture has the solemn, self-assured look of the vice-president of a Jewish fraternity at a state university: not too smooth, but knowing all the ins and outs, and determined not to take guff from anyone. He is of medium height, with a mustache, slightly receding chin and hairline, and a keen, dark-eyed stare—a stare I can somehow imagine in dusty black and white, in the grid of small portraits of the men of his year, inside a dusty black frame at the turning of a staircase in a quiet back hall of the frat house. Fingerman is not a hail-fellow-well-met type, but there is a gruff friendliness about him, a deep-down warmth beneath the prickly surface, that seems appropriate to his job. He works with dogs.

Beagles, to be precise. Fingerman is the leader of the Department of Agriculture's Beagle Brigade at Kennedy Airport, an organization born at Kennedy and now widely imitated at America's other major airports, an organization dedicated to preventing the entry of unwanted fruits, vegetables, meats, birds, and other plants, animals, and plant- and animal-related products into the United States of America. It is a solemn trust, and Hal Fingerman is solemn about it. "We're the backbone of Agriculture," he says, in his deep, carrying, college-sportscaster voice. "People don't realize how important this is. This is the first line of defense against insects and plant disease in this country. When we work, the airport works—all right? If we stopped, the airport would stop."

We're inside the Beagle Brigade's headquarters, an unprepossessing beige prefab aluminum building in Kennedy's cargo area. Not surprisingly, the room smells like a veterinarian's office—not surprisingly, because the beagle cages are just outside an open door. We are also surrounded by beagle sounds—beagles being beagles, the dogs are making their presence known. The aluminum walls echo with high-pitched howls, yips, bays, and barks. Fingerman, oblivious to the noise, is giving me the lay of the land. "I was an animal husbandry major at Penn State," he says. "I joined Agriculture in 1978, and worked as a plant protection and quarantine officer in New Orleans until 1981, when I came north to work in the Hoboken Post Office. In 1984 I came to Kennedy, and we started the Canine Brigade. It became the Beagle Brigade two years later."

I follow him outside, where we get into a green Department of Agriculture pickup: We're heading over to the IAB, to watch the brigade in action. "At first we went with the big dogs," Fingerman says, as we drive off. "Black Labradors. It didn't work out—their size scared people. We also thought about German shepherds, but they had too many bad connotations, with police and concentration camps and everything. Beagles were perfect. People thought they were cute, they were very trainable, and they had great noses.

THE AIRPORT

It's not the size of the dog, it's the size of the nose. Beagles have great noses—five million scent-gland nodules, compared to five hundred thousand in a human.

"Most of our dogs come from the ASPCA, or donations. We've never had a dog from puppy on up—they come to us with at least a few months on them. They can't start to acclimate to crowds until they're five months old. When they're nine months old, you can start to train them. And only one in fourteen works out. Some dogs are afraid of kids; some are scared of loud noises. Some are too aggressive. The only thing we require is that a dog be a chowhound." He pats a brown leather holster on his right hip, then snaps it open to show me that it's full of Ken-L Ration Special Cut dog treats.

"Customs uses shepherds and Labs," Fingerman says. "But then, they're macho—they like to carry guns and use the big dogs. If they were smart, they'd come inside here and take a look around. They're an antiquated service," he says, disdainfully. "But if you quote me, I'm dead meat." He glances to either side in the truck's cab.

"We are not an enforcement agency. We are a regulatory agency. We don't carry guns. If you lie to us, we give you a fine, starting at twenty-five bucks and going up. People have paid a thousand dollars for one apple. They don't realize—all it takes is one fruit fly to start an epidemic.

"Agriculture," Fingerman says, meaning his department, "is serious business at Kennedy. We have twenty-five to thirty inspectors in the cargo area alone, working from eight P.M. to six A.M., inspecting everything that comes in. KLM might bring in a planeload of tulips—we're looking at it for root and tuber diseases. We're watching for the Medfly. We're also the same outfit trying to stop the Africanized bee from coming up from Mexico."

We pull up on the tarmac on the airside of the IAB and get out of the truck. In his D-of-A uniform—black pants, short-sleeved white shirt—Fingerman has an important stride. He leads the way as we go in one of the building's back doors and proceed upstairs to the Agriculture officers' office. He pulls out a big ring of keys and opens the door.

In the center of the narrow room is what looks like a dissection table, aluminum-topped, with a kitchen garbage-disposal unit mounted in the center. All around this opening sit seized fruits of various sizes, shapes, colors, and states of ripeness. Guavas, mangoes, apples, oranges, kiwis, and some I can't identify. "We're gonna destroy all this," Fingerman says, waving his hand dismissively over the table. Pasted on the wall is a large collection of fruit stickers from around the world, and a sign that reads THE MORE PEOPLE I MEET, THE MORE I LIKE MY DOG. I look at the stickers, the sign, the fruit. "OK?" Fingerman asks.

Back out into the IAB. A pretty Air France flight attendant passes by, trailing a suitcase on one of those foldable chrome carts. "I got married too early," Fingerman says, deep-voiced. "This airport is full of beautiful women." We walk down the wide corridor, Fingerman's keys jingling. Ahead of us, by a crowded baggage carousel, I see another uniformed inspector, with a beagle on a leash. "I'm gonna introduce you to Canine Officer Brent Heldt," he tells me. "His dog's name is Bruce—that's short for brucellosis. You know, undulant fever. It can come in in meat. They're a good team, which means they make a lot of hits—maybe fifteen to twenty seizures a day."

Heldt is a mustached young man wearing tinted glasses that make him resemble the actor Don Novello as Father Guido Sarducci. Bruce is a cute, frisky beagle in a green nylon jacket that reads PROTECTING AMERICAN AGRI-CULTURE on one side and AGRICULTURE'S BEAGLE BRIGADE on the other. The carousel area is packed with travelers who look not even remotely like Americans. An Aeroflot flight has just arrived from Moscow. Suddenly, Bruce pulls Brent in the direction of a stout lady in a fur-trimmed coat, standing next to a Smarte Carte full of luggage. Bruce walks up to the cart and sits down.

The culprit is a green apple in a zippered flight bag. The red-faced lady gives up the fruit to Canine Officer Heldt, but not without reluctance and some confusion. "A lot of people don't bring in illegal produce on purpose," Fingerman says. "A lot of people just don't know what they're doing."

We leave Brent and Bruce to the Russians. I see Bruce sitting down again by another suitcase as we walk away. "We initially train the dogs on citrus, mangoes, pork, and beef," Fingerman says. "Then we broaden their repertoire. You find all kinds of things. The largest heroin, cocaine, and marijuana seizures have been made inadvertently by Agriculture. It can get hairy sometimes. We've been slugged, pushed; I've been stabbed. A woman took off all her clothes and chased me with a voodoo doll."

Down a hallway, toward passport control. "Human ingenuity is endless," Fingerman is saying. "People hide sausages in bandoliers around their body. I've seen a man trying to bring in an entire fig tree *on his person.* The roots were in his shoes, the branches were in his sleeves. One lady tried to hide her pet bird between her breasts. Another was wearing a big hat, with a whole hatband full of little finches."

Here is the processing area for new arrivals into the United States: not the Great Hall of Ellis Island, but what might be a warehouse storage area, cordoned into lines. A cold, gray space. Fingerman greets a pair of fellow inspectors already working the crowds as they churn through the chutes. These are not the international rich. They wear jeans and polyester, robes and babushkas, fake leather jackets. Metal teeth are much in evidence. The luggage looks sad and distressed. A rich polyethnic draft of body odor hangs in the air. The travelers nod and smile uncomprehendingly, or duck their heads and look aside evasively, as they are confronted by official America. A gray-haired man in a black vinyl jacket is holding a sign that reads: "I do not speak English, I going to Chapel Hill North Carolina Please help me If You can." Fingerman unzips the man's suitcase and expertly fingers the lining. Nothing. He nods grimly to the man, who smiles and rezips his bag. "I get maybe one out of twenty," Fingerman says. "A dog gets nine out of ten. I've seen a dog that can smell the difference between gold and silver. And I'll tell you—I was macho, too. I loved my big black Labs. But now I'm a convert to the beagles."

There's a commotion down the line: a black woman yelling at the two inspectors. Fingerman goes over to help his colleagues out. He stands listening for a minute, hands on his hips, then returns.

"What was it?"

"Some Indian lady from Trinidad. She declared nothing, and she's full of meat." He shakes his head. "Millionaires come through here, and they lie to save a hundred dollars in taxes," he says. Now his restless eyes pick out two men having their passports processed nearby. One is Italian, the other Venezuelan; they look as if they have on at least three sports jackets apiece. They have huge fake-Vuitton suitcases, and Fingerman leans on one of the bags as he says, in his carrying voice, "How are you gentlemen doing today?"

I leave a little while later. Fingerman, who has forgotten all about me, is contentedly removing dozens of pieces of fruit and wrapped sausages from the men's bags as they gesture and shrug.

13

Opsafe

An Ugly Airplane. Groaning Scouts. Doughnuts in the Rain

"**W**hat have I been doing? I've been busting my ass getting medical teams in line," Lou Abelson complains, a few days after I first meet him. He's sitting in his steel-gray BMW convertible in the Kennedy Medical Facility's number one parking space. The seaside sun is brilliant this afternoon; a light wind feathers Abelson's white hair, giving him the air of a fierce old eagle. Irritability keeps him young. "Why don't you come with me to the bank," he says. "I need to deposit a check."

He starts the engine. "A real disaster would take all day," he says. The car purrs into reverse, and we drive out into the sun. Abelson hasn't bothered to put on his seat belt. He never does. "Twelve hours at least—this is foreshortened. The last Opsafe was two years ago. It's a big deal to put one together. The main reason you're doing it is you get to meet the key people who'd be involved in any disaster—fire chiefs, police chiefs, EMS people, et cetera. It smooths the way. In a real emergency, if you come charging out and there's a 'Who the hell are *you*?' situation, it's not going to go very well.

"EMS has been a particular problem in that regard," Abelson says, as we pull out into light traffic on the home end of the JFK Expressway and head into the central terminal area. "They tend to come lunging out, with an attitude—anything that happens in the city of New York is their province. But we're *here*. We have to take care of anything that happens until the director of EMS arrives. *We* have to do the triage.

"If there's a plane crash, with the way the road net is around here, once the media gets hold of it, you can't get in or out. Forget about it. With Flight Sixty-six, we had to send patients to the hospital by taxi. Today it'd be different. We have the mobile hospital units; we would fly in medical teams by heli-copter from preestablished points.

"Back then we only had the one inflatable unit, which we towed out to the scene of the crash. We didn't use it for the survivors—there were only twelve, anyway. We used it for a morgue."

We drive onto the central loop, toward the IAB. Abelson, the old lion, leans his big head back and flares his nostrils sensuously. In the wind, in the sun, in an exquisitely wrought convertible, what is death?

"Tomorrow the Boy Scouts will be moulaged to look like real victims—you're gonna see intestines hanging out; you'll see an arm off," he says. "That's what you'll see. What I'll be trying to do is break in Dr. Parrinello. I'll be standing over his shoulder, watching every move he makes. Our team will take care of triage until EMS shows up. You know how triage works?"

"I think so, but tell me anyway."

"There are four categories in the triage area, including the dead," he says. "Number one is life-threatening, serious injuries. This is divided into two sub-categories—those who have no chance are literally abandoned. Those who have a chance are taken care of.

"Number two is less serious injuries. And number three is minor injuries. With Flight Sixty-six, there wasn't much to triage, because most of them were dead. There was another Eastern crash out here, on a foggy night in the late fifties or early sixties—a real pea-soup fog. We tried to triage, but there was no way to even tell where the roads were. It was chaos. The thing is, triage is actually rare in a real disaster. In a real crash, you skip around—you don't go from number four to three to two to one. You can't."

"If Flight Sixty-six happened today, what would be different?" I ask.

"Nothing. We may have some better means at our disposal, but that was a bad crash. The people that survived would still survive; the people that died would still die. We did hear rumors that a couple of people died on the way to Jamaica Hospital, but I don't know. I'm pretty sure we couldn't have saved them no matter what."

We pull up at the curb in front of the IAB. Abelson simply gets out of the car and closes the door, as the alarm gives a little yip. He likes doing this—parking the Beemer in strict no-parking zones around the airport, and just leaving it sitting there among the cops and hustlers as he goes about his busi-ness. The cops, of course, know his car; probably the hustlers do, too. Forty years at the airport buys you some respect.

Abelson swaggers his swimmer-swagger down the sidewalk, cutting a swath through the disoriented foreigners.

"Normal EMS response time is around thirty minutes," he says, thoughtfully. "The police have helicopters and boats; EMS doesn't. Now, I know the chairman of the Metro Marine ferry—he runs a surface-effect vessel, similar to a hydrofoil, from Inwood to Wall Street. The trip takes about thirty-five minutes. I'm trying to tie him into our red-alert systems. We're also thinking about putting a barge in the bay near runway Thirteen/Thirty-one. You could evacuate a hundred or two hundred people—just sail 'em straight across the bay to Jamaica Hospital."

We walk into the terminal and head up the escalators to the Citibank. As we enter the bank, Abelson spies a familiar face. "Hello, father," he says, to the tall, pale man in black. It's Father Devine, of the Catholic chapel across the hall.

"Hello, Dr. Abelson," Devine says, mildly. "Preparing busily for Opsafe?"

"Oh, sure," says Abelson. "Yeah."

"Will you be there tomorrow, father?" I ask.

"Yes, I'll be giving last rites to the victims and such," Devine says, with a quiet smile.

"And how are you doing in the IAB, father?" Abelson growls.

Devine sighs. "Oh, well, we're comfortable enough, I suppose," he says. "They tell us we're here temporarily. Who knows how long temporarily is?"

❐

The late-spring morning is sticky and threatening, a lull between two rainstorms. Bad weather for the spirit. I pull up in front of Building 141 in an appropriate state of mind: I am twenty-five minutes late for Opsafe, Kennedy Airport's seventeenth full-scale disaster drill, the biggest deal of the year here. The small veins in my temples are throbbing dangerously. I would have been—should have been—*way* early, I left my house when the sun was barely up, but the Van Wyck, of course, proved my undoing, *Van Wyck disfecemi,* as it has undone so many others. How was I to know that the borough of Queens, or the Highway Department, or whoever the hell it was, would take it upon itself this Saturday morning, of all mornings, to install an entire new overpass just past the fabled Kew Gardens interchange, not far from Richmond Hill ("Richmond and Kew/Undid me," wrote T. S. Eliot, presciently), to lower a huge piece of light-green steel into place with enormous cranes, cavalierly backing up traffic for something like fifteen miles, and threatening my clutch bearing, not to mention the lining of my stomach, with spontaneous combustion?

But I should have known better. Military operations may start on time— may—but how could any major maneuver involving not only the considerable bureaucracy of the Port Authority, but also those of the New York City

Police Department, Fire Department, and Emergency Medical Service, all of which said bureaucracies generally detest and distrust each other—how could anything like this begin punctually? And they're not the only ones in the act. As I get out of my overheated car, I spy a slim young woman in a familiar-looking dark uniform and hat (and those unmistakable *shoes,* black with very low foam heels), talking gravely into a walkie-talkie. On her shoulder is the insignia of the Salvation Army. She looks weirdly sexy in her long institutional skirt: like Sister Sarah. But the *Salvation Army*? With this many cooks—and at Kennedy Airport, yet—how could one expect crack efficiency? My entire Van Wyck mental meltdown—the swearing, the fervent meditating, the perspiring—was all for naught. Lieutenant Frank Tabert, a genial, slightly plump, light-brown-mustached Port Authority cop and an old stationhouse acquaintance, sees me and grins cheerfully. "It used to be like C. B. DeMille—'Be here at ten-oh-three,'" he says. "Now we just wing it."

We—the various reporters, family members, airline and airport industry people here to witness this key event, maybe a couple hundred of us in all—are given maps of the crash site, which I now see is to be near The Fuselage, which, as you know well by now, is that big metal tube (complete with dummy engine pods) that's periodically ignited for crash-and-fire-rescue practice, on a barren plot at the airport's northeast corner, just south of Rockaway Boulevard and between the feet of runways 22 Right and 22 Left, not far from the spot where Eastern Flight 66 crashed in June 1975. It's an appropriate spot, the most crashed-upon turf at Kennedy. Also significantly noted on the map is the location of the Portosans.

The only thing we've been told ahead of time about today's drill is that it will simulate an aircraft disaster of some sort. In keeping with an important tradition, the inner cadre of Opsafe planners have revealed to no one exactly what kind of pretend mishap will be postulated. The reason for this secrecy is simple: spontaneity must be preserved. If chaos is to be corrected, chaos must be allowed to happen. Such, at any rate, is the theory.

Oppressive weather aside, the atmosphere is festive, even jokey, as we witnesses—some preacquainted, most not—climb aboard the three packed-to-the-gills airport buses. It feels precisely as though we are going on a school trip and missing a day of classes. We josh each other; we wink broadly. A few people have even brought their children along for the show. There is nothing, apparently, like a feigned disaster to enliven the spirits and sharpen the curiosity without the complicated feelings of guilt induced by actual tragedy (guilt induced by perfectly natural morbid interest and pleasure at one's own survival). This, Opsafe, is low-cal *Schadenfreude.*

The buses pull out. I'm standing and holding a metal bus strap, my back and sides pressed into fellow celebrants. The bus's air conditioning is a wisp, a nostril-teasing rumor. No matter: we don't have far to go. Through a pair of unchained chain-link gates, onto the runway area—or, as it is known here, *airside.* Along the outer perimeter road, behind the American and British/ United and TWA terminals and parallel to 13 Left. Then a diagonal jog left on taxiway Echo, crossing the runway, and up to the site.

The area, in the middle of an old unused landing strip (runway 14-32), has something of the feeling of a religious rite-in-progress, at first glance: it might be an outdoor revival meeting. There are a couple of towable aluminum bleachers; over there, a hundred yards off, in front of an orange-and-white blast fence, sits The Fuselage, burned and rusted, looking like an altar or sacrifice, an Ogden Allied fuel truck perched ominously nearby. The air is heavy with moisture and portent. The tall clouds, orange-white-gray and dark around the edges, seem to stand on high in judgment. And there, looming just across from the bleachers, is one of the ugliest airplanes I have ever seen: a stumpy, stubby 747, with an unfortunate livery of green stripes, a plane marked for phony disaster.

The 747—one-tenth of the fleet of Evergreen International, a charter outfit that is, as the unfortunate neologism has it, "headquartered" at Kennedy— has been rented for the day. It is an unlikely-looking crash victim. You can paint up people to make them appear injured, but you can't really do anything to a ten-million-dollar airplane that wouldn't threaten to actually *be* a disaster. So there the ugly jet sits, perkily upright, defiantly fake, casting a shadow over the proceedings.

We de-bus. The bleachers are splattered with last night's rainwater. People—especially people with kids—do the best they can to mop up with newspapers, jackets, and handkerchiefs, but, a mile from the nearest janitor's closet, little can be done to avoid wet posteriors: Here is the day's first inopportune unpredictable. I elect to walk around. On the tarmac, under the plane's right wing, the uniformed Boy Scouts—many of them plump Boy Scouts—who are to play the victims are easing into their prearranged positions, lying on their backs here and there as clumps of Port Authority cops stand around chatting happily.

A PA spokesman gets on the public address system, after the requisite squeal of feedback. "Right now"—*squeal*—"right now the casualties are setting themselves up," the announcer says. "And now, if you look down toward the blast fence, you'll see several of our crash-and-fire-rescue-trained police standing by as five hundred gallons of jet fuel are poured around the fuselage mockup." The tank truck obediently begins to whine; a cop manning a nozzle begins to slosh Jet-A around The Fuselage. "When that fuel is ignited," the spokesman says, "that's the signal that the plane has landed with . . ." And then he pauses.

He pauses. For just a second, the words are *too terrible to say*. People who work at the airport joke about a lot of things, but plane crashes aren't one of them. The fear is too primal, the possibility too real. And the memories too fresh. Most of the employees I've met have witnessed one crash or another, and a real plane crash, just an unpleasant item on the breakfast menu for most of us, is, in person, an almost indescribably awful thing. Today's event, therefore, is laden with emotional meaning for many of the participants, and if much of the pageant is overtly artificial, even that artificiality carries its own significance. Euphemism has its uses.

". . . with—some mishap," the p.a. announcer continues, vaguely, "and Opsafe has begun."

Now the Scouts who are to portray the plane's on-board victims climb the stairs onto the 747, cutting up—giving noogies, giggling, and so on—as they go. Under the wing, among the runway Scouts, a guy in a blue nylon American Red Cross windbreaker is kneeling by a supine boy, carefully pouring red liquid onto him from a plastic jug marked DISASTER—ARTIFICIAL. Perhaps because of my presence, a few of the other Scouts lying around on the runway have jumped the gun a little bit. "Help me," a couple of them groan. "No, help *me*." The effect of all this preadolescent groaning is part chilling, part comic. I can't help thinking of the scene in Woody Allen's *Everything You Always Wanted to Know About Sex* in which one of the experiments of the mad scientist played by John Carradine is to put the toothsome Meredith MacRae in a room with a dozen sex-crazed Scouts. The boys playing the Scouts in the movie lurch and moan quite unconvincingly, and these Opsafe Scouts aren't very good actors either, nor are a couple of them above doing some furtive smirking.

But even bad acting is not unaffecting in its own way, and the plastic fake intestines spilling out of Scout shirts, and the fake blood and severed limbs here and there, all create a certain undeniable ambience on the runway. Some of the cops standing and waiting for the start signal look a little more thoughtful.

Another squeal of feedback. "We're gonna simulate that the plane's left gear has collapsed," the p.a. announcer says, in his standard-issue New York cop accent. "And the plane has come to rest by the side of the runway. When we give the signal, you'll see two F-29 pumpers and two RIV rapid-intervention vehicles speed out from the satellite garage."

Now the spectators are alive with anticipation: sitting up, scanning the field for cues. All at once, a fire-suited PA cop lights a flare, drops it onto the ground by The Fuselage, and quickly steps back. The metal mockup bursts into flame, and a few kids in the stands scream. The flame's heat can be felt even here in the cheap seats, a hundred yards away. The silken wall of orange fire—it looks organic, like a live monster, a demon—crackles and sends aloft great black shrouds of smoke. And then, in the distance, in the shimmering air over the field, I see the two chartreuse fire trucks and the pair of blue-and-white ambulances streaking toward us at what must be seventy miles an hour.✈

The big Oshkosh F-29s screech to a halt by The Fuselage; helmeted, shiny-coated cops jump out and quickly pull the big canvas hoses off the sides of the trucks.

The p.a. announcer can't help kibitzing. "The biggest problem we have on the field in an actual disaster is the water problem," he says. "Disasters don't happen next to hydrants, so the only water or fire-fighting foam we have is the water or foam we can bring to the scene."

The trucks' pumps begin to whine, and the cops walk up to the fire with the big hoses over their shoulders, sending billows of white AFFF foam toward the blaze, which—incredibly—immediately goes out, just as though someone had turned a switch. Scattered, vaguely stunned applause from the gallery: Was this supposed to happen?

Unfazed, the announcer continues his droning narration. "When we have determined all the survivors have been removed from the scene," he says, "it becomes a structural fire, and New York City's responsibility."

I meander over to the public address microphone, and see that the announcer is a gray-haired lieutenant whose name tag reads A. PRETZEL.

Now a squadron of cops from the ambulances bang up the staircase to the 747, tools and lifesaving equipment in hand. Lieutenant Pretzel speaks. "The Port Authority rescue personnel are now going aboard the aircraft to determine if any injured or critically injured persons"—he says *poysons*—"are aboard the aircraft."

And, a moment later: "There are eight injured aboard the aircraft."

A few minutes later, at 10:08 A.M., a Port Authority ambulance pulls away, full of somehow sobered Scouts. A minute later, two NYPD ambulances speed up. Not long afterward Lou Abelson's CHEM lumbers onto the scene. Now a brace of EMS ambulances appear. And three pumpers from the FDNY. For the next half hour it seems as though another emergency vehicle from another organization arrives every thirty seconds. I also sight:

✈ It is the mandate of emergency vehicles at Kennedy that the first vehicle out must be able to reach the farthest runway in three minutes or less.

- a Port Authority mobile command post
- an FDNY field communication unit
- an NYPD Emergency Service unit
- a Red Cross Disaster Services truck

Soon the grounds are packed with uniformed men and women, walking around with purposeful and important expressions, bumping into each other: It's like an enormous movie set, without a director.

Lou Abelson shakes his head. "We're into a pissing contest here," he growls, tight-lipped. "Jurisdictionally, the EMS has priority. But they're abusing the hell out of it." He turns to the EMS supervisor, a rotund, bland-looking young man with an elaborate uniform and square steel-rimmed glasses. "Your guys are out there before they're supposed to be on the scene!" Abelson snaps. "They're out there giving critiques, and they haven't been to any of the meetings!"

The supervisor smiles and shrugs.

Just then Inspector William Ferrante, head of the Port Authority Police at Kennedy, walks by, wearing full-dress regalia and his best glad-to-see-ya smile. "How's everything goin'?" he says.

"It's sort of hard to keep track," I say.

"That's the way it should be," says the inspector.

Under the 747's left wing is the morgue. An open black suitcase is marked NYCPD MISSING PERSONS SQUAD—DISASTER RESPONSE. The suitcase contains Polaroids of the dead—in this instance, Scouts with their eyes closed— attached to fingerprint sheets.

On the tarmac behind the plane lies a thin black Scout, being attended to by clinical trauma specialist Jane Smeland, of Jamaica Hospital. "He's having a penetrating abdominal injury—all his intestines are hanging out," she says. "All his extremities are OK. His shock seems to be progressing." She turns to a colleague. "Larry—we need a stretcher. He's becoming less responsive."

She smiles down at the boy, whose eyelids are fluttering. "Is it cold laying on the ground?" she asks. He nods weakly. "OK, sweetheart, here's a stretcher," she says. And two men in white suits carefully pick the boy up and carry him away.

The uneasy comedy of fake blood. Here's another kid with bandages on his head and arm, standing near Father Devine. "Is he going to make it?" I ask the priest.

"He will, he will," Devine says. "He's got a lot of courage—he realizes they've got to take away the ones with broken arms and legs first."

"I have a burn victim," says Jacqueline Almenor, nursing supervisor of the emergency room of Mary Immaculate Hospital, in Jamaica. Another pair of stretcher-bearers pick up a Scout with blackened face and arms and carry him off to the triage area.

"And this one has internal injuries," Almenor says, of a dazed-looking fat boy, to a Port Authority cop.

"Kid, whud you eat last night?" the cop asks.

It begins to rain, out of a bright sky.

A big orange-and-blue bus with smoked-glass windows, flashing lights, and various serious-looking antenna arms and emergency vents pulls up importantly, into what has now become a parking lot. The bus, which is covered with official badges, is marked CITY OF NEW YORK COMMUNICATIONS COMMAND CENTER, MAYOR'S OFFICE FOR MANAGEMENT, HON. D. DINKINS, MAYOR. No one gets out of the bus. It sits idling loudly in the rain.

In the triage staging area, behind the plane: rows of stretchers on the ground. "Anyone who's really cold, raise a hand," a nurse says to the Scouts on the stretchers.

I wander over to find a red-metal portable command post, a kind of lectern with a glass map of the site marked in grease pencil, standing unmanned. The rain comes down harder. NYPD, FDNY, PA, and EMS brass walk around, all looking intent but not, apparently, doing anything.

There exists a mind-set—I think of it as *fireman's mind*—that loves nothing in the world more than listening to police scanners for mishaps, and, when mishaps occur, jumping into a four-wheel-drive vehicle, clamping a suction-mounted flasher on the roof, and speeding off into the night, with big flashlights, to help. Is this help officious? What of it? We are all the better for this aberrant personality, which thrives on chasing the demons—of night, of chaos—and which, no doubt, is thereby grappling with its own inner demons.

Opsafe is the ultimate fiesta of fireman's mind.

Two big white Salvation Army Emergency Disaster Services vans, with red-and-white flashers, screech to a stop on the muddy turf. A panel pops open on each truck's side, revealing a sign that reads HOT COFFEE, SANDWICHES. Free food! Lines quickly form. The doughnuts are delicious.

*

A blood-covered kid with a hoarse adolescent voice, to open-mouthed medical technicians: "You let me die, people! You let me die!"

The p.a. announcer, cheerily: "The schoolbuses are here for the Scouts! All aboard, please!"

Opsafe haiku:
Helicopters circle overhead. I wonder how much all this *costs*.

❐

Having stayed too long at the party, I am the only passenger on the bus back to Building 141. We pull up to the taxiway and wait a long time as the Evergreen International 747 moves by. The driver, an angry man, mutters as the big squat jet rumbles its ponderous way down Echo. "Wonder if this . . . *guy* has a driver's license," he says, shaking his head. "See that? He can't go in a straight line! Must be one of the new breed—one of them *lady* pilots."

Hard to be a bus driver. But then it's hard to be a plane driver, too.

14

Bus Driver's Blues

Up and Down the Ohio Valley

C all him Dave. Dave Swanson. It's a pseudonym, but it'll give you the idea. His face is as undistinguished as his name. Fiftyish, plumpish, baldish, pleasant-looking. He wears thick glasses; occasionally his hands flutter with what appears to be a slight tremor. He is an airline pilot.

He lives in a modest house in rural northwest New Jersey, in a town called Sparta—a town thickly populated, for no apparent reason, with pilots, many of whom do much of their flying out of Kennedy. The view out Swanson's picture window is of trees: the next house is a hundred yards away. The lights and noise of Manhattan, fifty miles distant, attract flight attendants, single people mostly. Pilots like the woods.

We settle down in the plain but cozy den. Dave fiddles around for a moment with the controls for his satellite dish, finally settling on a soccer game from Brazil, which plays silently on the screen of the big wood-cabinet color TV as we talk. He offers me a beer, pours himself a Lite. I ask him why so many pilots have clumped around this precise spot. "My guess is that there was probably one first person that came here, and then through word of mouth, others followed," Swanson says. He speaks in flat middle-American tones, in the kind of mildly techie, emotionally leashed talk that I associate with certain midlevel executives and career soldiers—and that, so often, has fury and despair and deadpan humor lurking around the edges. "I moved here twenty-five years ago. There were several so-called pilot ghettos then— Ridgefield, Connecticut, was one. When I got out of the service I interviewed for a lot of jobs, and one was with Pan American. I was living in Pennsylvania at the time, and a college friend, a United pilot who lived in Sparta, put me up for the night. And the Lake Mohawk area had that country flavor, and yet it was close enough to the airport."

James Kaplan

Swanson had graduated from a large midwestern university in 1960, gone into the air force, and learned to fly. The killing machine in Vietnam was just cranking up, and had he been a better student or a better pilot, he might not be here today. Fighters, bombers, and helicopters were the plum assignments in those days. Swanson drew transport planes—specifically, the giant C-124, a flying warehouse. He spent his war at Hickam Air Force Base in Hawaii, transporting men and equipment and supplies to Vietnam, flying soldiers back to the Philippines for R&R. When he left the service, in 1965, TWA was in the midst of a hiring boom. It needed, not ace pilots, but simply men who could fly planes. Swanson filled the bill. He stepped onto the bottom rung of the seniority list, a happy and hopeful young 707 copilot, and moved to Sparta with his wife and small children.

He's on his second marriage now, a different man—fatter, balder, sadder, wiser: worn in if not worn out. Flying takes its toll. He's still copiloting, though on a bigger plane, the 747. "Do I enjoy my work?" he says. "Very much, yeah. It gets to be pretty routine, though. The long and short of it is, you really just go out to the airport, get in a plane, and fly away. It's hard for people outside of this to know what I'm talking about. I mean, if I complain that I have to go to Paris, people can't understand it. But I have to fly all night. And as you get older, the actual flying is still fun, but, it's more and more like, you go to work, you get there, you sleep, you get up and eat, then you sleep, then you come home. It's not like when you were young. In every city I've been in I guess I've done everything that a tourist would do—once. But I don't keep doing it. I don't go to the Louvre every time I go to Paris. Although I've always enjoyed going to the Tower of London,✦ for some reason. I bet I've been there thirty times. It's something I like to do to kill the time. Probably one of my rogue ancestors was beheaded there or something."

He sips his Lite and looks more serious. "We have a tremendous amount of early retirement," he says. "I don't know if there are any statistics on this, but I would say, as a rule, pilots' longevity hasn't been outstanding. I don't know why. Certainly you have international flying, with the time zones and the jet lags. You miss a night's sleep every time you go to work. What that does to your body, I can't tell you. Most of our international flights leave at night. You can imagine the Tel Aviv flight, which is our worst. It's scheduled to leave Kennedy at eight P.M. You're never on time, it seems like. So you leave at nine. And by the time you get to the Tel Aviv Hilton, it's like nine or ten in the morning on your clock. You've just been up all night. It might be

---

✦ Not anymore. In 1991, then TWA chairman Carl Icahn sold the airline's JFK-Heathrow routes to American.

two or three in the afternoon their time. So you go to bed, you're exhausted, you've got to get up at six o'clock or so to go eat, so you can get on their schedule. You just have to force yourself out. Then you get a call at five or six o'clock in the morning to head home."

He takes another drink of beer. "On most of our other international flights, the layovers are twenty-four hours," he says. "But the same thing applies. You fly to Rome, you get to the hotel at eight or nine in the morning, and then you sleep for five or six hours. Then you get up and do whatever you can. Get on their schedule, go to dinner. Then you come back and try and go to sleep. And then usually something hits you, and you wake up at one or two in the morning. So you miss one night, then you struggle the next night, then you come home and you're whipped. And it takes a day to recuperate. I don't know if there's been any studies, but I think it's tough on you, if you've done it for a career.

"That's why when you start flying domestic, everyone says, 'You won't believe how good you're gonna feel. You won't be as tired as you've been for the last twenty years.'"

"So what about you? How long can you keep flying internationally?"

He shakes his head. "I'm not," he says. "I'm going to go back and be reschooled on the 727, to fly as a captain. I could have been a 727 captain for the last five years, probably. I just chose not to because of the working conditions. See, we have to fly about eighty hours a month—so if you fly international flights, it obviously takes fewer flights to get your eighty hours than if you're flying up and down the Ohio Valley. Fewer flights, less commuting."

"Is that where you'll be flying?" I ask. "The Ohio Valley?"

"Well, we have, like, patterns—they tell you exactly what you're going to do," he says. He picks up his big TWA pilot's schedule and opens it on his lap. With his thick glasses down on the tip of his small nose, he resembles a plumbing parts supplier looking up an obscure flush handle, an auto-dealership service manager confirming a tune-up appointment—anything but a pilot. "Here's a pattern that goes La Guardia to Denver to St. Louis to Omaha to St. Louis to Palm Beach to La Guardia to Fort Lauderdale," he says. "That's the kind of pattern I'll be flying once I start flying 727s."

"It doesn't sound very exciting," I say.

Swanson shrugs. "It's all a trade-off," he says. "As a copilot on a 747 I might only have to make four trips a month to the airport. As a captain on a 727 I might have to make nine. But then you have that stress of international travel. And since my wife works, she wants me to take weekends off. Which, as a captain, I'll be able to do a lot easier than I would as a copilot."

"Nine trips a month to Kennedy," I say. I calculate the distance roughly in my head. It has to be at least seventy miles from Sparta, with the worst part—New York City—at the end.

"That's at the most. Usually it's more like six."

"The commute can't be great, though," I say.

"It's tough from here," he admits. "But we all get to be masters of it. You know, when to be on the Harlem River, when to be on the Cross Bronx. There was a period when there was construction out here on Route Eighty—I would go by way of the Verrazano Bridge. When they were working on the lower level, there was a period when I avoided the George Washington Bridge. I mean, I can tell you some horror stories about having to race through Manhattan.

"But I've never missed a flight because of traffic. I've been late. I've been caught in snowstorms. I've showed up when the flight should have left, but because of the conditions, they weren't gonna make it anyway. Still, the drive to and from the airport is, without a doubt, the worst part of the job. That's why the people that commute in would rather fly in than drive in.

"When you're starting, you're on call, so you have to live within two hours of the airport. But once you're senior, and you can make your own schedule, you can live wherever you want. We have pilots all over the place. I knew one who lived in Thailand. Probably sixty or seventy-five percent of our international pilots don't even live in the States. Some of them come in a day early. Still, of course they have to stay in a hotel, which is a tough life for them."

"Tell me about going to work at Kennedy," I say.

"I drive to the airport and park in a TWA parking lot," Swanson says. "For international you go into a flight planning room and get your computerized flight plan. That gives you the winds and the fuel burn. You study the weather, you determine how much fuel you want, you plan the flight. And this all takes about an hour.

"From that, you go over to the airplane, and do all your preflight. The flight engineer does what he calls a walk-around. He checks the exterior of the airplane, underneath the landing gears. He'll look in the engines. I was on a flight out of Kennedy this winter where the airplane we were about to get on landed, and, when they put the engines into reverse, there were snowbanks on the edge of the runway high enough so that the engine sucked in ice and snow and was damaged. Now, the crew that was bringing it in wouldn't necessarily catch this. They just taxied in, parked the airplane, and left. But when we did our preflight, the mechanic saw the damage. Which the flight engineer also saw. Between them, there's a built-in redundancy, to make sure nothing slips through. So we literally had to change airplanes.

"When you preflight, you have a ton of checks to do. We have a whole book full of them. And we know everything in the book. It actually leads you from when you get to the airplane until you leave the airplane. We have what's called a before-starting-engines checklist; the person that's going to fly the airplane does the check. And the person that's not flying the airplane reads the checklist to the pilot that's doing it. I'll read it to him, and then he'll go over it. He'll say, 'OK, checklist.' And I'll say, 'Gear, lever, and lights.' And he'll say, 'Down in check.' And I'll go right down the list, and he'll give me the answers.

"Then after you start the engines, you have another checklist. Then as you're taxiing out, there's another. In the last few years there's been a real emphasis on flaps. They've had two accidents now where they're not sure the pilots took the flaps down. There was one in Detroit; I can't remember the other one. But in both cases it was a checklist item.

"Now, I've heard of occasions where you get a faulty indication. Remember that fatal accident—British Midland? A two-engine plane. A lot of pilots can't understand how the guy could have made the mistake he made. I mean, he would have had his emergency engine-fire checklist, which, if you get an indicator, says, 'Throttle closed.' If you have an engine fire, there's a little handle that lights up red, and a bell goes off. And when you hear a bell and look up and see that that handle's red, that's the one that you obviously think's on fire.

"So he shut that engine down—or *thought* he shut it down—by pulling the handle that lit up. But what if one engine's on fire and *the other handle* lights up? What if the wires were crisscrossed? You wouldn't have any way of knowing. They think maybe that's what happened on that one." He stares at me through the thick lenses. "Pretty scary."

"OK," I say. "You've checked out the plane. Now it's time to push back and take off. What's it like to leave from JFK?" I ask. "Any different from other airports? Better? Worse?"

He puts his schedule back on the floor. On the TV screen, the soccer players in purple are jumping up and down, their arms in the air. "I think that to most pilots most airports are pretty much the same, even though there are different considerations for each one," Swanson says. "Certain airports seem to be more efficient and have better instrument landing systems. Some have a more organized schematic, easier to follow. It's just like cities. You can maybe drive through Manhattan and not be confused, whereas I might drive it the first time and be overwhelmed.

"Kennedy Airport is so big. But when you've been flying out of there for the number of years I have, it's just second nature. Still, I've often thought

175

about a Russian flight coming in, or, say, someone from Yugoslavia—I could see how they could get bewildered. We have little, like, road maps."

He picks up a smaller book from the floor and opens it for me. "This is the airport road map, with the runways," he says. He points a chubby finger to JFK's central terminal loop. "Here's TWA's terminal," he says. "When you get on the airplane, you listen to the airport traffic information service—it tells you what the wind and the temperature are, and which runway they'll be using for takeoff, and which for landing.

"These are our TWA gates; this is our international building, this is our domestic. So we might be starting our entrance here." He points to the back of the TWA domestic terminal. "The sequence of events is that when you're sitting at a gate, and you want to leave, the first thing you do is call up TWA tower, which controls this ramp area so you don't have airplanes pushing into each other. And you say, 'TWA so-and-so, Gate Twenty-nine, ready to go.' And they say, 'You're clear to push back.' And you push back, start your engines.

"And then you taxi up to this point"—his finger has moved slightly, to the foot of taxiway Delta Alfa, just northeast of the terminal—"and you call Kennedy ground controller. Now, ground control has to set up a flow pattern of all the planes taxiing out. So I'll call and ask for taxi clearance. I'll say, 'TWA's ready to taxi from Delta Alfa.' And the ground controller'll say, 'Taxi out Delta Alfa; turn left on the outer'—that's the outer perimeter road—'and hold short of November.' So I know that I have to come out here"—his finger moves to taxiway Delta Alfa, just behind TWA International, and its intersection with the outer perimeter road. Then he traces the outer perimeter in a counterclockwise direction, around the west side of the terminal loop.

"Come back, taxi around, and then hold short of November," he says. "Then I'd have to stop here." His finger is poised on the southwest side of the loop, just behind the former, soon-to-be-demolished Eastern terminal, Terminal One. "So you follow these instructions, and then they feed you in, and when it's your turn to go, he'll say, 'Turn right on Papa and call tower.'

"Then you turn there"—he indicates taxiway Papa, which parallels 13 Right—"and taxi down to the end. Then you change frequencies and talk to the tower. This guy in the tower is clearing airplanes landing on the left runway and taking off on the right runway."

"Does it always work that way?" I ask.

"When the volume gets so big, the way it does at Kennedy, they almost always have the landings on one runway, and the takeoffs on the other," Dave says. "But that's not chiseled in stone. If the traffic is kind of light, a Delta plane that parks over here"—he points to the former Pan Am terminal, at the bottom of the loop—"might rather land on the takeoff runway, One Three Right, so he wouldn't have to taxi as far. But usually at night at Kennedy, they have so many airplanes lined up at takeoff that they ask everybody to land on one so they can get the departures out on the other."

"So next you get cleared for takeoff?"

"So then he clears you for takeoff, you turn left onto Papa Delta, and left again onto the runway. And then after you actually lift off the ground and start flying your flight, the tower guy changes you to a departure controller, who controls all the aircraft leaving the airport. And then *he* turns you over to what's called a center control. When you leave the North American continent, you're talking to Gander in Newfoundland, and they control you to about halfway across the ocean. And *then* you talk to Shannon, the people in Ireland. This is all on high-frequency radios. You're always talking with someone."

"And what about coming into JFK?"

He takes off his glasses and wipes the lenses on his shirt. His naked eyes look small and startled. "Kennedy is relatively difficult, because so much of the traffic control is based on noise considerations. Now, they never land you on a runway that's not favorable to winds— that would be unsafe. But they can make you unhappy. The pilot always has the right to demand to land on what he feels is the safest runway.✈ You want a head wind, for landing and taking off. You always want to fly an airplane into the wind. For lift control, speed control. Tail winds are the worst. It's easier to land with a head wind. You get a nice, smooth landing—smoother than you usually get in a crosswind. On most airplanes, the maximum crosswind would be about thirty knots. But with so many different runways, you never really get a severe crosswind, because if the wind is that strong, the controllers just change you over. They don't use the noise factor if there's a strong wind.

"In a calm wind situation, they rotate the runways, so that the people in Canarsie don't have to hear the airplanes all day long forever. Just as an example, if the wind was two hundred at fifteen knots at Kennedy—that's a fifteen-knot wind from two hundred degrees, or roughly the southwest—they might use runway One Three, which would give you a crosswind. But if you came in and requested to land on runway Two Two—right into the wind—they wouldn't deny that to you. It might slow you down. This happens quite frequently. They'll say, 'This is the noise runway; please use it if you can.' Just for the convenience of traffic flow."

"Do you ever fly as a passenger?" I ask.

✈ See Chapter 5.

"Frequently," Dave says. "If I have a pattern that starts in Los Angeles, the company gets me out there—that's dead-heading. But if my wife and I want to go out to L.A. to visit her parents, then I'm flying strictly as a passenger."

"That's free, right?"

"Travel privileges are part of our fringe benefits," he says. "But we're the last ones on. All the paying ticketed passengers go first, and then they go down the list of standbys according to seniority. It's all space available. Airline employees are left at the gate quite a bit. It's a stressful way to travel if you have a schedule.

"And it's only totally free if you're in coach. If you want to fly business or first, you pay a surcharge—it might go from a high of sixty dollars to a low of twenty. It's not much, but it all depends whether or not you think it's worth it. It might not seem worth it to me, whereas it'd be very much so to you. I mean, if I do it all the time, I might feel nonchalant about flying first class. My wife prefers flying what we call Ambassador—she calls it *up in the bubble* of a 747, in the upper deck. I mean, that's where her comfort zone is. She kind of has a fear of flying."

It suddenly occurs to me that this pudgy man in the BarcaLounger is, in walking-around life, in the fabulous position of being where I am after two stiff drinks—absolutely unafraid to fly. Or is this true?

"Me?" Dave says. "Well, I shouldn't say I have no fear. I feel more comfortable when I'm flying the plane. I mean, are you as comfortable with your wife driving as when you are? My wife's an excellent driver, but I just prefer being at the controls. It's the same way in an airplane. I just would be more comfortable flying it, even though I'm very comfortable being a passenger. The other day my wife and I came in from Toronto as passengers, and we got into what I would call severe turbulence. And she was scared out of her wits. I think for a lot of people, turbulence is probably the biggest fear. Number one, you wonder if the airplane's gonna hold up. These wings—you look at 'em, you see the wings flapping because they're flexible. Well, what you have to realize is, they stress-test these planes to a point way beyond anything they ever encounter. And the guys in the cockpit know what they're doing. So I just sat there blasé, because I know those guys are doing whatever they can. I mean, I have a lot of faith in 'em."

He blinks through the thick lenses; I blink back. And wonder, just for a moment: *Do I feel the same way?*

15

The Tower

Pushing Tin

In October 1981, President Ronald Reagan summarily fired all 11,400 members of the Professional Air Traffic Controllers Organization (PATCO)—federal employees, forbidden by law to strike, who had had the temerity, in the wild and woolly days following deregulation, to walk out for higher wages nevertheless. The PATCO employees, proud professionals who had made the nation's airways run for forty years, who had lived and breathed their work, were stunned by the president's rough justice. When a high-stress job that demands utter commitment is replaced by unemployment, a dangerous vacuum results. Some of the former controllers committed suicide; many turned to drink. The ones who coped sold real estate, sold bonds, tended bar, worked at private airports, or even left the country to push tin overseas.✛ In the place of PATCO came a new breed of air traffic professionals.

John Pallante, the head of the Kennedy tower, is short, trim, dark-eyed, and intense in his blue blazer, conservative tie, and black cowboy boots, a former navy controller turned civil controller turned bureaucrat, but at heart simply a *controller:* aggressive, fidgety, commanding. He speaks in an authoritative staccato, the words emerging like small-arms rounds. "Air traffic controllers are responsible for the safe, orderly, and expeditious flow of air traffic," he says, peering at me sharply to make sure he has my full attention. "Note the sequence. Ninety-nine out of a hundred times, if you're safe you're orderly, and if you're orderly you're expeditious." We're sitting in his sunny

---

✛ In August 1993, President Clinton reversed the nonperson status of the former PATCO controllers, signing a bill that would allow them to go back to work in their cherished profession if they wished. The news, of course, came late. Most of the controllers were set in their new lives, and all had grown older, and controlling is a young person's profession. And while some reacted eagerly to the news, a hiring freeze on controllers existed contemporaneously with Clinton's magnanimous act, and it was doubtful that the edict would have more than symbolic meaning.

corner office on the tower's sixth floor. On a tabletop behind Pallante is a cautionary totem—a wrought-iron sculpture of a small plane that has crashed into the branches of a tree. Sinatra plays softly in the background (no, not "Come Fly with Me" or "Let's Get Away from It All," but "All the Way").

What kind of person becomes a controller? "Number one," Pallante says, "someone who is very self-confident. They are also normally impatient. When they're watching TV, they all watch two or three stations at the same time. When two controllers talk, they can't wait for the other one to finish— they all want what's in front of them to happen right *now*. There isn't a spouse that doesn't complain about it.

"They're used to issuing and receiving instructions with an instantaneous response—'Go eat lunch *now*.' If the heat in their house doesn't work, they want it fixed *now*. It gets in your blood. In the break room, they play Pac-Man and Lazer Tag. Most of them talk in their sleep.

"They have great recall," Pallante says. "They can remember eighty-five to ninety percent of the call signs they heard the day before. At work, they talk cars; at a bar, they talk planes. When they're playing softball, they have to stop the game to watch planes go by."

He paces around his office. "Controllers are paid by the number of aircraft they handle," he says. "We keep pretty busy here. Nine hundred operations a day is a lot of operations."

The bulk of it, of course, comes between two in the afternoon and ten or eleven at night, when a takeoff or landing every sixty seconds is light to average, and when the small cab of the old Kennedy tower may contain up to twelve controllers at a time, working in deodorant-commercial-like propinquity. And headache-remedy-commercial-like stress. I have visions of fritzed-out controllers—frozen rigid into chair shapes, smoke coming out of their ears—being yanked aside to be replaced by fresh meat. "What are the hours like?" I ask.

"Usually a week of days, then a week of evenings," Pallante says. "We have three shifts—seven A.M. to three P.M., which is light; three to eleven, where the majority are needed; and then eleven P.M. to seven A.M., where you have a skeleton crew.

"From midnight to seven, what you mainly get is a lot of cargo flights. Another part of it is shuttling planes to maintenance in the hangars. From six to six-thirty in the morning, there's a little flurry of red-eye activity, from L.A. and San Francisco. From seven-thirty to eight-thirty, there's another push, this time mostly domestic flights and commuters. From eight-thirty to ten, you have your departures for the Caribbean.

THE AIRPORT

"Nobody ever works for more than two hours at a time. And you always rotate from busy tasks to easy ones."

"Do you miss doing it yourself?" I ask Pallante.

He nods, it seems, the instant before I ask the question. "It's a well-kept secret—I'd do it for free," he says.

"I thrive on stress," says James Johnston, a controller for eight years. He is a smooth-cheeked, slightly moon-faced young man of thirty—he might be a pool player or a funeral director—with a nervous habit, à la Rodney Dangerfield, of shrugging his right shoulder and straightening his tie. In his off-hours, he serves as a lieutenant on the Baldwin, Long Island, fire department. But controlling comes first: It's in the blood. Johnston's father, too, pushed tin, starting his career in the Idlewild tower and eventually becoming the manager at Newark and area manager at Tracon, the terminal radar approach control facility for the densely air-traveled New York metropolitan region, in Westbury, Long Island. "My father loved his work," Johnston tells me. "It's like playing in the World Series every night—it's that important.

"At the academy, they describe controlling as hours of boredom punctuated by seconds of sheer terror. I don't agree about the boredom. There are too many variables—the weather, for one. Then you have emergencies, which are almost routine. Of course, whenever the media gets ahold of a hydraulic failure or blown tires, they make it sound like this plane's never gonna fly again.

"When you're in the tower with ten or eleven other people, a good sense of humor is imperative. Once British Airways was pushing a gate, and I got a call, 'Um, tower, this is Speedbird One One Four—we need emergency equipment right away.' When I asked what was wrong, he said, 'We were pulling back, and we just squashed a chap.'

"Another time, the pilot of a TWA 747 on its way to Paris requested permission to return to the gate. When I queried him about it, it turned out he'd left without enough toilet paper on board."

"Is there ever friction on the radio between planes and the tower?" I ask.

"Occasionally," Johnston says. "But it's never a question of anyone acting superior. You get to know people—you hear the same names, the same voices, again and again. If there are lengthy delays—say, on a summer night—sometimes you can hear the frustration in a pilot's voice. And we don't like it either. We're born and bred to move traffic—that's what we enjoy doing best. And then, sometimes on a difficult night, when you have fog and rain, for example, and you're sequencing"—lining up incoming aircraft at

181

intervals along a vector in the sky—and there's an endless barrage of radio transmissions, you might hear a pilot say, 'Thank you, tower, you're doing a great job.'"

On a busy summer evening, there may be as many as 110 takeoffs and landings per hour at Kennedy Airport. "That's one every thirty seconds, and you have to make a couple of transmissions for each," Johnston says. "Theoretically we are responsible in one hour for more lives than a doctor could be in his entire career, and billions of dollars in equipment," he says. "But it's an unspoken thing—we don't dwell on it."

"Do you ever remember your dreams?" I ask him.

He looks at me for a second. "I don't—not at all," he says. "It's very fortunate."

Mary June—the name seems to come from a musical comedy of the twenties, but in fact it belongs to an air traffic controller of the nineties. Six of Kennedy's thirty-three controllers are women: a little over the national proportion of 15 percent. Mary June grew up on a chicken ranch near Decker, Michigan, one of six children. She graduated from Ferris State College in 1978 with a degree in human services, got married, had a daughter, got divorced. Worked, at low pay, with retarded adults. Remarried and moved to New Jersey. In 1980, still working with the retarded, she earned fourteen thousand dollars.

"In 1981 I saw all this strike stuff about the air traffic controllers on TV," June says. "And they were crying about making forty to fifty thousand a year. So as soon as they all got fired, my husband went and got me an application."

She is a small, quiet woman with short, dark hair and matter-of-fact eyes. "I took the test in October of '81," she says. "I scored high—especially on abstract thinking and reaction time. But then I waited almost a year to hear. On August fourteenth, 1982, they said, 'We want you.' So I reported to controller school in Oklahoma City.

"I *thought* I was going to school to learn to be a controller," she says. "But in reality, it was a screening process. You get paid, and you get a per diem, and you go to school, and they don't teach you a whole lot at first—mainly basic weather principles and aircraft identification. You'd go to lab and wear a headset, while people behind you pretended to be pilots, giving you their call signs.

"I like challenge, but I was scared. It turned out high anxiety was the whole shot. You were always being evaluated. And being a woman, you had a lot more attention on you. There were about three hundred people at the school, and thirty of us were women. The old group of controllers, the ones who got fired, was a real old-boys' club—about one percent were women. Well, there were more of us now, but it was still hard. I couldn't get confident. Aircraft identification was never my strong point.

"I reported for work the day after Christmas, 1982, and I didn't know anything. The only plane I knew was the DC-10. So there was a lot of learning on the job, a lot of information particular to Kennedy—runway setup, runway lengths, radio frequencies. You train for the first three positions—flight data, clearance delivery, and ground control—for a year to a year and a half. Then you have to go back to school to learn local control—clearing planes to land and take off in the TCA, the terminal control area.

"More than a hundred hours into my ground-control training, my manager told me, 'Mary, give it up—you'll never be a controller. Maybe we can get you a job as a clerk-typist at the regional office.' I had all the knowledge, but I didn't have the confidence. They told me I was too nice. I got a letter saying that my training was terminated."

She smiles slightly. "That was like a red flag in front of a bull for me. I said I wasn't leaving. And it wasn't easy for them to let me go. I was a woman. And Kennedy had no one left after the strike—everyone was in training. So I managed to get twenty more hours of training, and then J.J.—James Johnston—trained me on local. In April of '86, I finished everything. I was a controller." Her smile broadens.

"Some people go home and listen to airport frequencies. J.J. does that. I love the work, but I have a life. There are other people in my life. I belong to the PWC—the Professional Women Controllers. I've done some work with Mercer County Community College, talking to women and minorities about what I do." She nods. "It's worked out well. And I didn't have to change, either—I have been angry at pilots, but my style of working is that I *am* nice. Nice, and firm."

Control tower: fraught phrase. Masculine, majestic, domineering, aloof. And yet—if there had been any thought that the control tower of one of the world's great airports would be any of the above, let alone an antiseptic hive of high-tech efficiency, the thought is quickly banished at Kennedy. The cab of Kennedy's tower, twelve stories above the IAB, gives little feeling of height, let alone majesty, and its octagonal interior, lit by eight big inward-canting tinted panes affording a 360-degree view of the airport and environs, is— especially at 11 A.M., the calm before the storm—a cozily messy den. Here is a large (open) box of Entenmann's Danish; there is today's *Daily News,* open to the sports section. Three men and three women, in jeans and sneakers, are on duty, sitting on ratty old office chairs. Long strips of white paper with flight numbers on them—traffic-count strips—lie around the floor. The ground-radar screen is acting up this morning; fortunately it's clear out. The conflict-alert beeper (a.k.a. ca-ca), which alerts the controllers to potential midair collisions, is silent. As are the two alarm bells on the wall, one a crash alarm, one a city fire alarm.

There are seven telephones on the wall of the tower, one of them red, one beige, two yellow, two black, and one white. The beige one is connected to FAA headquarters in Washington, D.C., and is used primarily to let CF2—the Central Flow Control Facility—know if one of Kennedy's runways becomes disabled.

The two yellow phones are connected to the New York fire and police departments and the Port Authority Police.

One black phone calls the sector supervisor in the terminal radar approach-control (TRACON) facility in Westbury, New York. The other is connected to FBI headquarters in Manhattan, and could be used by agents in the tower in the event of a hijacking or terrorist incident.

The white phone, used by Secret Service agents who come to the tower whenever a government VIP passes through the airport, is connected to the White House.

And the red phone is the one no controller ever wants to pick up. It rings, simultaneously:

- the Port Authority crash team in the satellite garage
- the NYPD at 1 Police Plaza, in lower Manhattan
- the FDNY on Woodhaven Boulevard, Queens
- the tower manager's office
- the Port Authority operations manager in Building 269
- the Kennedy Medical Facility
- skycap dispatch

But this is a quiet morning at Kennedy, and the phones hang on the wall like counters in a game that's shelved for the time being. Controlling, at this moment, looks like an easy business. It isn't.

Next to the phones hangs a hand-lettered sign that reads: QUIT PLEASE.

16

Concord(e)

The World's Priciest Airplane

So what's the alternative to the bus-riding blues? There is precisely one, and it's easy enough to find, if not to ride on. The British Airways terminal,✛ at roughly twelve o'clock on the central-terminal-area loop, is conspicuous among Kennedy's various edifices for its cleanliness. The building's white exterior, designed by Gollins, Melvin and Ward, P.C., a London firm, has a nice, crisp, successfully boxy look to it, and the interior is clean, too—well maintained and policed (by BA's own security people; every terminal lessee at the airport makes its own arrangements for day-to-day security, although the PA Police, naturally, will come if called). The reason for all this immaculateness is not hard to fathom. British Airways is the most successful airline in the world, in a time when financially sound major carriers are as scarce as hen's teeth. Hence its claim to be "The World's Favourite Airline"—a justifiable boast if pounds sterling are the sole criterion.

Drive by the BA terminal early some morning and you'll see, protruding above the building's white left flank, a tall airplane tail in the strikingly chevroned blue-white-and-red British livery. There is something different about this plane's tail, though: It's broader than a regular jet's, its leading edge more rakishly angled. It is, of course, the tail of the Concorde.

Ever since I'd first sat in Sammy Chevalier's pickup out by runway 4 Left and seen that rocket pass over, its exhaust ports blinding white, its rumble shaking the ground as well as my insides, I felt about the Concorde as one might feel about a beautiful girl walking into class on the first day of school: I had to get close to her somehow, whether we ever actually hooked up or not. For the Concorde was, quite simply, the only passenger plane around that still had the ability to quicken the pulse. Could one say this of the 747? The MD-

---

✛ Since 1989, BA has shared the building with United.

80? The L-1011? Hardly. In fact, the most popular new passenger jet in the world is called, by way of capitulation to the inevitable, the Airbus.

The Concorde is no bus. Everyone knows that. It is fast, sleek, beautiful, and expensive. The one adjective that might conceivably go along with those others, and the one thing that the Concorde in fact is *not,* is dangerous. Like Qantas—as of this writing, at least—the Concorde has never crashed. This is a not inconsiderable, if unspoken, part of its mystique. The ground tone of that mystique, of course, is that it will get you across the Atlantic in three hours (sometimes less), and that it costs an arm and a leg ($7,212, round trip, as of this writing) to ride on it. It looked as though a handshake with the beauty would be as far as I'd get.

Just fifteen working Concordes exist in the world, and they are all owned and operated by the companies that originally commissioned them in the mid-seventies, Air France and British Airways. (This isn't the way it was originally planned to be.) They are old planes, most of them built twenty years ago; in technological terms, they are dinosaurs. And they are scheduled to begin to wear out (and in the case of airplanes, don't you think a beginning is nearly as good as an ending?) at the end of this century—which, we hardly need be reminded, is only a clock-tick away.

Paradoxically, however, the plane *looks* new. The newest commercial planes on the airport ramps—those Airbuses and 747-400s and 767s and MD-11s—are visually only a jot removed from the 707, the plane that gave my generation a little flutter back in second grade (it had no propellers! it was streamlined!), at the end of the Eisenhower years. Swept-back V-wings with slats and flaps, engines in suspended pods: As an aesthetic, it is serviceable but hoary. Shades of 1959—of John Foster Dulles and Ingemar Johansson and the Kingston Trio!

The Concorde is no such thing. It looks—especially when its movable nose is pointed down—like a cross between an origami crane and a space shuttle. It looks like 1999. (It also, weirdly enough, looks like 1959: the year I learned to make paper airplanes.) It is as white as the white whale.

We have seen and heard it take off. Strange phenomenon. It shakes the earth, pierces the sky, all in the service of *luxe.* One gets goosebumps; but what, exactly, are these goosebumps about? Humankind's ever-questing mind, our ceaseless conquest of the skies? Or John Kluge's right to arrive in London unmussed?

Nevertheless, one wants to *ride* it. You look at that thing, and you think, *Holy shit. Wouldn't that be a kick in the pants?* And then, a moment later, it hits you: *And only thirty-six hundred dollars one way.* And that's it—that's the whole point. Of course you couldn't come close to affording it. You couldn't afford to go out with Claudia Schiffer, either. To the (even the only slightly) aesthetically minded, the best things in life are far from free. This is where envy comes in. Envy being the entire basis of glamour.

Things used to be so much simpler. *"People used to get dressed up to travel in those days,"* Captain Frank Fox, of the Port Authority Police, told me, of Idlewild in 1959. *"Men would wear hats and suits; women would wear hats and gloves. You'd never see a young couple with a kid."*

You never saw a young couple with a kid in those days, because all the young couples with kids were in apartment buildings or suburban tract houses, making eleven thousand dollars a year and pleased as Punch about it. And Idlewild was an international airport, and who the hell got on a plane to go overseas in 1959? Farouk! Vincente Minnelli! Ian Fleming! (Not my grandparents. Not anymore. Most of their money was gone by then. Not J. Paul Getty, either. Getty, who hated life and wanted to live forever, was terrified of flying.) This was still in the days when people climbed those movable staircases to get into silver-skinned planes, rich people squinting in the sunlight off Jamaica Bay . . . still in the days *when everybody knew his place.* Long, long before deregulation, before the days when international airports would be jam-packed with Swedish kids with shorts and backpacks, and Pakistani families, and Iranian families, and Russian families—squalling babies and saris and babushkas and pungent body odors everywhere. This was long before Ellis Island returned to existence in the form of Kennedy Airport.

This was also long before the days of what might politely be referred to as Upgrade Fever. In October 1978, when President Carter signed the bill forever and irrevocably removing this country's airlines from the constraints of government regulation—thereby permanently ending the genteel old days when high fares were fixed by fiat, and the airlines, like members of some kind of gentlemen's club, were only nominally in competition with each other—he unwittingly opened a Pandora's box of what might be called classlust. The airline price wars began. Fares plummeted. Suddenly, *anybody* could fly. And did!

And as long as the barricades were partway down, why not raze them? Just as suddenly, the masses began to discover all kinds of nifty tricks for sitting where their supposed betters used to sit—where the seats were bigger, the food and drink better, the attendants friendlier, the liquor and headphones free. Where the very air seemed pleasanter to breathe. How to get up there? There were frequent-flier miles. There were all kinds of scams, from the ingenious (tickets could be altered, travel agents suborned) to the blatant (a fuss could be made, at the gate or on the plane, about some supposed lapse of service; satisfaction would be demanded). "I'm a travel agent!" "I can't sit in smoking!" Given half a chance, people were, it seemed, limitlessly greedy about feeling—how else to put it?—classy.

Imagine my delighted surprise, my vast titillation, when, nearly from the jump, British Airways held out the possibility of a flight on the Concorde—*a ride on the rocket,* as the wonderfully stiff-upper-lip British phrase goes. Strictly for research purposes, of course. Of course. *And it was their idea.* Not being a particularly brazen or cozy reporter—I've never been on a press junket, for example—I would have thought it much too much to ask for. The idea was mentioned, in an utterly (disingenuously?) by-the-by fashion, at my initial lunch (on me) with British Airways' head of PR in America, John Lampl, and the man who was to become my BA liaison, Peter Horton, a former Concorde first officer (copilot), who, by virtue of taking an executive position a couple of years ago (flight manager technical, Concorde), had vaulted through the seniority ranks to become a Concorde captain, as well as that rarest and most uncomfortable of centaurs, a member at once of labor and management.

It was December. We ate at a fancy hotel on Park Avenue. Horton was a complete surprise. I had expected—well, *dash* was what I'd expected. The RAF manner. An ascot and a pipe, perhaps. Long, thin face. Distracted, aristocratic air. Piercing glances down the side of the aquiline nose. Peter Horton was not this person. A stocky man in his mid-forties with squinting eyes, rosy cheeks, and thinning red-blond hair, he was at once ill-at-ease and assured, diffident and forthright. His accent was firmly middle-class. He had never flown in the RAF—had never been in the military. Cosmetically, at least, Horton could have been a tour bus driver. The truth was more complex.

He is from Southport, Lancashire, the eldest of seven children. His father, who died when Horton was twenty, was a sales executive for British Rail. After Horton graduated from high school, he became a public-health inspector, testing the cleanliness of restaurants, shops, and houses. "I found it utterly boring," he told me, when we met for the second time, at an eminently health-inspectable-looking midtown Manhattan restaurant frequented by BA Concorde crews. (Cruddy restaurants would become a theme in my relations with British crews, who are fond of pocketing as much as possible of their meal allowance.) The health inspector job paid £264 a year—a little over $700 at the time. His dreams did not involve advancement in the public-health field. "I actually rather fancied flying, but couldn't afford it," Horton said. He also lacked the necessary qualifications for a career as a pilot, having never stepped onto a plane.

After a couple of years searching for mouse droppings, Horton had had enough. He slogged through another couple of brain-numbing British jobs— production controller for a building firm in Chester ("There was never any money left at the end of the week"), computer operator for a clothing manufacturer in Leeds ("a little more interesting"). As soon as he was making a little more money (around eight hundred pounds a year), he decided to pay for some flying lessons. His first flight as a student, on a Cessna 150, was his first time on an airplane. The price was three pounds an hour—about a fifth of his weekly salary. "I could only afford to do it once a month," Horton said. "Everybody else was there in Mercedeses and Jags. I figured that at this rate, I'd never solo."

It was 1968; Horton was twenty-four. Then he saw an ad in a flying magazine for a pilot training program at BEA and BOAC (the two companies would merge in 1974 to become British Airways). The cost of the program was beyond his means, but the companies were also offering a sponsorship. Horton applied and, to his amazement, was accepted into an expenses-paid, eighteen-month commercial aviation course at the College of Air Training in Hamble, Hampshire.

"That course produced twelve hundred pilots," Horton told me. "During the sixties, they recruited like mad. People who joined three months before I did are a hundred fifty places ahead of me now—they were recruiting at that rate. In the seventies they cut way back. There was the recession, the advent of 747s—they needed far fewer crews to fly just as many passengers—and the introduction of inertial navigation. There used to be a navigator in every crew; suddenly, there was a machine to do his job."

The course taught Horton to solo in single- and twin-engine Cherokees, and he came out with a commercial license. There were three levels of license: in ascending order, commercial, senior, and airline transport. (Horton also had to get a flight navigator's license.) With a commercial or senior license, you could copilot; only with an airline transport certificate could you captain a plane. Two thousand hours of flying and a set of exams separated each level.

Horton joined BOAC in 1969, a newlywed, and within six weeks was flying as a first officer. His plane was the Vickers VC-10. The VC-10 was built, in 1962, to fly the Commonwealth routes, the ghost of the British Empire—old outposts like Africa, India, and Burma, the domain of big khaki Gurkha shorts, old-fashioned Rolexes, gin and bitters, wog-bullying. These airstrips were commonly hot and high up. Hot air is thinner, as is air at high altitudes: Planes need more power or greater taxiing distance, or both, for takeoff. The problem with Commonwealth-route strips was that they were not only hot and high, but short. Enter the VC-10—with *two* Rolls-Royce engines mounted on either side of the rear fuselage, a unique configuration, never duplicated since.

James Kaplan

The VC-10 was much beloved, by crews and passengers alike: It was safe, powerful, and—because of those rear-mounted engines—extraordinarily quiet to ride in. It was one of those rare successes of postwar British engineering and design seemingly unvitiated by the once-great country's shrinking economic base, labor problems, and sagging currency—not to mention consequent dispiritment and failure of imagination.[✈] (Consider just briefly how *in spite of,* in every way, was the phenomenon of the Beatles. Consider the primitiveness of the equipment on which they first recorded.)

But the VC-10 was doomed from the start, a victim of the American Century. World War II had pumped up the aviation industries in both Britain and the United States, but America's advantage in capital, labor force, and aerospace technology was overwhelming. When Vickers, out of Weybridge, tried, in 1955, to sell BOAC its new VC-7 jetliner, BOAC wasn't having any: The design simply wasn't up to snuff. When Boeing, out of Seattle, came calling the following year with the 707, BOAC snapped it up. Country, after all, was country; business was business.[✈✈]

The British government saw the writing on the wall in the early sixties: America had sewn up the civil aviation market for the time being. England's one chance was to develop an SST—a supersonic transport—for the seventies and beyond. The cost of the project would be so huge that enlisting a partner would be critical. The United States was out of the running, having its own (short-lived) SST project under way. The answer was another European country; the only candidate with sufficient capital and technological experience with supersonic planes was, inconveniently enough, France. Who knows what anti-batrachian imprecations were muttered, what harrumphs harrumphed, within oak-paneled walls in Parliament—but in 1962, the two countries, ever-vigorous detractors of each other, shook hands. The project, appropriately enough, was entitled Concorde.[✈✈✈]

It would be one of the greatest financial disasters in British history. In its desperation to redeem its aerospace industry and regain world economic power,

---

[✈] The English national funk is certifiable. A recent survey found that *49 percent* of Britons would move overseas if they could.

[✈✈] The Comet 2, Britain's initial foray into the passenger jet age, suffered a series of disastrous crashes—the result of design flaws—after its introduction in 1952. Comet 4, an improved version, was introduced in 1958, but—*bad juju!*—nobody was interested. By this time, anyway, the 707 was thoroughly entrenched, and the British aviation industry was a dead duck.

[✈✈✈] So vehement was anti-French sentiment in the British government that the final *e* of *Concorde* almost became a deal-breaker. When the UK finally capitulated, Prime Minister Harold Macmillan announced, "The *e* shall stand for England!" Parliament cheered.

THE AIRPORT

England squinted at every crucial implication of (a) the cost of the project and (b) the deal with France. There is every evidence that Charles de Gaulle, having a better-developed aviation infrastructure and a sounder economy, simply bamboozled England into entering an ironclad, escape-proof agreement to develop a plane for which, in 1962, *no performance specifications existed.* It was therefore impossible to calculate how much the Concorde would end up costing British taxpayers (since BOAC was still a nationalized airline).

The initial estimate was £150 million to £170 million (roughly $420 million to $475 million, in 1962 dollars). Nor were voices of reason absent. As Peter Hall recounts in his brilliant chapter on the Concorde in *Great Planning Disasters:*✛

> Enoch Powell, a Cabinet minister at the time, later said: "One hundred and fifty million pounds down, a prospect of breaking even in the long run and an olive branch to the French who might let us into the Common Market after all. . . . You use a truffle hound to find truffles, and a foxhound to find foxes. You use politicians if you want a political result, and businessmen if you want a business result." And two weeks before the agreement was signed, in a House of Lords debate, a veteran air expert, Lord Brabazon of Tara, succinctly voiced the objections that were afterwards to mount. Quoting the Minister of Aviation as saying "Space beckons us with a golden finger," he commented acidly: "My Lords, it beckons us to the three brass balls of the pawnbroker." The cost, £6,000,000 [$17 million] a plane, against £2,000,000 for a Boeing 707, he correctly predicted, would "put civil aviation in the red forever" and would fail to attract extra traffic. The time savings were largely illusory since they would be greatly reduced by ground access [*vide* the Van Wyck!]. Worst of all would be the problem of noise and sonic boom: "From a political point of view, I cannot imagine a better vote-catching stunt than smashing all the windows of two or three streets in the middle of a cold winter's night; people would then really appreciate the advantage of technology." He concluded, prophetically: "We are guessing—we do not know. I do not mind guessing, but you are guessing with the taxpayer's money. You are going to make this machine. Good luck to it! I only regret that when it is finished I shall not have the

✛ University of California, 1982. Other calamities covered in this excellent book include the San Francisco BART rapid-transit system; the Sydney, Australia, opera house; and the *London* airports.

privilege of saying, because people will not listen to me, 'I told you so.'"

We may proceed after duly heaving a sigh at the qualitative chasm between British and American political discourse. All hail, Lord Brabazon of Tara!

Perhaps Harold Macmillan really did see this gigantic—and he didn't know the half of it—outlay as the price of England's ticket, at last, into the Common Market. In any case, six weeks after England and France signed the Supersonic Aircraft Agreement, de Gaulle, with supreme Gallic irony, vetoed British entry. And when Harold Wilson's Labour government came in, in 1964, it found itself in a Brer Rabbit–like briar patch, from which escape was impossible.

The situation was not dissimilar to the aviation-averse William O'Dwyer's inheritance of the seventy-million-dollars-in-the-red New York International Airport upon taking over the mayoralty from the grand dreamer Fiorello La Guardia. Except that Harold Wilson had no New York Port Authority to bail him out. He was locked into co-producing Concordes, no matter what the cost.

First, however, the damn thing had to be *designed.* It wasn't easy. Citing one Mr. Thornton, secretary for aerospace and shipping at the Department of Trade and Industry, Peter Hall notes:

> The total weight of the plane, as originally designed, was 170 tons, of which the structure alone was 70 tons. The fuel took another 90 tons because of the extremely heavy fuel consumption per mile. This left only 10 tons for payload (passengers and baggage). If for any reason a modification were needed, a 1 per cent increase in the weight of the structure meant a 7 per cent loss of payload; half a ton more fuel meant a loss of 5 per cent on payload. So the "constant attempt" to rectify the structure or the engine performance had a "totally disastrous" effect on payload and thus on the plane's commercial prospects.

As the design was fine-tuned, R&D costs kept rising. Steeply. By 1964, the cost had gone from £150 million to £170 million to £275 million. The British cabinet asked the French government about the possibility of pulling out. The French government informed the cabinet that in this event, it would sue England for £100 million, the amount England had already committed. Research and development continued. By 1967, total costs had risen to £450 million. A 1968 redesign raised the 1969 total to £730 million. In 1969, both the English and French prototypes were flying. It was time to try to sell the plane.

For a while it seemed people might actually buy it. It was originally thought that the Concorde was the natural successor to the 707, but meanwhile the 747, the DC-10, and the Lockheed TriStar (L-1011) were developed, and then the airlines did their math. The 747, which first came into service in 1970, was the deal-breaker. It was no beauty, but it was, from a commercial (if not an aesthetic or technological) viewpoint, an amazing plane, by virtue of the sheer number of people that could be stuffed into one. It kicked the hell out of cost per seat-mile on long-haul trips. Airlines were, after all, a business, and by the late sixties the business was starting to decline. Part of the reason for this was that they were buying new equipment before the old planes had totally paid for themselves. In 1969, as we have seen, Pan Am spent $550 million on twenty-five new 747s. In 1970, therefore, it canceled one of its eight options on the Concorde. Pan Am's bellwether status in the business led other carriers to follow suit. Then, in 1973, came the Arab oil embargo, and the quadrupling of jet-fuel prices. By the end of the year, all the non-nationalized airlines that had put in options on Concordes—at one point seventy of the planes were on order, Pan Am and TWA being the biggest potential buyers—had withdrawn them, leaving England and France, in lonely splendor, holding the bag.✦

Peter Horton copiloted the VC-10 for seven years. Then, one day in 1976, on a flight to Singapore, he saw his future, shimmering out of the air like some surreal giant white grasshopper. It was the British Airways Concorde, then on one of its commercial testing trials. Ridiculous cost aside, the first sight of the plane is electrifying to everyone, and Horton was no exception. His first reaction was simply that he wanted to *fly it*. His ordinary path of seniority would have taken him to copiloting, and eventually piloting, 747s. Instead he chose, at that moment, to cast captaincy to the winds and train for the Concorde.

The seniority structure of British Airways was such that there was virtually no chance Horton could ever become a captain in the Concorde fleet. There were too few planes, too many pilots ahead of him in line. But if his only chance to fly this thing was to fly it as a copilot, then that was all right with him. "I'd rather drive a sports car than a saloon car," Horton told me, using the quaint British term for a large family sedan.

✦ By 1978, when the sixteenth and final Concorde had been manufactured, the total cost of the project, including R&D and production, had come to more than two billion pounds, a cost mostly borne by British and French taxpayers.

It is safe to say that all pilots become pilots because they love to fly; it is equally safe to say that the advent of sophisticated avionics and inertial navigation has taken most of the flying out of piloting large passenger jets. The next time you're aboard a 757, take a peep into the cockpit. What you will see will remind you of nothing so much as a large, two-screened video game. There are commercial airliners already in service that can perform an entire trip themselves—takeoff, flight, and landing. This is not to say that pilots are quickly becoming useless—systems will, for the foreseeable future, always need human backup—but any time spent among commercial pilots will quickly convince you that the Right Stuff is not a part of their flight kits.

No, as we have discovered, airline pilots—however tan, noble-profiled, deep-voiced, and assured—are very often depressed people. Their salaries, compared with those of the executives they fly around, are strictly so-so. Their livelihood is perpetually threatened by the airline wars. Their domestic lives are a joke. They feel defensive, deep down, about what they actually do and don't do. For they *don't get to do much flying.* What they mostly do is a lot of riding up front, while the machines do the work. It is not for nothing that the term *automatic pilot* has less-than-positive connotations in our culture.

Concordes, too, have autopilots. But the men who sit in their cockpits (and one woman now, as of this writing) are—domestic and financial worries aside—a cut above. There is a spring to their step. The plane they fly may be an anachronism, but by God, it's a great anachronism. And, despite the fact that it's outfitted with computers designed to make it feel just like a standard passenger aircraft, it's no cinch to pilot. Peter Horton had to take a six-month course to figure out to handle it—in the classroom, then in simulators, and finally in the thing itself, first learning how to fly it in the air, then how to take off and land. The latter maneuver is referred to by the Brits, in pricelessly BA fashion, as *circles and bumps.* (Wasn't that a dish I saw in a working-men's restaurant in Lancashire?)

Concorde is, first of all, a very different plane from anything else in commercial aviation. It has to be. It flies at twice the speed of sound, almost twice as high up as standard commercial aircraft. As Christopher Orlebar, a BA Concorde first officer, writes in *The Concorde Story:*

At Mach 2 it experiences a freezing wind of such force that the fuselage is heated to the boiling point of water, shock waves tear at every angle on its airframe, and all this occurs at an altitude where the atmospheric pressure is a tenth of its value at sea level. Only military aircraft flown by pilots, equipped with sophisticated oxygen supplies and wearing pressure suits, had ventured to these extremes and then usually only for minutes at a time. The SST was designed to carry ordinary airline passengers in complete comfort and safety for hours at a stretch. Could the fusion of British and French philosophies possibly produce such a craft?

Phony drama notwithstanding (and billions of bucks into the bargain), the trans-Channel adversaries managed. What they came up with was an extraordinarily complex yet beautifully simple-looking plane: a delta-winged (rather than swept-winged) configuration with no horizontal tail surfaces, which relied on a change of vertical attitude, rather than flaps and slats, for deceleration. In other words, the Concorde dropped its butt to slow down. In fact, it did quite a number of things differently than regular passenger jets. It shifted its entire fuel load from fore to aft, in flight, to maintain its center of gravity as the fuel was expended. It pumped that shifting fuel through a network of capillaries just under the plane's skin, in order to air-condition the aircraft's interior and prevent its occupants from being roasted by the air friction of Mach 2. At that speed, the plane expanded several inches horizontally. There was a crack between the engineer's instrument panel and the rear bulkhead of the flight deck that became, at twelve hundred miles an hour, an eight-inch gap. You could put your hand in it. (You wouldn't want to keep your hand there, however, as the plane slowed down.)

Flying the Concorde, piloting it, wasn't like flying standard jets, either. The four Rolls-Royce/SNECMA Olympus 593 Mark 602 turbojet engines delivered a total of 152,200 pounds of thrust at takeoff. "When you open up the engines and the thrust hits you in the backside, it's a hell of a feeling," Peter Horton said. "I mean, you're doing naught to one hundred in twelve seconds. It's a bit shattering to be on the receiving end of that kind of performance—and supposedly in control.

"The first takeoff is—" Horton, given to understatement, searched for a word. "Indescribable," he said, at last. "It's never the same after that."

Horton sat in the right-hand seat for ten years. His pay went up and his children grew. No pilot ghetto for him: he bought a house in the sleepy village of St. Olaves, on the Waveney River, two hundred miles northeast of London. His wife, Judy, taught nursery school. His daughter, Carrie, became a champion swimmer. Horton learned sailing. Often—now that he could afford it—he went to local flying clubs on the weekends and took up a Robin for a couple of hours. "Fun flying," he said. "Instead of going down the freeway, you're on back roads." But more than amusement was involved: "It takes just as much skill, of a slightly different kind, to fly a small airplane as it takes to fly a big one."

James Kaplan

While Peter Horton drove the rocket, his company changed radically and
irrevocably. In 1976, when he first started on the Concorde, British Airways
was still a nationalized carrier. Overstaffed and underachieving, the company
had run as a kind of boiled-beef barrel for years, costing England a steady
$200 million a year in the late seventies and early eighties, and earning the
pointed enmity of the flying public. (An old chestnut held that BA stood for
"bloody awful.") Twenty-five years of postwar economic and social malaise,
combined with the influx of dislocated minorities from former outposts of the
empire, had shaken apart the ossified old English class structure, playing
havoc with the grand British ideal of service. In the nationalized BA, the customer was an inconvenience, an afterthought, an object upon whom the
British national cafard might be acted out.

Then, in 1981, Margaret Thatcher, champion of free enterprise, appointed
John King, a bulldog-faced millionaire industrialist and loyal Tory, as chairman of the company. King immediately axed 40 percent of the work force, as
well as several of the old boiled-beef-barrel suppliers—companies that, it
might easily be imagined, were not exactly knocking themselves out to bid
competitively for BA's business. He also hired Saatchi and Saatchi to spiff up
the carrier's image. One of the ad company's first moves was to coin a new
slogan—"The World's Favourite Airline"—which might, at first glance, have
seemed a bit premature.

In the first year after John King's deep personnel slashes, BA lost *$920
million*—much of it in severance settlements—and worker morale hit bottom.
King brought in a seasoned marketing pro named Colin Marshall as CEO,
and Marshall immediately set about instilling the previously unknown concept of marketing in the barnacled organization, as well as ruthlessly expung-
ing all traces of the national bad mood in its BA branch locations. Planes were
repainted in the new British Airways livery, with a rakish (and somewhat un-
British) blue-and-red chevron motif. Workers' uniforms were redesigned
around the same aesthetic, and, it being an English company, a coat of arms
was created: a winged lion and a winged horse rampant and leaning on BA's
chevroned shield, which was topped by a garland, a jeweled crown, and a rising (or was it setting?) sun. Strange symbolism, in the post-twilight of empire.
All stood atop a pennon bearing the new BA motto: "To Fly, to Serve." And
a strange sentiment. One would hope the first infinitive to be true of any airline; as for the second, given the heretofore depressed and surly state of BA's
service—well, one could always aspire to better things.

Or one could push, hard. Marshall also brought in a Danish(!) management consulting firm, with the aim, as it was said, of "instilling in workers the
ethos of service." Some fairly forceful instilling was in order. Soon people

196

were attending touchy-feely workshops; people were walking around wearing "Putting People First" buttons. People were also grumbling. But then came the riveting thought of those twenty-three thousand cashiered employees. Ticket agents, service managers, and cabin crews began to wear strained British smiles, nearly indistinguishable from the real thing.

What was more, in 1987 Mrs. Thatcher—with the full agreement of John King and Colin Marshall, who were shortly to receive, respectively, a peerage and a knighthood for their efforts—kicked BA out of the nest. Unlike Air France, Air Jamaica, Lufthansa, Sabena, SAS, and El Al, et al., British Airways would no longer be a national carrier but a publicly held corporation, responsible for keeping itself aloft. And by God, it was beginning to do the job. Staff cuts, competitive suppliers, aggressive marketing, enforced niceness (not to mention employee profit sharing) . . . it all was having its effect. Lord King and Sir Colin, ace industrialists, were no dopes. They rode hard, but they got results. In 1987, British Airways ran in the black for the first time since the 1974 merger. All was peaceable in the kingdom. So, at least, it seemed.

Peter Horton had his own, now changed, game plan. Just before British Airways denationalized, he de-Concordized. As BA employee No. 980, he knew he could never rise by natural seniority to a command in the Concorde fleet, so he decided to aim for the next-best thing: a 747 captaincy. "There's only one seat to sit in on an airplane—that's the front seat, left-hand side," he says. "Every pilot worth his salt wants to be captain of his airplane." Money had nothing to do with it. BA captains are paid strictly according to seniority, whether they fly the 737 or Concorde.

It works differently in America. Here, captains are paid not by seniority but—in what somehow seems like a gloss on nineteenth-century whaling practices—according to the weight of the plane they fly. One pictures the directors of the various U.S. airlines as steely-eyed Peleg and Bildad types in chin beards and stovepipes, sitting around calculating the profits down to the last American Tourister, the nearest barrel of jet fuel. As I once overheard the steely-eyed Colonel Frank Borman, former astronaut and former head of the former Eastern Airlines, remarking to Peter Horton, in the Concorde lounge at Kennedy, "It's hard to beat the economics of a fully loaded 747." Nevertheless, the Concorde, a mere sylph at 400,000-odd pounds fully fueled and loaded, to the 800,000 pounds of a packed 747, is an interesting exception, the vertiginous fare being calculated to offset the plane's relative petiteness.

And in any case, there are arguments to be made for the English pay system. "The advantage is that people can actually fly the plane they want, the routes they want, without having to chase the money," Horton said. "It means that a very senior captain on a 737 can stay doing that—otherwise everyone would end up on a 747. And it saves BA money, because we're not involved in continual training." This is Horton the manager talking. Horton the pilot sings a slightly different tune. "What seniority does for you," he said, "is let you pick your routes"—the better routes being the ones for which a higher travel allowance is allotted. "If you fly to the Middle East or the U.S., you can take hard currency home," he said. This is an ambivalent phenomenon. For one thing, BA pilots, Horton included, don't like to talk much about taking hard currency home: Inland Revenue is listening. And even if a resourceful senior pilot can take home an additional ten thousand dollars or so, in cash, a year—"You get a certain amount for meals; if somebody decides to go on a diet, good luck to them," Horton said—the sight of Concorde captains scrimping on beers and eating at cheap Manhattan coffee shops does not add to their mystique.

For Peter Horton, getting a 747 command would mean once again working his way up through the ranks; at the beginning, he would pilot 737s. The decision was a difficult one, but once he made it, the break was clean. "I thought that was it—I'd never fly Concorde again," he told me. He had had his ten years on the rocket.

The transition was not easy. It was a boom time for leisure travel in the new hard-marketing BA, and Horton found himself expelled from Heathrow, flying tours out of Gatwick to various locations throughout the Continent. "It certainly improved my knowledge of European geography," he said, dryly. His new passengers were as different from the old as the plane he was flying was different from a Concorde. "It was the opposite end of the spectrum," Horton said. Again dryly. These were retired schoolteachers, grannies from East Anglia—in short, the very people whose ranks Horton had risen from. Not that he had taken on grand airs as a Concorde first officer; quite the reverse. True, he owned a nice house up north and sailed a boat and flew on the weekends, but the house was modest, its distance from London made it relatively inexpensive, and Horton drove a Ford Sierra—and this last was the key. Horton was in every way a Ford guy, or at least the British equivalent thereof. He was—or seemed—stolid and uncomplex, a meat-eater. It might tickle him to have Rod Stewart riding in back of his plane, but it didn't set him aflutter. Then again, with a plane full of electricians and car dealers and housewives, the tickle was pretty much gone.

He put in one year on the package-tour milk run, then got kicked upstairs, to an office position as assistant flight manager technical for BA's 737 fleet. He liked the work, which primarily consisted of monitoring pilots' use of their equipment to ensure BA was making the most possible money in the safest possible way. A big plus was that he got to fly on a regular basis, both to keep his skills sharp and to stay current on procedures and hardware. Then the unforeseen happened. The flight manager technical for the Concorde fleet retired, and Horton, who had both Concorde and managerial experience, was tapped for the job. "I was in the right place at the right time," he said. He was back.

Yet being both a pilot and an executive often produces schizophrenic results. "When I'm a pilot," he said, "I'm not a manager. If I do something wrong, I've done it as a pilot." And as a pilot of two decades' standing, he is a member of BALPA—the British Airline Pilots' Association. "Every year, management and the union have a negotiation," he said. "Management tries to get salaries down, and I try to get them up." His own two-headed salary works out not quite to his benefit: A manager at his level doesn't make as much as a senior captain. Then again, he usually gets to pilot the rocket on three or four transatlantic round trips a month. For wearing his two hats, Horton earns £73,000 a year, about $100,000. This places him squarely in the hard-pressed upper middle class. Yet his distance from London allows him to live like a small-scale country squire, of the heavily mortgaged variety. He has a house with a big garden, a swimming pool, a mooring on the river, a small sailboat, two horses. The house, which is under two thousand square feet, is worth about $260,000 on the current market.

Most of Horton's St. Olaves neighbors have no idea what he does for a living. "They see me in jeans and a sweatshirt; I don't fit the image," he said. His son, Paul, a college student, appears to have taken his father's bootstrap success to heart. "I think he'd like to work in the stock market," Horton said. "I think he would love to be a yuppie." His daughter wants to be an airline pilot.

For years, Horton barely saw his family. "There were a lot of years flying on weekends," he said. "It was lonely having Wednesday and Thursday off." He would make the long drive up from London on a weekday night, tumble into bed exhausted, kiss his wife and children good-bye as they went off to work and school the next morning, then head back to work himself as the weekend began. These days, however, his seniority and management status have made him a weekdays-only man, just like any office worker. The difference being that this is an office worker who periodically gets up from his desk and flies the world's fastest passenger jet, the coolest plane in the world, across the Atlantic and back at twice the speed of sound.

If Peter Horton's story is the triumph of the former health inspector—roach eggs and mouse droppings, farewell!—not every Concorde captain subscribes so ardently to the bourgeois ideal. There are twenty of them, and their personalities and styles fit no template. Nevertheless, there are those who are precisely what you'd expect. Horton suddenly stopped his narrative midsentence and listened. "There's Nigel," he said.

"Who's Nigel?"

A minute later, I was being introduced to Nigel, who was possessed of precisely the right name, not to mention a long, sharp face, an ascot, a pipe (looking back, I can't be positive about that pipe, but I'd swear to at least one, if not several), a background as an RAF captain, and easily the plummiest voice on West Fifty-fifth Street. As we shook hands, I detected within myself an effervescent mixture of intimidation and amusement. Here he was! The Concorde Pilot! I glanced over at Horton's tour-bus-driver's face, which looked amused. It took me a moment to figure out why. "He has got a very distinctive voice, hasn't he?" Horton said, once Nigel had left. "He's gotten better, though. Now he calls *me* sir." He smiled. Dryly.

Naturally the pilot who adhered *most* closely to the boys'-book concept of jet captain would possess one more crucial quality. For jet planes are not shaped like saucers or spheres or doughnuts, but instead happen to be modeled after the primal questing instrument of man's ambition—in the case of the Concorde, it might be argued, even more so. Thus it would only stand to reason that there are those pilots who identify with the ithyphallic rakishness embodied by the plane itself. Sure enough, some time after Horton introduced me to Nigel, I got wind of a certain legendary Concorde captain—Ian Saxon. A name redolent of rutting, blue-painted, fur-wearing Picts and Sassenachs.

It all began, oddly enough, in the course of a fairly arid morning checking out the Concorde lounge in the BA terminal at Kennedy: *lots* of rich-looking guys reading their salmon-colored *Financial Times*es; one excessively wan and moneyed young Brit couple with wan infant in tow (Nanny, it goes without saying, was traveling on jumbo, with the luggage); one long-haired guy who looked as though he ought to be somebody, but I was pretty sure wasn't. Not a luminary in sight, in other words, and the atmosphere couldn't have been more parched. A couple of rich folks circumambulated the elegant breakfast buffet, breezing by those pricey Concorde pastries and that fresh-squeezed Concorde juice with scant interest. Food didn't seem to do it for them. Of course not! They're rich! They're thin! They're jaded!

But where, I wondered, was the sex in all of this? For isn't glamour, with its inherent enviability, a crucial element in some of our more pervasive fantasies about sex? *The rich have it better.* The rich do kinky stuff. Look at Claus von Bülow; look at Roxanne Pulitzer. Where was the sex in the Concorde lounge? That rich young couple—he in his soft gray bespoke suit and twelve-hundred-dollar Lobb's shoes; she in her pink dress with Peter Pan collar—how, precisely, had they managed to reproduce? (My thoughts turned, quite unavoidably and unpleasantly, to his boxer shorts, which I was positive had been pressed, pleat by pleat, by some long-suffering lackey.)

When boarding for Flight 001 at 9:30 was announced, these forty-two rich folks (*fifty-eight* seats on the morning flight would go empty; why oh why, I wondered, couldn't I—or, of course, any other curious and worthy party—simply hop aboard?) rose as if to answer the phone. Where was the excitement? The slight tension of putting one's life on the line (even if under these most actuarially positive of conditions, riding a plane that has never once crashed)? Oh sure, I thought, these people spend $3,600 to fly twice the speed of sound *all the time.* Then it occurred to me immediately, depressingly, that many of them probably did. The rich people strolled jadedly on board, and suddenly the lounge was all but empty, the pastries and juices scarcely touched.

Two women in BA uniforms—one thin, dark, and bespectacled; one short and blond—started to put the food away in the kitchen behind the lounge. I introduced myself. The two were service managers for BA at Kennedy; between them they had some thirty years of employment here. Katinka, as I'll call the short one, was Dutch. She was humorous, slightly coarse, a chain smoker. The punch lines punctuated by puffs. She was quitting BA in a couple of months to go back to Holland and get married; she had a pleasantly coarse, dissipated, bachelorette-party air about her. The taller, thinner one— call her Betty—was *thoroughly* Queens, and the older hand. The two women exuded professional competence; at the same time, they seemed to have a giggling acquaintance, a conspiratorial air. I wondered what it was all about.

❏

We met, one rainy afternoon, in the first-class lounge, which was empty between flights. Betty and Katinka had brought along a colleague I'll call Rhonda, who, like Betty, was from the outer boroughs, and who had also worked for BA at the airport for twenty years. Rhonda was cute and dark-haired, with a kind face, but as we sat down around a glass table, I quickly found that kindness was not the order of the day. Rhonda was as vehement as her colleagues, and the object of her animus was her employer.

"You see," Betty said, setting a little dish of Pepperidge Farm Goldfish on the table, "something sad happened here over the past ten to fifteen years— since deregulation. When the British government subsidized us, the concern was quality. We grew up with a feeling of being nurtured. We used to be the highest paid on the airport. We were the crème de la crème.

"But then, when this airline was restructured, people who knew nothing about the airline industry were brought in. Five years ago they had this program called PPF—Putting People First. They spent tens of thousands of dollars on it. And now management has gone against everything in that program. Now you have people going into therapy because of the stress of negotiations. During our first negotiation—"

"You're in a union?" I asked.

"IAMW," Betty said. "International— What is it."

"Aerospace—" Katinka said.

"Machinist Workers?" Rhonda said.

"Yeah. I think," Betty said. "Rhonda and I are both shop stewards. Anyway, it was an ugly negotiation. Things like, your pension is based on your base rate, but your raises are given in a lump sum, so they don't affect your pension. Then, at the height of the bargaining, at the most sensitive point, Lord King got a two hundred percent raise."

The sweet-faced Rhonda then said something unrepeatable about Lord King.

"They're so worried about the morale at this station," Betty continued. "This station is the moneymaker for North America. It's all about making money now."

"One girl swapped a day with another girl, and on the way to work she had a miscarriage—she was penalized," Rhonda said. "One girl had bronchitis—she was penalized."

"You know about yield control?" Betty asked.

"Could you slow down a second?" I said.

These were unhappy women, and the picture they were giving of the World's Favourite Airline, the airline that was widely looked upon as the leader in the industry, was hardly a favorable one. But, in a way, wasn't it really airlines in general they were talking about? Deregulation may have opened a Pandora's box, but nobody knew yet whether all the critters let out were monsters or not. That is to say, was it good for capitalism, or not so good, for airlines to feel the sting of real competition, with the result that more and more of them were dropping off the map every month? Was it good that many more people were flying, yet flying in a manner that—largely because of the narrowing of airline services, as a result of the tighter competition—felt progressively more inconvenient? The answer, in each case, seemed to be *good and bad. Yield control*—a.k.a. yield management—as described by Betty, Rhonda, and Katinka, was nothing more than a business's attempt to stay in business. What could an airline do about people who called up and reserved seats, never to show up and claim them? Everybody has, at one time or another, booked seats on four different flights, not out of caprice, but simply to cover one's options. Airline people have, no doubt, done it themselves. But flights, after all, have to be planned in advance: Equipment and personnel must be committed, and enough fuel bought to carry a given number of passengers, calculated by weight (the average avoirdupois of a passenger and his baggage is one hundred kilos), plus freight. "You base your fuel upload on booking," Betty said. "You can't take the fuel off."

What's an airline to do about all this profligate reserving? "There's no way to penalize passengers for no-show," Betty said. Yet while this may be true in terms of criminal prosecution, there are ways. One answer is to make the cheaper tickets nonrefundable, thus driving the Mad Reservers to pay, one way or the other, for their choiciness. Another is yield control, which mainly means, in the case of BA, that the people in London oversell like crazy. "Airlines are allowed to oversell by a certain amount—there is a formula for each day and each flight," Betty explained. In short—every man for himself! It's a kind of low-stakes gambling, based on a simple principle: Only rarely does everybody who's reserved a seat show up to claim it. And supposing everybody does?

"Betty, remember the night we were minus ninety-five [ninety-five oversold], and we broke even?" Rhonda said. The world's most successful airline can get really creative. Especially if it's first class that's oversold.

"You're talking about giving back twenty-four hundred dollars," Betty said. "We'll offer a downgrade to M [business] class and vouchers for further travel."

"If business class is oversold, troubleshooters go through and pick people to put in Concorde," Rhonda said.

"*They* don't complain," Katinka said, tapping her cigarette on an empty peanut dish.

"The guy paying seventeen hundred dollars is paying less than half of what he'd pay for a ride on the rocket," Betty said.

"For the seven P.M. 747 flight to Heathrow, we try to sell business-class passengers on the seven forty-five TriStar flight to Gatwick," Rhonda said.

"Then you have your voluntary offload scheme," Betty said. "They get DBC."

"DBC?" I said.

"Denied-Boarding Compensation," Rhonda said. "We pay for a hotel room or taxi home, and they fly the next morning."

"But you wonder," Betty said. "Why do you want to do this to your regular customers?"

The obvious answer—that it was corporate self-defense—seemed inopportune, given the militancy of the proceedings.

"No-shows skyrocketed during the Gulf War," Katinka mused.

"How could you blame them?" Betty said. "There's no safety here. There's no safety at any American airport. Everybody knows security's a joke. Anybody can get on the ramp here. Anybody can get on the ramp at Heathrow."

Rhonda nodded. "We had to fight for lockable doors to the ramp," she said.

"Maybe El Al's the best," Betty said. "They pressurize their baggage. But the Lockerbie bomb had a timer detonator—pressurizing wouldn't have changed anything." ✈

There was a silence as the rain pelted the big windows. We might be cozy and dry for the moment, but the world, clearly, was large, cutthroat, and perilous. The kabuki of flying—the histrionics of getting people to pretend that the whole process of paying to fly isn't degrading and frightening—seems formidable: from the bulletproof cheeriness of ticket agents, to the cool aplomb of service managers, to the remote, collected, only mildly sexual tease of flight attendants, to the noble reserve of pilots. Most of us buy it all, hook, line, and sinker, even as we know in our heart of hearts that it's inch-thick mummery. We *need* it! Flying is just too scary otherwise.

Now the whole works was unraveling in front of my eyes. (Lockerbie was the moment when the whole works unraveled in front of everybody's eyes. But the human capacity for self-deceit, self-protection, and useful forgetfulness is infinite: Lockerbie—except for its victims' friends and relatives, and the managers and employees of Pan Am—could be, and was, and has been, mentally swept under the rug.) Here, however, were three service managers for the World's Favourite Airline—a fatuous claim, but one, don't you see, that that splendid, thoroughly hard-won bottom line could pretend to justify—breaking down the fourth wall, casting aside mummery, and telling me that commercial aviation was the *shmatte* business all over again, with the addition of life-threatening jeopardy and the subtraction (so it seemed, at least) of the Mob.

BA's relentless cost cutting, according to these women, was not only removing human value from the business, it was removing necessary humans. And the continuous paring of personnel meant that the survivors had to take up the slack. It used to be that Betty and Rhonda and Katinka were simply responsible for dealing with the public at the gate. Now there were a

---

✈ As it turned out, that detonator was barometer-triggered.

few other things to do. "They had Betty and I doing body searches!" Rhonda told me. "We didn't know what we were doing! If the detector went off, we had to take them behind a screen and do a search.

"We had to take our weights-and-balances certification test. You have to give a notification to the captain for everything he's carrying. Once I was told to sign a form saying I had visually checked the cargo when I hadn't. I refused to sign."

"And now we're learning operations," Betty said. "Navigation, meteorology, restricted runways, ILS limitations, alternate airports. You have to study six manuals. Ops One—it used to be a thirteen-week course; now we have one month to study. The passing grade is ninety-five. But you can bet your bippy if we don't get ninety-five, we'll go to London anyway for Ops Two."

In other words, Betty and Rhonda (Katinka was leaving the business) are now going to be responsible not only for dealing with screaming babies and complaining, class-hopping fakes at the gate, but for actually *charting the courses* of the jets those babies and fakes are boarding. No, those aren't highly skilled, engineering-school-trained technicians plotting wind velocity and storm activity and fuel upload—those are the unwilling graduates of a one-month crash (pardon the word) course. . . . All of a sudden, the seemingly skewed and melodramatic view of BA top management as a bunch of money-mad, drunken pirates was starting to make all too much sense. To console myself, I thought of the crash-free Concorde—of the roar of those rockets, of that incredible silhouette. Of glamour, of *luxe, calme, et volupté*.

"Tell me about the Concorde lounge," I said, in one of those pointed changes-of-subject beloved of society hostesses.

"In the Concorde lounge," said Betty, "you see the rich and the famous and the people who run the world. And God forbid if there's a delay. My God, is the fate of the world in these people's hands? We had a couple-hour holdup the other day; these guys fell apart."

"They're babies—they can't do anything for themselves," Rhonda said. "Tony Curtis had me call his agent in L.A. Actually had me dial the phone."

"Henry Kissinger," Katinka said. The three women, as one, shook their heads.

"What about him?" I asked.

"He doesn't travel under 'Henry Kissinger,'" Rhonda said. "He travels under an alias—as if anybody cared."

"He has this little guy in his twenties who goes everywhere with him," Betty said. "Some poor, nerdy-looking little guy who carries his briefcase for him. He flies as a technical on the Concorde." She put her hand to the base of her throat and snorted a laugh. "Oh God," she said. "One time Kissinger went to London to make a speech to Parliament, and his bag got lost. So he made some London men's store open in the middle of the night, so he'd have something to wear. Next time he traveled, there was management standing all along the baggage belt."

"You get two types of wealthy people here," Rhonda said. "Quiet and low-key, and people who throw their weight around."

"We get called names," Katinka said. "There was a guy flying first-class on the 747, and we'd sold his seat. He stood up and beat his chest, screaming, 'Do you know who I am?' I said, 'No, sir—have you lost your memory?'"

"What about sex?" I said. For wasn't this, after all, what I had come to talk to them about in the first place? Sex? Luxe? The ithyphallic Concorde? And wasn't this what they'd promised? *You want stories? I'll tell you stories.*

"Never with the passengers," Betty said. The others nodded solemnly. "Oh, Eric Clapton'll give you that cute sexy smile. But that's the extent of it. But that's not the crews. The crews come on to you. That is rampant."

"Ian," Rhonda said.

"Ian?" I said.

"Tell him about Ian," Betty said, smirking.

"Captain Ian Saxon," Katinka said, exhaling smoke and narrowing her eyes. "Of Concorde. Oh, Ian has a woman in every port. He's quite notorious. And relentless."

"He won't take no for an answer," Betty said.

"Barbara Carson brought on the load sheet," Katinka said. "And Ian said, 'Give me a peek, or I won't sign.' So she opened her blouse. He has a sheep farm up north in England. He came on to me, and I said, 'What's wrong, Ian? Aren't you getting enough with your sheep?' To get back at Ian we sent a guy in drag onto the plane with the load sheet."

Rhonda: "One Halloween they had a Flight to Nowhere, for rich people, and Ian was flying. We were all in costume—all the service personnel. I was supervising at the gate, dressed up like a character from *La Traviata,* with a low-cut peasant blouse and a push-up bra. And everybody was laughing and drinking, and Ian was attacking me. He said, 'Would you like to take Willie out to play?' I was yelling for help through my microphone."

So there was this, and then there was the story of Captain Brian Walpole, BA's first Concorde pilot, who is pictured twice on the foreword page of *The Concorde Story,* the airline's PR-handout book: once standing in full four-stripes-on-the-sleeve uniform (the BA captain's hat, however, is unfortunate in its contour, the wide curve of its peak somehow conveying a certain British dowdiness, or maybe it's merely the lingering rigidity of the class structure; in any case, the visual message is *driver* rather than *pilot*) in front of a Concorde, hands folded, grinning, the portrait of confidence. "Captain Brian Walpole, General Manager, Concorde Division of British Airways," the caption reads. Nice blue eyes, with those epicanthic folds at the corners called Norwegian flaps—but complicated eyes, too. In the lower image, Walpole, sans cap and jacket, with headset in place, is turning from the controls of his plane to face the photographer on August 6, 1985, a red-letter day for BA. For in the jumpseat behind him is HM the Queen Mother, in triple strand of pearls and yellow hat with turned-up brim, roses, and veil, taking a birthday trip (where?) courtesy of British Airways. What a splendid present! What splendid PR—for BA, for the Crown, for British industry! Queen Mum goes supersonic! And she's not afraid, either!

Not long after this picture was taken, Walpole was flying from Kennedy to Heathrow, with his first officer at the controls, when the plane, upon entering British air space, was found to be low on fuel. This can happen if the plane is forced, for any mechanical reason, to fly at subsonic speed for any amount of time. When a Concorde goes subsonic, it must descend from its Icarus-like altitude of sixty thousand feet to a more mundane seven or eight miles, the air up high not being dense enough to support less-than-bulletlike performance. Thicker air, lower efficiency: big burn. Concorde generally has about fifteen hundred kilos of fuel left as it approaches its destination—just enough to go to an alternate airport. Walpole had somewhat less than this. His first officer advised him to divert to Shannon, but Captain Walpole, G.M., C.D., of BA, clenched his jaw and said to press on to Heathrow. The plane landed on fumes.

After some shilly-shallying and foot dragging—Walpole, after all! our top man!—the case was reviewed. And Captain Brian O. Walpole, G.M., C.D., of BA, was forced to give up flying and concentrate on his ground duties. *Not* cashiered, mind you—reassigned. Out of deference to years of service, and so forth. And, one imagines, out of deference to appearances, too. For the thing never got out. It was like one of those suboceanic volcanic eruptions that only get picked up on geological instruments. Yet inside BA, the reverberations were profound, the transatlantic buzz insistent. Was the incident, I asked Peter Horton, a cautionary example for the rest of the Concorde crews? "You bet," he said. "There was an awful lot of stable-door closing after that."

It is a door, as we have seen, that closes late pretty frequently around airports and airlines.

◻

And so it came to pass that, with all this contradictory and overstimulating information revolving in my head and heart—viz., that the clean white box of the BA terminal was just a facade; the coolest plane in the world was a super-annuated boondoggle with a fancy paint job; The World's Favourite Airline was also the world's meanest; pilots, even Concorde pilots, were only human beings, and not especially distinguished ones at that—I would finally get my own ride on the rocket . . . but not yet.

17

Cops and Robbers

A Brief History of Crime

Back to earth. OK, OK, we've seen some genuine JFK squalor. But aren't we overdue for a look at the *real* airport nitty-gritty? Which, as everyone knows (or seems to know), is crime? Which is—as everyone seems to be certain—the Mob?

The world's image of JFK is highly colored by *GoodFellas,* Martin Scorsese's movie adaptation of Nicholas Pileggi's *Wiseguy,* the account of the heist of $5 million in cash and $850,000 in jewelry from Lufthansa cargo in December 1978. Tell people you are writing about Kennedy International, and you will be asked, often, if your life is insured. The impression is of an airport under constant, ubiquitous siege by fiendishly clever mafiosi, who would shoot your kneecaps off—at least—if you revealed their diabolical secrets.

The truth is that the Lufthansa heist took place in the dead of night, in a part of the airport most passengers never see—the cargo area, a mile from the central terminals—and, while it has attracted attention by being the single largest cash robbery in U.S. history, it was an utter fiasco. Everybody involved went to jail or was murdered in the crime's aftermath. The heist was a singularly foolish, greedy, incompetent, and ultimately petty inside job, the last gasp of the dying art of grand theft at Kennedy. John Gotti may have earned his stripes hijacking freight at the airport, but these days the Mob has found better ways of making money. Or, more correctly, the Mob briefly branched out to large-scale cargo theft, but stuck all along with—and now, in its twilight years,✢ has reverted almost exclusively to—time-tested, harder-to-

---

✢ FBI prosecution, coupled with the Mafia's own brand of corporate downsizing, has reduced the Five Families' hierarchy to a shell, loosening its iron grip on organized crime in the New York area and enabling the ascendancy of such groups as the Russian *mafiyeh,* now firmly entrenched in Brighton Beach's Little Odessa; the highly active, frequently murderous Colombian drug cartels of Medellín and Cali, rampant in Jackson Heights and Elmhurst; and the Chinese gangs of Queens: the Green Dragons of Elmhurst, the White Tigers of Flushing.

prosecute ways of making money: gambling, loan-sharking, and—most especially—labor racketeering. Mafiosi, never very clever people to begin with, finally got it through their heads that stolen loot and large amounts of purloined cash are simply *hard to get rid of.* And that a single hit—even a six-million-dollar hit—is peanuts compared with what can be siphoned off, over time, by less dramatic means.

You want to talk drama? (Quiet drama.) Consider two moments. The first, in the summer of 1956, was when Idlewild's quickly growing cargo-handling operations (soon to be the world's largest) were removed from the main terminal and shifted into their own complex—consisting of a group of one-story sheds and a two-story beige-brick structure, Building 80—on a then far-removed eighty-acre site at the northwest corner of the airport. The cargo area's splendid isolation quickly made it a Shangri-La of crime: a place where, as Pileggi writes,

> wiseguys who could barely read learned about bills of lading, shipping manifests, and invoices. They found that information about valuable cargo was available from a stack of over a hundred unguarded pigeonholes used by shipping brokers in [Building 80], a chaotically run two-story structure with no security. . . . There cargo brokers, runners, clerks, and customs officers dealt daily with the overabundance of paperwork required for international shipments. There were over forty brokers employing a couple of hundred runners, many of them part-time workers, so it was not difficult to slip orders from the shelves or copy information about valuable cargo, to pass on to whoever wanted it.

The second moment of drama was Harry Davidoff's arrival at Idlewild.

He didn't come by plane. In 1960 Davidoff was named secretary-treasurer of Teamsters Local 295, a union representing cargo handlers, truck drivers, and other ground workers at Idlewild. It was a nice change from his previous job as president of Toy and Doll International, AFL, Local 130—a post Davidoff had left expeditiously when it was found he'd been milking the union's welfare fund for a "salary," an expense account, and money for new cars.

Born in 1916, Davidoff—currently a resident of the federal prison in Sandstone, Minnesota, where he is scheduled to abide until 1999—was, in his walking-around days, what used to be known as a *colorful character,* or, as a *New York Post* article quoted in the report of a 1976 Senate subcommittee on the corruption of the cargo handlers' unions at Kennedy put it: "a tough-looking, tough-talking man with a sixth grade education, [who] has been shot, arrested, questioned by Congressional panels and investigated by the FBI. His convictions, dating from the 1930s, include burglary, extortion and gambling. Numerous arrests for felonious assault with a knife, possession of a gun, grand larceny and extortion are listed on his record."

Davidoff once told a *Life* magazine photographer who had the temerity to snap his picture, "I could have you killed." Angry as he might have been, he was making a simple statement of fact. Davidoff was once a member of Murder, Inc. He worked for the Luccheses, one of New York's famous Five Families of crime, and his first boss there—insofar as Harry Davidoff ever had a boss—was a capo named John (Johnny Dio) Dioguardi. After Johnny Dio went away, the task of reining in Davidoff fell to another Lucchese capo named Paul Vario.

After a slow start (the volume wasn't there at first), cargo theft turned into a growth industry at Idlewild in the late fifties. By the time Davidoff arrived, the airport had become a vast, slack goody bag, with larceny going virtually unchecked. Cash, gold, jewelry, watches, fur coats: If it looked good, it walked, and there was little the shippers could do about it except to pay fat insurance premiums—and report as little theft as possible, to keep the premiums from going any higher. The extra cost was passed on to the consumer.

The cargo theft business at Idlewild was a kind of dark twin to the cargo business, running, if anything, even more smoothly. The Lucchese and Genovese families kept careful tabs on inventory. And labor. "The workers—the cargo handlers, the truck drivers. There's a whole city out there—thousands and thousands of people work there," says Ed McDonald, who, as a member of the U.S. Justice Department Organized Crime Strike Force for the Eastern District of New York (the Brooklyn Strike Force, for short), helped prosecute the Lufthansa heist, and, as head of the strike force from 1981 to 1989, stemmed the tide of labor racketeering at Kennedy Airport. "I had spent five years in the Manhattan DA's office, dealing with a lot of poor people," McDonald says. "Who were, for the most part, members of minority groups. When I started dealing with these cargo workers at the airport—most of whom were white—I said, 'Where the hell do these people *come* from?'

"These people were really at the very low end of the socioeconomic ladder. And gambling was just *pervasive*—I mean, *everybody* was gambling like crazy. You know, sports betting and numbers and craps games—whatever. And of course all these gambling operations are run by organized-crime figures. And when a guy is down twenty-five thousand dollars, and can't afford to pay his bookmaker, his bookmaker becomes his loan shark. So gambling and loan-sharking go hand in hand. Those were the two big bread-and-butter operations for organized crime."

With the advent of containerization in the late sixties, the fine old art of hijacking began to decline. Distribution of stolen goods had always been a challenge, and cherry-picking loot from a sealed trailer was simply harder than taking it from an open truck. Although crooks weren't averse to stealing an entire containerized shipment, trailer and all, now and then, things just weren't the same.

"In the old days, ninety percent of hijackings were give-ups—phony hijackings, where the driver knew what was coming," says Detective Sergeant Carmine Spano, head of the Cargo Crime Unit at Kennedy. His office, poignantly, is in the old crime center, Building 80. Spano, a small, thin man with a long, slightly mournful face and direct dark eyes, has thinning hair combed over artfully, not blatantly, on top, in a neat, squared-off shape. He somewhat resembles the actor Jerry Orbach, although he lacks Orbach's enthusiasm about the nostrils, his quality of seeming always about to break into raffish song. Spano tends toward quiet. He has twice turned down promotions to lieutenant, because a glitch in his contract would have removed him from the detectives, putting him back in uniform and robbing him of his fiefdom. "I run my own unit," he says, in a soft Brooklyn accent. "Nobody calls me up and says, 'Why'd you do this?' or 'Why didn't you do that?'"

Sergeant Spano's card reads simply "Detective Sergeant," but he makes top lieutenant's pay for leading a unit whose specialties are cargo theft and organized crime. He is well versed in his subjects. It would be tempting to say he knows every trick in the book, but as crime is a book that is constantly being rewritten, its repetitions and variations are a source of concern and delight to Spano. Delight because he loves his work, and concern for the obvious reasons, as well as one less obvious: Like many cops, he could easily have gone the other way.

I approach the subject tentatively, given his ethnicity. "I don't mean to be facetious, but was there any sort of—romance to organized crime when you were growing up?" I say. I'm sitting across from Spano at his desk. He lights a Merit. My suburban politesse was unnecessary. Spano nods at once, with force. "Absolutely," he says, exhaling smoke. "As the saying goes, 'Only by the grace of God . . .' My neighborhood was Canarsie. Paul Vario lived there, and the Amusos, one of whom is a capo today.

"It was all in the climate of the fifties, and hanging out at candy stores," Spano says. "Of course, this was when I was sixteen, seventeen years old.

THE AIRPORT

There were the Club Cadillac Boys—these were guys twenty-five, twenty-six years old. The Parkway Boys. Tough customers. There were the usual street fights, some gang activity. I was involved.

"But finally, when I was seventeen years old, I looked at these guys who were twenty-five or twenty-nine, and still hanging out. I had a friend, Dicky Messina, who was shot in the head in an armored car robbery. I wasn't brought up that way. My father would've kicked the shit out of me if I had gotten mixed up in anything like that. My father was a hard-working guy, and he expected me to be, too. So when I was seventeen, the way I looked at it, my playtime was over with."

Spano, who joined the PA Police in 1968, transferred to airport duty after his rookie assignments in the Lincoln and Holland tunnels literally made him sick. "It was two in, two out," he says. "Two hours in the tunnel, and two out. The soot and dust just got to me—after three months I was ready to pack it in."

Nineteen sixty-eight was the year that a longshoremen's strike in the Port of New York caused the air-cargo business at Kennedy to start to climb sharply; volume has gone from $4 billion that year to a current level of $90 billion per annum.

"At that time there were certain colorful characters," Spano says. "Like Frenchy McMahon, an Air France employee. A very stand-up guy—you were wasting your time trying to get him to talk about anything. And there was another Air France employee, whose name I can't mention because he's still at large. Call him Mr. X.

"These were guys who were exceedingly tail-conscious." Spano sounds positively affectionate. "Talking about this second individual, Mr. X—every day when he was leaving work, he'd make a complete visual inspection of his car. Inside and out, and underneath. He was that worried we'd plant a bug on him. When he drove home, just to make sure we wouldn't flake him—"

"Flake him?"

"Put a tail on him. He'd drive thirty-five miles out of his way going home. At one point, we had an eight-car tail on this guy. We put so much pressure on him—and perhaps OC [organized crime] put so much pressure on him—that he left the job after eighteen years. This guy was a lead man, a foist-line supervisor. He had access to every shipment coming in.

"As a result of the cash hit on Air France," Spano says, referring to the 1967 theft of $480,000 from a locked storage room, engineered by Henry Hill, of *Wiseguy* and *GoodFellas* fame, and Frenchy McMahon, "Air France was starting to build a high-value storage room to meet our standards. I mean, a chain-link fence with a padlock is not our idea of a secure high-value area.

You need a double lock for mail shipments and currency. So Air France was starting to comply. Meanwhile, Frenchy McMahon was telling Henry Hill, 'You gotta hurry up with whatever you've got planned—the high-value room is being finished.'

"So they finished the room. This was a cinder-block enclosure within their cargo area, just big enough to drive a forklift into, with a double door and a double-key system to get in. That is to say, two separate people had to open two separate doors to enter—the system was virtually impossible to compromise. Remember, the big cash hit in '67 had succeeded because there was only a single key. And this new room not only had a double key, it had a closed-circuit TV camera that was activated each time the door was opened.

"But then we discovered that the closed-circuit TV camera's field of view was limited. And Air France didn't want to hear about it." Spano shakes his head. "To get airlines to spend money on cargo security is extremely difficult. It's just not their foist priority," he says. Out of sheer self-protection, shippers of valuables began long ago to insure themselves, thus ridding the carriers of one incentive to protect the goods.

"Now," Spano says, "just outside of the camera's field of view was a wooden box containing silver coins. This was a post-entry item, meaning it had been brought in by courier. And on top of that box, someone had inadvertently placed a box the size of a cigarette package, containing a hundred eighty thousand dollars' worth of emeralds. The emeralds were logged in, so this second individual—Mr. X—knew exactly what was in there. He entered the high-value room legitimately every day. And then, one day, the box of emeralds is gone."

Spano stands up. This may be as excited as he gets. He walks around in back of my chair, where there's an ashtray, about two and a half feet high, with a flat-black cylindrical base supporting a brushed-chrome dish. I turn around. "Say this base is the box of silver coins," Spano says. "And this"—he takes the dish out, turns it over, mounts it back on the base—"is the box of emeralds.

"We look at the videotape over and over. What we see is Mr. X, with a clipboard, supervising a guy on a forklift who's coming in to pick up the shipment of silver that's stored there. That's all we see. Then we notice Mr. X puts down the clipboard, *just outside the camera's range.*" Spano mimes putting a clipboard down on top of the ashtray. "He motions the forklift guy in. Then he picks the clipboard back up." Spano picks up the phantom clipboard, along with the ashtray. "That's how we think he did it."

Magic. The Lufthansa heist, facilitated by Louis Werner, a Lufthansa employee addicted to gambling and deeply indebted to Mob loan sharks, was considerably less artistic. It was, in fact, a kind of climactic pig-out: An old era of crime had ended, and a new one had begun.

Ed McDonald didn't just prosecute the Lufthansa robbery; he appeared in the movie. McDonald played himself in a brief scene in *GoodFellas,* telling Henry Hill, as portrayed by Ray Liotta, how he might save his own hide by cooperating with the investigation. Not introverted by nature, McDonald had a convincing screen presence. He looks like exactly what he is: a smart, tough, Brooklyn-born, Irish-American, Catholic-educated attorney, with a prosecutorial turn of mind. "It was an oddball case for us," McDonald says. "The U.S. Attorney's office was handling the Lufthansa investigation, but the FBI decided that they needed electronic surveillance to be done. It seems strange to think, now that the U.S. Attorney's office does so much electronic surveillance, but in the late seventies they had very little experience with it. And we had had a lot.

"[Then strike-force head Tom] Puccio was asked if we could devote some people to the Lufthansa case. And he chose me to conduct the electronic surveillance. You know, to try to get the wires up as quickly as possible—to get the paperwork done over a weekend. Which is what we did. So that's how I got involved in the Lufthansa case. But that was sort of the only street-crime-type organized-crime work we were doing. And we only got into it because it was the largest robbery in the history of the United States."

"The prosecution was really a failure in many respects," McDonald says. "I could argue that it was a success, in that the people who were responsible for Lufthansa—the ones who weren't murdered—ended up going to prison in cases that we developed as a result of our investigation. But only one person in the Lufthansa case was ever convicted, and that was Lou Werner, who was the inside man.

"Jimmy Burke, who Robert De Niro played in the movie; Paul Vario [played by Paul Sorvino], who was the main guy—these people were all convicted on the basis of offshoot investigations. Primarily as a result of turning Henry Hill. Which we did in the context of Lufthansa."

Handsome, magnetic "Jimmy the Gent" Burke—a former resident of Howard Beach, at the western edge of Kennedy airport—happened to be a kingpin in the subsequent Boston College point-shaving case, in which McDonald sent him to prison for twenty years. While there, he was also found guilty of the less gentlemanly misdeed of garroting one of the minor confederates in the Lufthansa robbery—one of nine men murdered in the heist's aftermath, either to prevent them from talking or to decrease the number of shareholders, or both. Burke will not be out of jail soon.

Paul Vario died there. As did Vito Genovese. As did Johnny Dio. Vario, who masterminded (if the term can even apply) the Lufthansa theft, was finally brought to ground by Ed McDonald in 1985, not for Lufthansa but for a much larger crime: for racketeering in the cargo-handling business at Kennedy. Also convicted in the same investigation was Harry Davidoff.

Davidoff was a pioneer of labor racketeering at the airport. Johnny Dio and Vito Genovese knew how to use guns to rob, but Harry Davidoff knew how to use unions. And as theft at Kennedy became more problematic for the Mafia, Davidoff's way began to prevail.

"In the late seventies, we realized—from intelligence, from informants—that organized crime was having a significant impact on the air-freight business at Kennedy Airport," Ed McDonald says. "They were making millions of dollars, and they were causing the cost of goods coming in and out of the country to go up. I think the low-level people saw there was more money to be made in drugs; the high-level people saw that there was a lot more money to be made in sophisticated types of crimes—in labor racketeering and in running businesses out there. It's a lot more difficult to get caught. When you hijack a truck, you gotta use a gun. Unless it's a give-up. But then you have the risk of including in your little conspiracy the driver, or somebody else in the company who's basically a legitimate guy and probably can't be trusted.

"But when you shake down a business, and you're using the labor union as your gun, and the businessman is really sort of getting a benefit because he's not having any labor problems, there are no telltale signs. It's a lot more difficult to prove those kinds of cases, and you make a hell of a lot more money. So organized crime realized that they could go quasi-legitimate, and get involved in the legitimate businesses out at the airport.

"Basically the way it works," McDonald says, "is that there are two unions at Kennedy Airport. Sister locals, or brother locals—851 and 295. It's really one union. Two Ninety-five basically represents the truck drivers and warehouse workers—you know, the guys who do the lifting. And 851 represents, more or less, the clerical employees. And Harry Davidoff controlled these two unions forever, in conjunction with the Lucchese crime family.

"Paul Vario ran the airport for the Lucchese crime family. It was the most significant family at the airport. They had their numbers operations and their gambling and their loan-sharking and their truck hijackers. But they also controlled Harry Davidoff. Which meant that they controlled the two unions out there—851 and 295. And basically what they did was, they'd go to the air-freight companies—or to the trucking subcontractors of the air-freight companies—and say, 'If you guys want to do business here, you're gonna have to pay.'

THE AIRPORT

"They were talking cash payoffs. And of course the threat, the clout that they have, is not the gun, it's the labor union. Either they'll walk out, or they'll enforce the terms of the collective-bargaining agreement. There's so many of these organized-crime-dominated businesses or industries in New York, and the terms are so onerous, that if the collective-bargaining agreement is enforced to its letter, there's no way a company can do business. You would have to charge a much higher rate—you'd have to put, like, three workers on a truck. Or they might say, 'Look—if you don't do what we want, we're gonna walk off the job.' Or 'We're gonna send you derelicts to come work in your cargo operation.' Everybody understood it to be labor peace."

"OC has diversified, if you will," Sergeant Spano explains. "Kennedy is a closed shop. So OC, which is heavily in the unions, proposes that on the very next job, if a company doesn't stir the pot—if the next contract doesn't go to us—we're gonna strike. If a freight forwarder or an airline does not do the right thing—pay no-shows, lease nonexistent equipment—we're gonna strike, and tie them in knots. We're gonna do all the warehousing and trucking, getting paid a premium for it, plus controlling the goods.

"Say you're a freight forwarder, and you need ten people and eight trucks to run your warehouse. Organized crime would come to you and say, 'I'm gonna charge you for fifteen people, ten of which are union; I'm gonna charge you for twelve trucks. And if you pay me, I will guarantee you labor peace. All you gotta do is tack on a few extra dollars to the customer.'

"The legitimate businessman was just as much to blame for this as the criminals," Spano says. "A businessman would say, 'I don't want any trouble from the Teamsters, so all I have to do is charge a couple of extra bucks to the customer, and I succeed.' But then organized crime got greedy. They started asking for more. That's when we got some businessmen cooperating with Kenrac—the Kennedy Airport racketeering investigation."

Infiltrating the Mob wasn't easy: Just remembering it, Ed McDonald rubs his forehead with the heel of his hand. "We had an undercover operation out there run by the New York City Police Department, which went absolutely nowhere," he says. "This was back in the late seventies. We started a trucking company that would be a subcontractor for an air-freight company. There's a special sort of undercover organization in the police department—some of these guys had worked at infiltrating the Black Panthers and these other groups in the seventies. So they put these guys to work running this trucking company at the airport. But nobody would do business with them. They didn't trust them. They didn't know who they were. All of a sudden these

217

guys appear out of nowhere. They were great undercover cops—we made a couple of gun cases: stolen guns and stuff like that. But we were never able to get into the labor unions through them.

"In the case we had against Harry Davidoff, we developed informants—we and the FBI—and they got a pretty good sense of what was going on out there. So we started subpoenaing people from trucking companies, who told us they were making payoffs. And then, very often in this business, the extortion victim, somewhere along the line, becomes sort of a briber. There's a very fine line between an extortion victim and a bribe-giver.

"Say the organized-crime figures who are backed by the union come to a businessman and say, 'Look, unless you pay us five hundred dollars a month'—or five hundred dollars a week, or whatever, depending on the size of the business—'we're gonna put you out of business. We're gonna create problems; we're gonna enforce the terms of the collective-bargaining agreement.' The guy's an extortion victim. Well, you know, two years down the road, the guy's paying his money, and he's saying, 'Look, I don't want to have to pay overtime on the books, so we pay overtime off the books. That way I don't have to pay into the pension and welfare fund.' Pension and welfare fund payments can be really substantial.

"So the union guys say, 'OK, fine. Pay an eight-hour day for these workers, but all the overtime, you pay them cash.' And now the guy who started out as an extortion victim is getting a benefit from this corrupt bargain he has. There's a fine line—it depends how closely connected the businessman might be to the organized-crime figures. A lot of these people are really in bed with the organized-crime figures. Vario and Davidoff worked together for thirty years."

Tom Puccio and Ed McDonald knew what Vario and Davidoff were up to for a long time before they could do anything about it. "We began to bring some of these people in," McDonald says. "Trucking company executives and air-freight company executives. It was very difficult to get anybody to cooperate. We were making a few half-assed cases here and there. But eventually, we got enough intelligence to the FBI that we discovered a guy named Frank Manzo—who was called 'Frank the Wop' Manzo. Manzo was an Italian immigrant who owned a restaurant near the airport, in Queens. Vario hung around there. And he discovered very quickly that Frank Manzo was a sort of financial genius. They actually made him a member of the family. He hung out with them more and more. And soon it became pretty clear that Frank Manzo was running the labor racketeering for the Lucchese crime family at the airport, and was controlling the unions.

"The FBI was doing surveillance, and it showed that Frank Manzo's home was a meeting place. All these guys would come in and sit down and talk about what they were doing. So we put a bug in Frank Manzo's home. And we just hit paydirt. Just a real bonanza. We had him talking to Paul Vario; we had him talking to Harry Davidoff; we had him talking to representatives of the air-freight companies. And we turned a couple of people based on the wiretaps that we were doing. It was an absolutely remarkable case."

"How'd you get a bug into his house?" I ask.

"He was away—I think he went to a wedding," McDonald says. "And nobody was at the house. His was pretty easy." McDonald smiles. "The FBI—they never tell you how they do it. They don't trust the prosecutors—they see the prosecutors are gonna go into private practice, and they don't want to give up their secrets.

"There was a guy by the name of Heino Benthin, who was a freight forwarder," McDonald says. "A German guy. And we indicted him, because he was being used to launder money—payoffs for Davidoff and these people. He cooperated. And he told this story, which he testified to, about how when he first met Frank Manzo, Manzo was sitting there with some other guy, and he began to argue with Manzo at this diner—the Airport Diner. And Manzo took a fork and went *boom!*—smashed right down into the guy's hand!" McDonald laughs, still astonished.

"Benthin hadn't really been too *sure* what was gonna happen at this meeting. You know, probably somebody said, 'I'm gonna introduce you to this guy Frank Manzo, and he's gonna help you in your business.' And this is a guy put a *fork* in a guy's *hand!*" McDonald shakes his head. "Benthin knew *exactly* what he was involved with at that point. Nobody ever had to utter a *threat.*

"So this was how we developed Kenrac. At one point, Consolidated Freightways—CF—was gonna merge with Air Express International—AEI—to become the largest air-freight company in the world. And Manzo and Vario and Davidoff said, 'Look, if you guys wanna do this, you're gonna have to pay us a half a million dollars.' Vario and Manzo wanted Manzo's trucking companies to be CF's trucking subcontractor. Which would've meant millions. And because they controlled the union, they went into court to block the merger. They said that their union would be out of business, because Consolidated Freightways had an effective bargaining agreement with a union from New Jersey. It was complicated.

"But while the case was going on, Manzo was dictating how the union would handle the litigation. And depending on what steps would be taken in the litigation, the price of the stock of CF and AEI was going up and down. And Manzo was trading on the stock in substantial amounts. He was *manip-*

ulating the stock. So we had an inside-trade case on top of the whole thing. There are these great lines in the wiretap transcript where Manzo tells his stockbroker, 'I see the headlines now—"The Mafia's on Wall Street."' It was great stuff. They all pleaded guilty, except for Davidoff. Vario pleaded guilty, and Davidoff went to trial and was convicted, and he got ten years. The labor-union officials were all convicted.

"There was a follow-up case—sort of a Kenrac Two—that we filed just before I left. Where the guys who replaced Davidoff and the other people in the union were all indicted, and I think most of them have been convicted. And the upshot of the whole thing was sort of strange. Under the RICO [Racketeer Influenced and Corrupt Organizations] statute, the federal government used the civil provisions to go into court and get a trustee appointed to take over the unions—295 and 851. And so there's a court-appointed trustee who is really sort of running the unions at this point. And that trustee happens to be Tom Puccio."

"Did Kenrac extirpate organized crime at Kennedy Airport?" I ask McDonald.

"Well, I'm not gonna say that," McDonald says. "Let's put it this way. I think hijacking is down, no thanks to what we did. I think that narcotics is still flourishing at the airport. I don't know enough about what's going on with complicit employees, but I'm sure the stuff is coming through Kennedy Airport in large amounts.

"I think as far as the business crimes out there—the shakedowns in the air-freight industry—my sense of it is that we've had some impact. Because Puccio's running the union. And the organized-crime figures who were running the union are all in the process of being removed from the union. Either because they were kicked out under court decrees, or they've gone to prison. So if you don't have the labor union as your tool of extortion, or your weapon, you're not able to run these labor-peace extortion schemes.

"On the other hand, a lot of the people who got involved in the air-freight businesses and the trucking companies were organized-crime figures—either Mafia members, or brothers-in-law of Mafia members, or whatever. The industry has a significant organized-crime presence. Not every company. But a significant number of people are organized-crime figures.

"I think we had some impact," McDonald says. "What's gonna happen when Puccio's term runs out—it could be extended, but it's certainly not a permanent position—remains to be seen. Local 560, the Teamsters over in New Jersey, was run by Tony Provenzano. A trustee was appointed to clean up the union, and he's been there for about ten years now. And they had free elections about two years ago, and Tony Provenzano's *niece* was elected president of the union. Tony's long dead. It's pretty hard to drive these people out."

Harder still when the Port Authority—the steward of Kennedy Airport, the holder of the keys—refuses to acknowledge the problem exists. "There's a lot of fooling around with figures," McDonald tells me. "The NYPD probably is not going to do that, but the Port Authority is *notorious* in what they *report* about the level of criminal activity at the airport.

"There's a tendency in law enforcement," he says, "to provide statistics that sort of serve their ends. When they want to get more money for their budget, they're gonna say hijacking or labor racketeering or narcotics is a serious, serious problem. They tend to shade it to make the problem look worse.

"Or if they're trying to make it look like 'We've accomplished so much,' or whatever, they tend to shade it so it looks less significant. Port Authority is a business. I'd have these meetings with these people—" McDonald shakes his head. He still recalls vividly, a dozen years after the fact, an audience with then PA chief Peter Goldmark: "He barely even gave me the time of day. He had to go take a helicopter somewhere—he was going to go give a speech to his underlings. I was like, 'You invited *me* here—what kind of bullshit is this?' He was just going through the motions to make it look like he was interested in trying to stop labor racketeering and organized crime at the airport.

"Even later, when we got the big labor-racketeering prosecutions involving the airport going, there would always be a little exposé. Where *The New York Times* would do this story about this terrible problem of organized crime controlling the air-cargo business. And then there'd always be this sort of *required piece*—"He laughs. "You know, they had to go to somebody who was a spokesman on behalf of the Port Authority to get some facts and figures about how this was total bullshit.

"All the law enforcement agencies out at Kennedy—New York City Police Department, the FBI, the DEA, Customs—everybody was trying to pitch in. We had the IRS working. The Port Authority cops were there. And some of these people were really, really interested in getting on board. They would contact us informally, and we'd go over. I met with [Peter Goldmark's successor, Stephen] Berger and talked to him about getting these people involved. And he talked about organized crime like it didn't exist at Kennedy Airport.

"There were some people there who I had met and I kind of respected and liked, and they convinced me that they really wanted to actively get involved in the anti-racketeering activities at the airport. And it never happened. They never participated in any of the activities. Because they didn't want to acknowledge the existence of organized crime. They didn't want to do something that could be construed as saying that the Port Authority agrees there's a serious organized-crime problem.

"Were they pressured not to get involved?" I ask.

"There's no question that's what happened. The cops were sincerely interested in becoming involved in this, and they were blocked by their superiors. The PA's concern is that if somebody is bringing freight in from Germany, they'll say, 'We might as well go to Baltimore.' Or 'Might as well go to Philadelphia and truck it up.' Which is exactly what they *do*. But the truth of the matter is that organized crime is a terrible problem at Kennedy Airport. And they just sort of ignore it. They not only deny its existence, but they do very little to combat organized crime. Their focus is on [freight] hijacking.

"And even the hijacking stats, going back to the seventies, when hijacking was a serious problem—I used to talk to cops and FBI guys, and they'd say, 'This is a complete farce. We know that hijacking is much, much worse than the Port Authority is letting on.' Also, some of the companies didn't want to report all the thefts, for insurance purposes.

"Berger—I thought the guy was a total asshole," McDonald says. "Sitting in his office was like being in this *fantasy* world. I'm talking to this guy—and, you know, I had a *lot of experience* of Kennedy Airport at that point. I knew pretty well what the problems were. And Norman Bloch—a guy who had spent a good part of his professional career fighting organized crime in the air-freight business—was with me. We knew what we were talking about. And here was the head of the Port Authority telling us that organized crime *did not exist* at Kennedy Airport. It was like talking to the wall."

"Our track record in cargo theft is very, very good," says Al Graser. Graser, the manager of the airport's Security and Landside Services Division—i.e., the top security man at Kennedy—is tall and almost comically grave-looking: gaunt face, strong nose, and bushy eyebrows over rectangular silver-rimmed spectacles. His dress tends to dark, sacky suits that give him the look of a not particularly prosperous undertaker. But Graser entirely lacks the undertaker's oiliness; instead he has a detective's stone deadpan and restless eyes that always seem to be looking someplace else. Which, in all likelihood, means that the second before you looked at him, he was looking at you. At the Opsafe disaster drill, Graser was talking about a police officer I didn't know. When I asked if the man was present, Graser very rapidly pulled open one side of his suit jacket, pointed backward through the fabric to a cop standing a few feet away, and closed his jacket again. I instantly forgot the man and remembered the gesture forever.

THE AIRPORT

"We track theft; most airports don't," Graser tells me. For the moment, I have his entire attention—the effect is somewhat unsettling. What Graser doesn't say is that most airports, if not all airports, lack Kennedy's unique concatenation of qualities: huge cargo volume; multiplicity of carriers; New York–style wide-open scruffiness; close proximity to Brooklyn, Queens, and Long Island, the New World omphalos of organized crime.

"But the fact is that many companies don't report thefts," Graser says, understating the case considerably. In fact, even in these days of containerization, the vast majority of cargo theft is still factored in by carriers and freight forwarders as part of the Cost of Doing Business: If any company reported all the larceny it actually incurred, its already high insurance premiums would go through the roof. "First of all, they have an insurance deductible to meet," Graser says. "Second, is the cargo lost or stolen? The carriers don't always know, or if they know, they don't say. We've had one hundred twenty reported thefts this year, for a total of about three hundred thousand dollars. That's out of ninety billion dollars in cargo volume. You figure it out.

"The stress time is September and October. Then it's Christmas shopping time on the ramp. If, say, Alitalia gets hit, we let everybody know, so they can watch out. But if the carriers don't tell us about it, we can't tell anyone. Most cargo is lost from the front door, not the ramp. It's easy to get it out of the airport."

"I'm not gonna paint a rosy picture of Kennedy Airport," says Sergeant Carmine Spano. "But it is not a mega–candy store. And we do have a damn good record of catching thieves.

"The perception out there is that anybody can come in here and take whatever he wants, whenever he wants. That is not the case. First of all, a full eighty-five percent of cargo theft is employee theft. That includes pilferage, and collusion with someone on the outside—say, a trucker. A very small percentage of theft is committed by people from outside. They generally come in two categories.

"There's the drug abuser, the opportunist. Sometimes there are boxes unattended on the truck docks. And these thieves come in from time to time and knock our block off for a while. And the overburdened court system being what it is, these cases are not a priority. So these individuals get low bail; they cop a plea. And a person with a six-hundred- to one-thousand-dollar-a-day drug habit is gonna be back.

"The second category is organized crime, or people who are affiliated

223

with organized crime. Say an airline employee has a gambling problem or a drug problem, and is into a loan shark, and his salary is not sufficient to meet that weekly vig. So he will help to set up a load.

"There is a different type of individual involved in cargo theft today than was the case in the past," Spano says. "Prior to the first oil crisis in '73, most airlines had their own employee groups. But when the oil crunch hit, the airlines started eliminating their own employee rolls, and contracting work out to service companies. You went from employees earning fifteen to eighteen dollars an hour—which didn't mean they were all honest, by any means—to minimum-wage, part-time people, with no benefits, no career path, no light at the end of the tunnel.

"You have a different type of criminal today." Spano looks regretful. "What we have now is the part-timer. He's supposed to work a six-hour day; he's actually working a sixty-hour week, trying to make ends meet. And he can't make ends meet on four fifty an hour. These guys become strictly opportunists. If you dangle that carrot in front of them, these guys steal. These contract service companies that operate the warehouses—Ogden Allied, Triangle, Hudson General, AMR, DynAir—they're all looking to cut costs wherever they can, and salaries is where they cut first. Which directly leads to theft.

"We had one warehouse supervisor who *gave* an undercover guy two hundred eighty thousand dollars' worth of wearing apparel. Gave it to him. All he got out of the deal was two thousand bucks. When we finally arrested him, I axed him what I always ask—'Why did you do it?' And he told me, 'Every time they promote in the organization, they go over me and get someone from the outside. I just wanted to get back at them.'"

The "them" in this case being the encrusted, inextirpable, organized-crime-associated hierarchy of Kennedy's cargo companies and unions. "The FBI asked me about relatives of organized-crime figures involved in the cargo business at Kennedy," says Mike Moroney, Tom Puccio's assistant in the trusteeship of Locals 295 and 851. "I said, 'You're kidding me. It would be easier to find who's *not* related. The sons, the daughters, the nieces and nephews—they all have nice, cushy clerical jobs in 851. Harry Davidoff's son Mark ran 295 before he was sent to jail, for threatening a truck driver. Frankie Manzo put his kids in eighty-hour-a-week no-show jobs. AEI, the freight carrier, has seventeen people on the payroll directly related to Paul Vario. Jimmy Burke's daughter works for Amerford.

"You have to understand," Moroney says, "there are two levels in the air-freight industry. The good jobs—the ones that pay eighteen dollars an hour, with double and triple overtime—these jobs are bought, or given to relatives of organized-crime figures. Seniority is completely rigged. There are two Local 295s. In what is known as Big 295, the Italians receive top wages and benefits. In Little 295, the blacks and Puerto Ricans receive low wages and no benefits."

In other words, the world of cargo theft at Kennedy these days is one in which the little crooks are committing crimes against the big crooks. And the police?

"The PA cops are totally ineffective," Moroney says. "They're a non-player—which usually means that they're paid off. But really, when it comes down to it, who needs to bribe anyone? Organized crime still controls the industry lock, stock, and barrel."

❒

The Port Authority Police Department—the law enforcement arm of this singular private/public organization, comprising some fourteen hundred men and women who patrol Kennedy, La Guardia, and Newark airports, as well as the Lincoln and Holland tunnels; the George Washington, Outerbridge Crossing, Bayonne, and Goethals bridges; the PATH trains under the Hudson; the Brooklyn and Manhattan piers; the World Trade Center; and the Forty-second Street bus terminal—is not exactly a Praetorian Guard. It is, as a matter of fact, tonally virtually indistinguishable from that world's scruffiest police department, the NYPD. Ask the man or woman on the street what the difference is between the cops who patrol the airports, tunnels, bridges, and bus terminal and the cops who patrol the city's streets, and you'd likely get an annoyed shrug. A cop is a cop. Especially in New York.

And yet there is, within the blue sector of the public spectrum, all the difference on earth between city cops and PA cops. PA cops make more money, for one thing: Because they work for a semi-private concern and not the state, and because of the extraordinarily effective collective bargaining of the Port Authority Police Benevolent Association, PA cops earn an average $49,000 per annum, not including overtime, as compared with the $44,000 of a veteran New York City cop.

Furthermore, there is, within the PA Police spectrum, all the difference in the world between working the bus terminal (the lowest of the low), working the tunnels (not much better), and working the airports, where an average patrolman may ultimately be trained for elite crash-and-fire-rescue duty (CFR), and in any event leads the kind of relatively clean, placid, and ordered existence that drives his or her confreres—not to mention city cops—to fits of envy.

And Kennedy is the plummiest plum of all. Newark is boring; La Guardia is small. Yet—even at Kennedy—a policeman's lot is not a happy one. There is a fly in the ointment. A worm in the apple. For the Port Authority considers its airport police departments a barnacled nuisance, full of overpaid, quite possibly useless, crybabies. And the displeasure of the PA hierarchy, however defused by the PAPBA, hurts the cops' feelings, and makes up for any tension that the job itself lacks.

It's touchy stuff, tinder that occasionally bursts into flame. The PA—which a cynic might say is public in its sanctimoniousness and private in its accountability—is not renowned for fiscal austerity, especially when it comes to the comforts of the top brass. Nor is the existence of a police force specific to the airport by any means a given in everyone's mind. *Glorified security guards.* This was how a former U.S. Attorney who had handled many airport crime cases referred to airport cops, in my presence. *Keystone Kops.*

"Having a police force for a specialized organization and having one for a government are not the same thing," former PA director Stephen Berger told me, before leaving office. "The reason for having a police force must jibe with the mission of the specialized organization," he said. "When I was a kid on Kingsbridge Road in the Bronx, I used to ride the subway all the time. Robert Wagner was mayor, and his promise was to put a cop on every subway car. Now, he didn't want the cop there to make arrests; he wanted him there for his presence."

He narrowed his eyes. "*I don't want these guys at Kennedy making nickel busts,*" he said. "It takes their presence away. The mayor of New York said, 'I'm not gonna have cops giving traffic tickets.'" Berger puffed on the cigar. "Why the fuck are these guys giving traffic tickets?

"When I post an ad offering mobility assignments," Berger told me, referring to temporary transfers off the airport for PA Police officers, "the union grieves. They grieve at everything. They've isolated themselves behind a blue wall. Whenever anything comes up, I say it's a matter for negotiation. Their union cannot negotiate. The executive committee is composed of present, former, and future union leaders. So what does that tell you? With every diddlyshit thing, they have to go into arbitration because of the shame that giving anything up would bring on them.

"We have a lot of good cops," Berger said. "A lot of very well educated cops doing mundane jobs. There are some smart guys who would be good managers in other contexts. Here they are, writing traffic tickets at the airport."

And yet, not long ago, an edict came down from on high forbidding the PA Police at Kennedy to make drug arrests. PA cops should be deterring pickpocketing and luggage theft in the terminals, Port Authority brass claimed; Customs should be making drug arrests.

THE AIRPORT

But Customs—deterred by federal and state district attorneys who won't prosecute because of the sheer volume of drug cases clogging the court systems—has been letting first-time smugglers go with a $500 fine. All first-time smugglers. Two summers ago, a man who was caught at JFK with a pound of opium—worth $100,000 on the street—fainted when Customs agents told him he was being fined and released. If the state had successfully prosecuted him, he could have been sentenced to twenty-five years to life in prison. So the Port Authority Police Benevolent Association filed a grievance against the PA—claiming not that they had too much to handle, but too little.

The front desk of the Kennedy Airport headquarters of the Port Authority Police, Building 269, is as unprepossessing as most police desks around the world, even though it features the weird amenity of a waiting lounge. (One entire wall of which is devoted to a display of faded color photographs of PA Police greeting various dignitaries at Kennedy; in one of the pictures someone—not unimaginably, a cop—has inked a beard and mustache over the eager, glad-to-see-you, recessive-chinned face of the number-one man here, Deputy Inspector William Ferrante). Nobody's waiting in the waiting lounge when I come in. Two Hispanic guys are standing at the desk, not looking very hopeful: One of them is talking, through the right-hand porthole in the glass partition, with a Hispanic sergeant about the slim possibility of getting his car back. The guys are hustlers, and their cars have been impounded. It's the kind of rhetorical conversation where the supplicant can't quite look into the eye of Authority, and Authority does not have very good news. You need a DA release, the sergeant tells the hustler, who looks blank for a couple of beats, then goes into useless conference, in fast Spanish, with his associate.

Over the desk, engraved in brass, is the honor roll of PA officers fallen in the line of duty (A POLICE OFFICER DOES NOT HESITATE TO PLACE HIS OWN LIFE IN DANGER SO THAT THE SAFETY AND RIGHTS OF HIS FELLOW MEN ARE SAFEGUARDED). It contains seven names—seven names too many, obviously. Still, it is not clear whether the roll is just for Kennedy or for the entire jurisdiction of the Port. One of the names, etched impossibly but incontrovertibly for posterity—look once, look twice; it doesn't change—is Hitler McLeod, Shield No. 897, who died in action on November 3, 1961.

I clear my throat at the left porthole. Behind the partition, on the pale-green wall—the color seems to have been distilled out of a bad nightmare of fluorescent light and cigarette smoke—is one of those loud public-service posters, reading, DON'T PUT YOUR WEAPON UP FOR GRABS/SECURE IT IN THE PROPER HOLSTER. There's an empty beige Kenmore coffee maker, deeply dirty, and an open industrial-size carton of Pepperidge Farm Goldfish. When I state my business to Desk Sergeant Bomengo, whose short sleeves are rolled up over biceps the size of Virginia hams, a short, dark officer whose name tag reads M. PALERMO leans over to the porthole. "You're writing a book?" he says. "You should note that we're working eight months without a contract. And that morale could not be lower. And that we attribute this directly to [then] Executive Director Stephen Berger."

Noted. Cops may come in all shapes, sizes, and dispositions, but the spirit of pained official dignity, worn with light-opera brio, is fairly universal. (Especially in New York. Cops in New York are like cops everywhere else, only a little more so.) We tend to think of the police as creatures apart, somehow worse or better than the rest of us; in fact they are the same as the rest of us, except for this perceived apartness, which they believe in and take to heart, which makes them lonely. This loneliness makes them like to talk. And talk. Much of the talk is complaint, of which cops have made a fine art.

"It's a continuing war between the PA and the cops," Patrolman John Brant, a tall and uncop-ishly lean young cop with a dark mustache and close-set dark eyes, tells me, once I've been admitted into the dispatch room, whose windowless four walls full of medium-tech electronic equipment are hooked up to burglar and fire alarms all over the airport. "I mean," Brant says, "they want us to be more public-oriented, not law-enforcement-oriented. They want the cop to look pretty. You know, white gloves. A presence. They don't want us making arrests, because that creates overtime.

"OK, we got some really good contracts in the eighties," he says. "Maybe we're a little spoiled. You know, we get a hotel room if there's less than eight hours between tours. Stuff like that. But the PA wants to bring in private security, for God's sake. You can't get the job done if you're not a cop. But they won't let us be a cop.

"And I'll tell ya, the airlines are spoiled rotten," Brant says. "I mean, they call us and we're there in like five, ten minutes. In the city, what kind of response time do you get?"

M. Palermo, the desk officer, pokes his head in. "You want to know something else?" he asks. "I been on the force for seventeen years, I been at the airport for seventeen years, and I been on CFR for nine years," he says, "and not once has any of the pilots for any of the airlines ever come here to ask about the equipment."

I ponder this for a moment. "Maybe they don't want to think about it?" I say.

"I don't want to think about dyin'," says M. Palermo, "but I got life insurance."

THE AIRPORT

Brant and Palermo and a small cop with a high voice, Mike Greco, discuss the recent unsuccessful contract meeting with Stephen Berger. "That son of a bitch doesn't even think we exist," Greco says. "He calls us a security force."

"We're a necessary evil to the Port Authority," Brant says to me. "They realize that if the NYPD came in here, there'd be much more corruption."

I ask why.

"We're run by civilians—we're not a police department per se. We don't have our own budget. The NYPD is run by police officers, so there's no oversight. The airport manager—what's-his-name—"

Rowe, I say.

"He's basically our mayor. He dictates all policy, including our budget. If city cops came in, they'd have no one to listen to. The way it is now, if there's a problem on the airport, if a cop was taking money, you could tell a civilian. They couldn't bring the city in here," Brant says. "The city couldn't cover it."

A cop sitting in the back, making out hack summonses, sees Brant. "Busy today, John?" he asks.

"The calm before the storm," Brant says. He turns to me. "You really want to see something, come here on a Thursday or Friday before Memorial Day. You got gridlock, you got cardiacs, you got ambulances that can't get through—*you'll* be doin' CPR out here."

This, I will later find—on a Friday before Memorial Day—is something of an exaggeration.

As, apparently, is the existential jeopardy of the airport cops. Stephen Berger, after all, was taking his strong opinions out the door with him. And as for the corporate bête noire of the nineties, downsizing? "The Port Authority does periodic budgetary analysis," Captain Frank Fox, JFK's then second-in-command, tells me. "We go down [trim] certain posts, but never critical ones. And mostly it's not in the nature of firing people. Mostly it's in the nature of not refilling the posts of people who have left. For instance, management identified sixty jobs that could be civilianized—things like fire marshal, abandoned-car detail—but that would have to be passed through the union. And those positions are locked in."

Translation: Management loses.

"So why do the cops complain?" I asked.

"It is the nature of cops to complain," Fox said.

❑

Anonymous cop: "The trouble is, ninety-nine point eight percent of police work is boring, boring, boring. Then there's that one time, it's four-thirty in the morning, you're in a cargo building, and suddenly a guy's pointing a gun at you.

"Guys handle it all different ways. Some have what we call tombstone courage—there's a bank robbery in the IAB, they run in there with their guns drawn, all macho. Others are more careful.

"But as you get more time on the force, your guard definitely goes down. Definitely. Like, I got a call the other night from Lufthansa. Lufthansa! I mean, you gotta think, right? And I go over to the Lufthansa cargo building, and Charlie Kellner—he's been on the force forever—is walking around, saying, 'Hello? Hello?' I mean, some guy gets the drop on him, he's dead."

John Brant, the handsome cop: "I'm not scared to die. That's nothing. The thing that scares me, especially these days, is bombs. Some bomb goes off, and you're mutilated, a quadriplegic for life. I couldn't imagine what that would be like.

"There's a lot more bomb threats now. Fortunately, they've all been false alarms. We had one yesterday: a guy was meeting his daughter at TWA. He had adopted this Korean girl, maybe seventeen, eighteen years old. And he said, 'I'm not leaving, I got bombs on me.' It was very unfortunate; he had to be arrested. We had to strip-search him, but he asked that we search him inside this secluded men's room. And we found he was wearing a bra and a teddy under his shirt. It was really pathetic—it was like a child's bra."

I ask what it's like to work the IAB. In response, Sergeant Tom McKinney tells me a riddle: "What's the difference between the Indians with the turbans and the ones with the dot on their forehead?"

"Well," I say innocently, "the ones in the turbans are Sikhs—"

"You almost have it right, Jim," Sergeant Barry McCarthy says.

McKinney: "The turban is pull-start, the dot is push-start. If they got nothing, it's a jump-start."

Patrolman John Brant: "Cops are strange. Strange things make different guys want to become cops. You get some people in here, they must've gotten pushed around when they were growing up. They walk in in their outside clothes, and they're sort of hunched-over and puny-looking. Then they put on the uniform, and their chest is puffed-out. They have an attitude. It's a whole macho thing. You're making an arrest, and your backup comes, and he's gotta get in on it, whether it's verbal or pushing the guy around. It's called getting a piece of the action. Everyone wants to get a piece of the action."

THE AIRPORT

*

Tom McKinney tells me the tale of Sergeant Gillette: "His real name was Sergeant Bob Liebling. He was from the old school, Jim. Just come in and get your paycheck and go back out. He never believed there were really any bad guys out there. So one night Liebling picks up this psycho, and he throws him in the backseat of the cruiser without putting any cuffs on him. Why bother? He's just a nut. And Liebling and his partner are bringing the psycho back in, and they're gabbing, gabbing, gabbing in the front seat, not paying any attention to the psycho. They get back to headquarters, and Liebling turns around, and his mouth drops open—the psycho has cut his throat. He wasn't cuffed, and he had his bag with all his effects, and there was a safety razor in it. So from then on, whenever anyone called Liebling on the radio, they'd hum the first few notes of the Gillette jingle: Ba-bum-bum-*ba*-bum, bum bum bum *bum* bum bum."

And Sergeant Liebling forever became Sergeant Gillette.

❐

Airport lore, I will later discover, is replete with Airport Bill stories, the gist of most of them being that Bill—a.k.a. APB, a.k.a. Officer William Curtis—is eerily, assertively omniscient in virtually all matters relating to Kennedy. There were, for example, the stolen Italian ballet slippers. This case of ballet slippers showed up in a cargo area, and no one was sure how to valuate them for the records. And APB stated a figure, off the top of his head, that turned out to be within pennies of the actual price. Then there was the time a small earthquake hit Kennedy, and APB—instantly, authoritatively, instinctively—stated that it had been a 4.3 on the Richter scale. It turned out to have been a 4.4. There was the time a bunch of Bill's fellow officers decided to call him at home in the middle of the night and ask him the best way to fly from New York to Canberra, Australia. Without the slightest hesitation, APB gave them a complete itinerary, with schedules, and an accurate fare. There was the time . . . It goes on.

All this would, theoretically, make Officer Curtis the ideal riding companion for one whose job is to learn as much as possible about the airport. And yet. The charms of omniscience have their limits. APB, when I meet him, turns out to be a round-faced, sandy-haired man in his middle forties with a slightly distant manner—as though one were conversing with him through a pane or two of glass—and a deep, orotund voice. (APB is, of course, also police jargon for *all-points bulletin*—especially appropriate in this case, since APB's every utterance sounds like an APB.) He also smokes. There are more pleasant ways to learn the airport, I quickly learn, than driving around and around and around it, late into the reaches of the night, in a smoky Plymouth, in the company of a deep-voiced, orotund, relentlessly informative companion. Very soon, with many hours left to go on the shift, I find myself clawingly eager to escape Airport Bill's police cruiser.

And yet—as the Zen dictum has it, boredom passes into fascination. (Especially in retrospect.) My pencil stays busy as I ride with Airport Bill. I learn, among many other things, that half of all cargo flown flies on passenger flights. That once a Sikh deportee, having attempted to enter this country illegally, and having been detained by Immigration in the Travelodge (which is under government contract for this very purpose), attempted to escape by lowering himself out the window on his own turban. That APB himself grew up in Brooklyn in the early sixties, and that he used to come out to Idlewild with a date and walk around the Fountain of Liberty, or go up in the control tower when civilians were still allowed to do so ("That was before terrorism got its foothold," he says, in his curiously ornate fashion), or stand on the observation deck and wave to departing or arriving passengers (there were no jetways in those days).

"The airport has changed," I say.

"Quite so," says APB.

He's really not a bad fellow at all. He used to manage a Hills supermarket, he tells me. (I can imagine him in the white smock: "Soy sauce? Aisle four, fancy and foreign foods, Kikkoman or La Choy. Now, the soybean is an amazing bean. . . .") And he can do these great riffs. Just say "cargo theft," for example, and Bill can give you ten minutes. Or twenty, or thirty. This is, after all, his specialty: His steady beat is Sector 2, Kennedy's cargo area. His steady shift, three to eleven. Afternoons and nights, all alone, cruising these deserted warehouses . . . *Hello? Hello?*

"Most of your theft happens the minute the cargo doors open," Curtis announces, his ringing voice nicely filling the cruiser's interior. He's got the acoustics down pat. I suddenly wonder if he ever talks to himself. For some reason, this is a plausible and terrifying thought. I quash it. It's very dark out here in the cargo area; the only illumination comes from scattered crime lights and the occasional lit warehouse. I stare through the wide-open garage door of a warehouse, at boxes sitting on pallets under fluorescent light. Nobody at all seems to be around. How could anyone possibly secure all this?

"Nintendo games," Bill says.

Nintendo games?

"Just lately, a number of airline employees were walking off with Nintendo games. They lost about a million dollars' worth." APB looks around and shakes his head portentously. "The temptation out here is great," he intones.

THE AIRPORT

We're rolling alongside runway 13 Left. A blue-and-white 747, whose only marking is the single word CARGO, is taking off. "That's El Al," Bill says.

"Unmarked for security," I say.

"Correct," Bill says. He shakes his head. "We've led a charmed life out here. At any time, if a terrorist wanted to, he could take out any plane he wanted to. C-4; shoulder-fired Stinger missiles . . ." He shakes his head again.

"C-4 is—?"

"Plastic explosive."

"Like what they used on Pan Am One Oh Three?"

"Correct."

At this moment we pass a Northwest 747 being towed down a taxiway, its engines churning. A flame leaps out of one of the engines. I jump. "What was that?" I say.

"That was what you call a hot start—the pilot gets a warning light on one of the engines and hits the thrust to blow it out," says Airport Bill. He clears his throat, a big sound in the small car. I will later find that the flame we saw was a transitory tailpipe fire, the result of a tiny leakage of burning fuel, and that a hot start is something else entirely.

"Will there ever be an end to crime out here?" Bill asks himself. Then answers himself: "I couldn't really say." It is several hours later. We have made the circuit of Sector 2 a half-dozen more times, and APB is considering cargo theft from yet another angle. I am semicomatose. We are touching the essence of police work. "This Ogden Allied guy was carrying a box of suede jackets," Curtis booms, his late-night energy unflagging. "He was caught by a postal employee at night, throwing the box over the fence."

I take notes to keep awake. *Suede jackets* . . . We have passed into the deep watches of the night; the air in the cruiser seems composed of stale cigarette smoke, stale talk, cold fog, sleep, and mercury-vapor light—an atmosphere conducive to a Beckett-like assessment of the human condition.

"I'll show you something," Bill says. We pull up in front of a chain-link fence bearing a sign that reads LONG-TERM PARKING—LOT 7. Behind the fence are hundreds and hundreds of automobiles, sitting beneath pathetically dim crime lights. Whose cars are these? We are miles from the terminal buildings. No one who wanted to keep an intact vehicle would ever put it here, and yet here are these hundreds of cars. *Whose cars are these?* This is The Place of Dead Roads, the Last Lot. "The PA Police used to patrol Long-Term Lots Seven and Eight," APB says, "but then the Port Authority, in its wisdom, gave the job to Alert. There are two to three Alert guards to every PA policeman, and crime in the lots has increased threefold.

"It's like special order," Bill says. "You need a Blaupunkt? No problem. An Alpine? No problem." He pulls into the lot, cruises slowly over the broken asphalt. There, sitting in the dark, somewhat apart from the other cars, is a black Cadillac limousine, whose rear window is ajar. And Bill stops the cruiser and gets out.

My mind shifts from sleep-fog to yellow alert; my heart begins to thud. Do I stay put or get out? If the essence of police work is hour upon hour of drudgery punctuated by infrequent but emphatic peril, it seems likely that what we have here could at least tend toward the latter. Suddenly I have wiseguys on the brain: This limo, I cannot restrain myself from thinking, has a distinctly mobbed-up look about it. And there's old big-bellied Bill, peering in the windows. It's too reminiscent of a hundred movie scenes, and my legs won't move. He doesn't look like a hero. He's the guy who gets it. "See anything?" I call weakly out the window. This would be when the sound-track music would get into subwoofer range, blatant in its portent, but nonetheless quite effective on a visceral level.

Now APB is down on all fours, examining the pavement under the limo. I hold my breath. He gets up and brushes his hands on his pants. "Well," he says, "there's nothing on the ground"—*Blood,* I think; *it's blood he's talking about*—"and there's no smell coming out of it. So there's no bodies in it. I hope." And Airport Bill, good old paunchy, loud-talking APB, my hero and shield, the not-so-thin blue line, gets back into the car. My adrenaline has metabolized into disappointment. When this happens a thousand times, you're a cop.

A little later we drive by a darkened, muddy, storm-fenced plot on the out-skirts of the long-term lots. A sign reading DEVELOPMENT AREA, and bearing the JFK 2000 logo, leans back on the distressed fence. It feels like a testament to the folly of man: as if we were far in the future, looking at a development area that never developed. "This is gonna be the employee lot in the year 2050, or whatever," Bill says, reading my mind.

"So you don't have high hopes for an on-time finish?" I say.

"I don't think Kennedy has ever been completed," he says, philosophically. And then, as we drive off, "JFK 2000 is a thing of the past. They don't even promote it anymore. The Port Authority tried to get the airlines to pay for it. And the thing is, the airlines can go to Newark."

18

Riding the Rocket

The Ingrate

The morning was unseasonably warm, the air as still as death. It was the kind of hazy, polluted sunlight in which colors are flat and shiny objects glint ominously. I drove through the contorted fandango of the airport's under-construction roadway system, all gravel and buckboards and neon-orange safety cones; negotiated a banked, one-lane, amusement-park-like temporary overpass; and descended to the parking lot in front of the BA/United terminal. There, looming behind a barrier, was the unmistakably low and wide tail, with its unmistakable blue-white-and-red chevron design.

Never crashed, never crashed . . . I kept hearing Dustin Hoffman's autistic crow-squawk, from *Rain Man,* playing over and over in my head. Never crashed—did that make your odds better, or worse? Obviously, the answer was neither, but it didn't stop me from thinking this way. Surely there must be some X factor at work (or X, Y, and Z factors): the construction of the plane or the skill of the pilots (*Brian Walpole! Ian Saxon!* I couldn't help thinking) or, maybe, even the relative paucity of Concordes. Fewer flights, fewer incidents. *Its number is coming up. Stop that,* I told myself.

It wasn't that I didn't want to make this trip. I wanted it very badly. It was the very dreamlikeness of the proceedings that troubled me. *It was the idea of the Concorde.* I had taken hundreds of airline flights, but I had never flown on a plane that was also an idea. There was the idea of flying—troubling in its own right—but a plane was always a service, a means to an end. Here there was no precedent, no standard operating procedure. It was all very well for the rich to strut on and strut off, to take this plane back and forth, back and forth, over the Atlantic, but it was the essence of richness to accept and take for granted, after the brief initial tickle, the most outlandish services—the

235

James Kaplan

Concorde being one of these. It was fun, it was necessary, it was noblesse oblige, to take the Concorde for granted! Mach 2? *Mais oui! "They're babies —they can't do anything for themselves,"* Rhonda had said. But it's not that they *can't;* it's that they *won't.* Why should they? That's what *you're* there for! That's what *it's* there for.

I parked my Rabbit in the small, dilapidated BA lot among others of its ilk, family sedans mostly. These were, of course, workers' cars. As we have seen, only truly desperate or ignorant travelers park their cars at Kennedy. I was neither, and yet something superstitious in me wanted to have my own dowdy old VW waiting for me when I returned, unimaginably transformed, tomorrow morning, after having ridden the rocket to London and back again.

To get to the Concorde lounge, you ascend a windowless, up-sloping, shiny-floored corridor reminiscent of nothing so much as the General Electric or the IBM pavilion at the 1964–1965 New York World's Fair. To my thirteen-year-old self, then, there seemed something innately, unquestionably, good and important about the idea of a *pavilion,* and, indeed, about the world's-fair concept itself: I don't recall the concept of irony ever creeping in amid the awe. My now three-times-as-old self appeared to be equally impressed—despite the public-relations minuet in which I was now irretrievably locked; despite the more than slightly repellent sociology of Concorde travel. The thing about those old world's-fair pavilions was, whatever they meant in advertising or informational terms, they were great *rides.* The exact same thing was true today. As I joshed hollowly with the security guards at the X-ray checkpoint at the slope's top; as I glanced at the very pricey-looking duty-free shop and the inner-lit billboards for purple-sacked Chivas Regal and unattainably pricey Chopard watches, realizing I would never, ever be here in the course of my normal life, that's what hit me: No matter what the atmospherics, this had to be the Ride of Rides.

It was a good thing to remember, for now, in the lounge proper, I was confronted with the tiresome sight of leather pantsuits, Palm Beach straw hats, and blazers: the cock-a-hoop, Thurston-Howell-III-and-Lovey-like equipage of the International Traveling Rich. But then, to my surprise, another sociological stratum appeared to be mingling in among the jaded countenances—suddenly I was starting to see excited eyes and flashing cameras. Clearly, this was not your ordinary weekday-morning Concorde crowd. And soon I found out what it was. These were charter people.

Those forty-two empty seats I had remarked on my previous visit to the lounge were no freak occurrence: The bald fact is that at $3,600 one way, the

THE AIRPORT

Concorde doesn't usually pack them in. Hence British Airways does what it can, one measure being tour packages, and one of those packages being the Cunard-BA *QE2*-Concorde round-trip parlay.✛ The present occupants of the Concorde lounge—this observer included—were, therefore, *Concorde outsiders.* For a moment, I cursed my sociological luck—*naturally, the people in BA PR were no dopes; why shouldn't they throw their cut-rate passengers together?*

But then things got even dicier when my friend Betty showed up (she had kindly offered to see me off) and told me that the plane was chock-full, all one hundred seats taken by semi-paying customers.

I had a vision of slogging back out to the crummy BA parking lot: clearly my fate lay with the Sammy Chevaliers and the George Murphys and the APBs of the world; I was a terrestrial sort of yearner, shooting here simply too high. But then the Palm Beach set, those very leather pantsuits and blazers, proved to be my backhanded salvation.

A tiny BA captain had materialized to my left, five two or three at most, the four gold stripes on each navy-blue sleeve looking disproportionately massive. He had a long, inquisitive nose and a crinkling irony at the corners of his eyes. He was very tan. All at once Betty, rustling Betty, BA service manager, my friend, my informant, materialized on my right, in all her Queens glory. "This is Mike Riley," she said to me. Riley looked up and shook my hand. I had about a foot on him. Betty explained to him that I was booked but placeless: Riley, his eyes crinkling, simply said, "Well. He can sit in the jump seat, can't he."

Naturally it was a statement, not a question. It was his plane! Betty nodded. "Sure, Mike," she said. And to me, "So. You'll sit in the jump seat."

"Great," I said, without much conviction, at once visualizing one of those rickety-looking pull-down affairs, humiliatingly facing the passengers, into which the flight attendants strap themselves during takeoff and landing. I pictured the tan Palm Beach faces sneering at me as I sat at the head of the cabin: Who's *he*? Great—a transatlantic pillory. At least it would be quick.

Then there was a commotion at the lounge's front desk, where a harried-looking service manager whose black-and-white, chevroned name tag read

---

✛ Once BA denationalized in 1987, it hit the ground running with its marketing of the Concorde: the thing might have been a royal waste of money, but now, by gad, it would pull its weight. Which it hasn't, but not for lack of trying. Besides the *QE2* package, BA has sold round-the-world trips, Halley's Comet trips, one-day trips to the Pyramids, to the Bolshoi in Moscow, to Lapland to visit Father Christmas, and so forth. In a pinch, the plane can be stuffed with blue-collar couples who shell out a hard-won five hundred dollars or so to fly from Heathrow back to Heathrow on a one-hour Trip to Nowhere.

237

James Kaplan

JOANNE had passed beyond the point of placation with a low-to-the-ground, pantsuited and bejeweled matron. From time to time the matron, whose tan brow was furrowed ominously, emitted a tense sigh and tapped her multiringed fingers on the counter. Was she, perchance, a travel agent? Had her doctor forbidden her to ride in the smoking section?⁺ Finally Joanne could take it no longer. "Ma'am, will you please just keep your hands *off the desk,*" she said. The woman sized her up, narrowed her eyes as though to say *I'm remembering this, girlie,* turned around, and returned to her blazer. "Everybody wants to change seats," Joanne told me, "and it's impossible to change seats on this plane when it's full. Everybody wants to change, and nobody wants to move, and it gets to a point where I can't handle it anymore—I just want to get the hell out of here."

Which was precisely what we, the fortunate passengers of BA Flight 001 (no messy high numbers for Concorde people), did a couple of minutes later, when Betty crowded in next to the delaminating Joanne behind the counter and, in her best service-manager purr, announced boarding. I didn't want to sit in that jump seat any longer than I had to, so I hung around and chatted with her until every last rich person had walked onto the plane. All at once the lounge was very quiet. "Have fun," Betty said. "You will. It's a real kick in the ass."

I ducked to enter the plane (I had already seen—having been given a walk-around of cabin and flight deck a few weeks before—that the Concorde was, inside and out, well, *compact)* and started to turn right, explaining apologetically to a stewardess⁺⁺ that I was sitting in the jump seat. And she pointed me left, toward the flight deck.

⁺ On the Concorde, from row 7 to the back of the plane. In other words, a lot of rows — nineteen! Smoking, as we know, is prohibited on American carriers for flights of six hours or less. Which means it is allowed, in certain sections, on transatlantic and transpacific trips. The size of the smoking section on any given flight is up to the airline—yet another delicate equation in the myriad of delicate equations that each carrier must juggle in order to stay in the black. (Did you realize, for example, that the exterior paint on a 747 weighs a total of four hundred pounds? Not so negligible when the price of jet fuel is taken into account! Nor is dirt—hence the airlines' fastidiousness about washing their planes' skin. And hence the financially troubled Northwest's decision to leave its jumbos nude, their sparkling sheet-metal epidermes a glittering reminder of aviation's glorious past.) Every seat row more or less of smoking section alienates one vociferous group or the other. Whom to please? You can be certain that BA's decision to give 76 percent of its Concorde cabin over to atmospheric nastiness was not lightly arrived at. Is it that the whole-wheat-and-alfalfa-sprouting of America is peculiar to this country alone, a function of advanced consumerism and creeping Californiation? Or is it that the international rich are still living in an anachronistic, Charles Boyer-esque world of sterling-silver cigarette boxes and gold-foil-lined packs of Dunhills? As APB would say, quite so.

⁺⁺ This word has unfortunately been politically corrected out of acceptable usage, to be replaced by the infinitely grayer, groaningly boring *flight attendant.* All right, sure, *stewardess* had all kinds of spicy coffee-tea-or-me connotations, but if the truth be told, have those connotations been entirely effaced with the word? Yes, there is a whole new generation of male and female cabin personnel working the skies today, many of them—OK, *most* of them—serious and responsible people (some of them *older* people), spiciness

238

THE AIRPORT

*

As I ducked and hunched myself down the narrow companionway onto the tiny flight deck⁺ of the Concorde, all I could think was *Oh my God, I'm going to ride up front,* and *Do I really want this?* Then I thought of HM the Queen Mother. That granite jaw under the lace veil. She had brought it off! By God, I would, too.

Mike, Captain Riley, was in his left-hand chair, turning to greet me, his tininess quite lost in the sitting position—or, rather, transformed into pure capability. For how many cooler things are there to be at the controls of? Think a second. Not many. Yet Mike wore it well. There was a mystical reserve to his eyes that spoke more of poetry than self-importance. And, just as there was no foolishness about his size, nor was there any about the coolness of his command. Nor was there any phony laid-backness. He was, simply, *there.* It was his plane, and his aspect neither ignored nor overemphasized the fact. Rather, he suspended it ever so slightly to introduce me to the rest of the crew.

On his right⁺⁺ was the first officer, Dick Routledge, whose bland Brit handsomeness I faintly distrusted. And directly in back of Routledge, facing the wildly begauged right wall of the cockpit, sat the flight engineer, Ian Fellowes-Freeman, one of those long and bony English types whose gaunt faces would not look amiss on the Battle of Hastings tapestry. It was a good face, for it was as plain as the prominent nose on it that he loved his job utterly.

The jump seat was directly in back of Mike and across from Ian, facing front. I put my knapsack on the floor behind the seat and sat down—and found my knees in tight contact with the captain's chair. Ian reached over and showed me a lever that would slide the seat back on its track, far enough for

---

the last thing on their minds. And flight-attending can be dog work, especially on the Concorde, where meal and wine service of a high order must be performed in an extremely short time, in ludicrously cramped circumstances. And I spent many off-the-job hours with a number of BA cabin-service people, and, frankly, most of them weren't people to fantasize about. (But this edges into the whole aesthetic question of Britishness, a separate matter.) Yet it seems to me, from a fairly extensive experience of present-day commercial flying, that there are still any number of male and female attendants for whom the cabin-service kabuki includes a good dollop of sex, and I'll bet an upgrade certificate that *that* fourth wall is broken from time to time.

⁺ A harmless bit of pseudo-nautical rodomontade. I prefer the less humorless, quasi-nasty *cockpit,* with its connotations of intimacy and swaggering, Right Stuff penility (there is a famous New York leather-jacket store that gets a good deal of mileage, intended or no, from the double entendre).

⁺⁺ Why does the captain in a British plane not sit on the right? I can only guess that this near-universal configuration has to do with the overwhelming influence of American aircraft manufacture.

even a long-legged type such as I to be comfortable. But I noticed at once that the farther back I went, the less access I would have to the captain's side window. How I wanted to look out that window! For my only frontward view was over the shoulders of the captain and first officer, and I couldn't exactly ask either one to lean over so I could see better. Yet by compromising comfort just a bit, I was able to bend forward and press my nose against my very own square of Perspex. It was an important adjustment.

As was the fastening of my safety harness, a confusing three-part affair that went between my legs and over my shoulders, and had an anachronistic, RAF-in-the-Battle-of-Britain look to it. In fact, as I finally settled (as much as was possible, for I was feeling anything but settled) back into the jump seat, what struck me immediately was that the whole flight deck was—how can I put this tactfully? (I can't)—*low-tech*. It was, in all its lineaments (too cruel, but true), *1976*. Or earlier. For the Concorde's instrumentation was designed in the late sixties and has not been significantly modified since. And even then, well . . . *British technology*—it's not an oxymoron, exactly; that's nasty. Still, there is about the term, and the thing itself, something very . . . what? *Bakelite.* Bakelite tonality. Black-and-white. Chipped gray enamel. Metal instead of plastic. And that squared-off, ineffably noble-looking, ubiquitous official British typeface, white on black—you see it everywhere in London: on bus signs, in the Underground. And on the gauges in the Concorde.

All at once I was reminded, quite pleasantly, of the cockpit of a British-racing-green MGB I drove in the late seventies. Black dashboard, Smith's gauges, divine leathery smell. It was, the whole gestalt, a whiff of the pre-high-tech past—a time before Bauhaus and Japanese microprocessor design conspired to change the look of the world.

As was, somehow, the flight deck of the Concorde. A World War I airman brought back to life would not feel completely mystified by it: there were, after all, rudder pedals, control columns, throttles. Put the same airman in the video-game cockpit of a 767 or an A320 Airbus, and he would instantly return to a spectral state.

Ian clapped a pair of headphones over his large ears. Mike was on the intercom, talking to the passengers: "I don't want you to be alarmed if you feel us dipping sharply to the right immediately after takeoff," he said. "It's a perfectly routine turn we take so our noise won't disturb the people living below."✈ On the back of his seat hung a blank chart describing, I presumed, the plane's four routes out of New York:

✈ For four years after the Concorde began flying between Europe and the United States in 1976, it wasn't allowed to land at Kennedy—the result of vigorous and orchestrated protests by antinoise activists from

THE AIRPORT

SID	R/W	ROUTEING	ALTITUDES
Kennedy 4		(incl. min. noise routeing)	
Breezy Point Climb			
Bridge Climb			
Canarsie Climb			

Breezy Point Climb! Canarsie Climb! It sounded . . . *fun.* I felt calmer. For a second. Mike rung off and turned to his crew. "What's holding us up?" he said, mildly. It was 9:34, four minutes after our scheduled push-back time. Minutes are money on Concorde, whose high-strung passengers have been known to erupt over even slight delays. Ian, who had taken off the headphones and hung them around his neck, shrugged. Mike shrugged, too.

"How was Barbados?" Dick asked.

"Oh, lovely," Mike said. "Just lovely. I mean, you just wear shorts—nothing else. That's how it was the whole week."

That explained the tan. Barbados chat continued for a while, Riley's whole English demeanor reflecting a pleased incredulity at the existence of such a sun-shot antipode. After a couple of minutes the radio crackled. "Speedbird Oh Oh One, you can push back," said the Queens-accented ground controller.

Riley turned back to work. "Ready to go," he said. "Ready to hit it." Whistling something tuneless, he reached over, flicked a couple of toggle switches. A dull roar began somewhere behind us. My pulse began to hammer.

Ian clapped the headphones back on. Dick turned to me. "We start two engines now while we push back," he said. "The other two when we're cleared for takeoff." Now that my life was at least partly in his hands, he didn't seem such a bad fellow after all. We were backing up and slowly wheeling around to face frontward. "Once we're up, we'll take that gentle right turn Mike mentioned," Routledge said, with an ironic glance at Riley, "then a long left turn as we climb to altitude. We try to maintain two hundred

---

neighborhoods adjacent to the airport. Having spent hours of my childhood cowering as 707s going into and out of Kennedy roared over my grandparents' Hewlett house at what looked like a couple of hundred feet, I find it hard to blame them. The Concorde is *unbelievably* loud—much louder, it seems, than any Boeing or Lockheed. The tide was finally turned when special noise-avoidance maneuvers such as the one described above (a right turn, immediately after takeoff, so sharp that if a 747 were to try it, its wing would scrape the ground) were worked out.

241

fifty knots until we're up to ten thousand feet, to keep the noise down. And then we just point towards Nantucket, and we're off."

Now we were rolling out on taxiway Bravo, away from the terminal. We held for a moment at what I now knew to be the hold-bar light, then we crossed 31 Right and turned right onto taxiway Xray. A very short man in a blue apron—BA insists on calling it a *tabard*—leaned into the doorway with a salver of rolled hot washcloths. "Thanks, Freddy," Mike said, taking a cloth and wiping his hands and face. Dick and Ian followed suit, and then Freddy extended the salver, with one rolled cloth left, to me. Freddy then plopped a tray of wheat biscuits on Ian's little flight engineer's desk, and retired. Ian offered biscuits all around. I took two. I could, I thought, get used to this.

I looked over Ian's shoulder at his gauges. One in particular caught my eye: TOTAL FUEL REM., it read. The red electronic digits (the gauge was a relatively recent addition to the cockpit) were changing as we rolled—8,430 . . . 8,429 . . . 8,426. I did a quick mental calculation and realized the gauge was moving in ten-kilogram decrements—that we were using twenty-five to fifty pounds of fuel every three or four seconds as we taxied down toward the foot of 22 Right. The very runway where I'd sat with Sammy months ago and watched my first rocket launch.

Ian turned to me from his gauges. "Look at that Class Four jumbo on the runway," he said, nodding toward the foot of 22 Right, where a Northwest 747-400, identifiable by its stretched upper deck and uptilted winglets, was about to take off. "Only two crew and a big CRT screen," he said. He shook his head. "Fourteen hours in the air to Tokyo—can you believe it?"

As I watched the 747 roll down the runway, something caught my eye: There was a gnat on the inside of our windshield. A gnat flying the Concorde. We turned onto the foot of 22 Right.

Dick pointed out the windshield. "Look, there's the French Concorde coming in," he said. "It's quite late today." The white-and-blue plane, its livery only subtly different from BA's, sailed across our purview, tail down, nose up.

"What's the plane like to land?" I asked.

Dick pointed to Mike. "He knows more about landing this thing than anyone around."

Glad to hear it, I thought. But then Mike shook his head. "Don't say that," he said, mildly. "There are fifty ways to do it wrong." He whistled his tuneless song again for a moment. "Actually," he said, turning to Dick, "the whole success of the week in Barbados depends on who you're with."

Dick smiled faintly. "Look at the birds," he said. He pointed to the white-gray sky up to the right. We all stared. I could just make out, I thought, a haze of something up there, certainly not anything like individual birds.

"Geese," Mike said. He picked up his radio microphone and pushed the button to speak to ground control. "We're seeing some bird activity over the bay," he said.

"Roger, Speedbird, thank you," said the crackly Queens voice on the speaker.

Mike clicked off. "I should think they'll be at about a thousand feet," he told us. "We'll be higher."

We waited. Ahead of us, at the entrance to the runway, sat three lesser entities: a corporate jet, a little Cessna, and an American Eagle prop commuter.

The jet took off.

Beneath the window on Mike's left, I noticed, was a window crank, and a sign that read DO NOT OPEN WINDOW IN FLIGHT.

Dick pointed out the windshield again. "There's another crowd," he said. I squinted at the sky. I couldn't see a thing.

The Cessna trundled down the runway and was aloft.

"They say these Canada geese can be about forty pounds, don't they?" Mike said, smiling slightly.

The commuter took off.

"All takeoff checks are complete," Mike said. He picked up the microphone and pushed the intercom button. "This is the captain again," he said. "We're all lined up and ready to go. We're about to give it all we've got."

I tried, somehow, to prepare myself for *giving it all we've got.* I knew, abstractly, that the Concorde's takeoff was much faster than a normal jet's: that we would be accelerating from 0 to 250 knots in about thirty seconds. Should I go into a tuck? I tried to relax. Mike pushed up the throttle, the roar behind us grew, and we began to move. *Move.* My back and neck pressed into the jump seat. And pressed harder. As we hurtled down the runway, I noticed an absurd detail: Mike was checking that window crank on his left.

And then, just like that, we were up.

Never crashed.

❐

I would like to be able to report that crossing the Atlantic at Mach 2 in the cockpit of the Concorde was a transforming experience, one that brought my feelings about the history of aviation—and in particular the history of Kennedy Airport, with all its cross-currents of money, safety, and departed glamour—into crystalline focus. I would like to be able to speak of my mystical feelings as I broke the sound barrier for the first time, and flew higher than I had ever flown.

I would like to, but what I must say instead is that, besides the fun of riding on a flight deck (which I had never done before), and the pleasantness of the company, riding the rocket was a profound anticlimax.

When the mechanical-digital Mach gauge clicked from 0.96 to 0.99 to 1.00—nothing happened. No sound, no light, no smell, no popping of Champagne corks. The gauge just proceeded on up in a blasé way—1.06, 1.12 . . . Had it really happened? Was this what dozens of test pilots had perished for? What Chuck Yeager had almost augered into the earth for? I felt disappointed, almost angry. *I wanted something to happen.* Was it possible the gauge was broken?

Mike was minding his flying; Dick was resetting the altitude selector. Ian was logging his gauge readings. I cleared my throat. "Nothing happened," I said. "At Mach one."

"Nothing does," Dick said. "We're leaving our boom behind us, and off to the sides, but we don't get any of it at all. We just keep on flying."

"Even at Mach two?"

"Sorry."

I can report that at eleven miles up, the view out the plane's front windows was breathtaking. Cloud-flecked blue-green below, deep blue ahead, the earth's grand camber subtle but noticeable in the horizon line. And blue-black above: space.

And what suddenly occurred to me at that moment was that *anticlimax was the whole point.* This was what successful technology was all about. What was allowing me to take in this view in calm comfort was an entire history of sacrifice, error, and death. Climaxes are for pioneers, and the climaxes of exploration are grand—but of course, often as not, fatal.

I can report that at fifty thousand feet over the Atlantic, the crew and I discussed the cockroach population of a luncheonette on West Fifty-seventh Street.

That the Concorde food was better than I remembered British food to be and not as transcendent as I imagined Concorde food might be.

That I walked off the plane at Heathrow almost giddily unexhausted.

And that the trip back home the next morning was exactly the same.

All of which, I guess, is just what those who can afford it fork over the $3,600 for. (Worth it? I don't know. Worth more than I paid? Definitely.)

In the end, the most exciting thing about the beautiful girl was watching her walk into the room. In the end, the most exciting thing about the Concorde was watching it take off from Sammy's truck.

19

IAB 3

Landing There, Living There

Give me your tired, your poor,
Your huddled masses yearning to breathe free,
The wretched refuse of your teeming shore,
Send these, the homeless, tempest-tossed, to me:
I lift my lamp beside the golden door.

—EMMA LAZARUS, 1885

We hate every ethnic group here. When the Third World flushes, it
comes through the IAB.

—PORT AUTHORITY POLICEMAN, 1993

Marina Belotserkovsky's last name means "white church" in Russian, and she is not entirely sure just how her ex-husband's family came to acquire it. They are, and she is, Jewish. She happens to be—it cannot be overlooked—an astonishingly beautiful woman: blond, blue-eyed, not "Jewish looking" in the stereotypical, and erroneous, sense. Nevertheless, she completely lacks the self-conscious grandeur or defensiveness or humorlessness of many beautiful women. She also lacks any trace of coquettishness or—most amazingly—of bitterness. In her mid-thirties, she has been through enough in her life to have made her looks a side issue or even, perhaps, a hindrance. She came, after all, from a place where appearances are not worshiped as they are here, and since she arrived in this country, she has had many things besides beauty to think about.

She arrived in the United States—point of entry the International Arrivals Building at Kennedy Airport—on September 28, 1989, along with her ten-year-old son, Gyorgi, and two thousand other Jews from what was then still the Soviet Union. Divorced from her husband, who remains in Russia, Marina and her son now live in Crown Heights, Brooklyn, like so many others, trying to make a new life for themselves.

Her story, too, is like so many others: singular and poignant enough to bear repeating, and typical enough, as well. She was a resident of Leningrad (before it reverted to its tsarist name of St. Petersburg), with a facility for languages, an excellent school record, and a certificate as a simultaneous translator into Spanish and English.

"Why did I want to leave Russia? Even now, being here, I cannot tell you exactly," she says, in only faintly accented English. We're sitting in an office at the Hebrew Immigrant Aid Society (HIAS) in Manhattan, where Belotserkovsky works helping those who have come after her. "But being Jewish, I reached everything I could reach being Jewish. I got tired of knocking on the closed door. For one thing, for simultaneous interpreting, all jobs involve contact with foreigners, and suspicion automatically arose toward Jews in this profession. Not to mention that career opportunities were very limited, since I couldn't travel—the government wouldn't allow Jewish people to go abroad.

"Also I didn't want my son to face the problems I had always faced, and which he was beginning to face. Anti-Semitism is very strong in Russia, by tradition and in the present culture. *Zhid*—it's like *kike*—this is the word for a Jew, even between two Russian kids. It's so strong that I really don't feel myself to be Russian—maybe out of revenge, maybe just because this is the way I was made to feel. For Americans, we're Russian. For me, I'm Jewish.

"My maiden name was Kooperschmidt. Belotserkovsky is my ex-husband's name. We were divorced five years before I left Russia. My husband was thinking of leaving, too, but he decided not to go. It's a very big decision—something you should think about for a long time. You don't just wake up one morning and say, 'I want to leave.'

"And there is no one family who could leave without vast difficulties. For one person it's money. For another, it's leaving family. For another, friends. For me, as for everyone else, it was a very difficult decision. My parents and grandparents are still there. Here there were some friends I used to talk to, but basically, there was nobody here for me. My son and I were leaving everything behind.

"I first applied to leave ten years ago, with my ex-husband and my parents. Brezhnev was in power then—this was supposed to be the 'golden century' for the USSR. My application was turned down, with the words 'It is not in the interests of the state.'

"I reapplied in 1988. Now Gorbachev was in power, and things had become much easier, but even then, and for a long time afterward, there were still refuseniks—people who had dealt with state secrets, people who were very active politically. For a long time—even with Gorbachev and *perestroika* and *glasnost*—they were trying to sell these people, if you know what I mean.

"We had to apply to the Department of Visas and Permissions in OVIR—the Soviet version of the U.S. INS, the Immigration and Naturalization Service. They deal with anybody who leaves, even tourists. We wanted to try to speed things up even more, but *blat*—the old favor system of bribery and cronyism—had become more difficult to use, *because* of *glasnost*. My son and I had applied along with some acquaintances, and we were amazed to receive permission within three months.

"But this was only permission to leave the Soviet Union, not to come to the United States. Then we heard about an organization in America called HIAS that helped Jewish émigrés come into this country. Their money came from charity, and also from U.S. government aid. At the time there was a HIAS office in Vienna and one in Rome, and the procedure was that HIAS would receive you and help prepare your papers for the INS, brief you for your Immigration interviews, et cetera. Later it changed, and the INS started interviewing people directly in the U.S. Embassy in Moscow.

"Then it wasn't so direct. We left Pulkovo Airport in Leningrad on December sixteenth, 1988—a Friday—and flew to Vienna. We were interviewed by HIAS in Vienna, then we flew from Vienna to Rome. We would have to be someplace for a while before there was any possibility of getting to the U.S., and I didn't want to stay in Vienna—even though it was the West, it was too close to Russia, and even though it was the West, I knew there was anti-Semitism there, too. Rome had a better history." She smiles. "And it was warmer."

The smile fades. "After we'd been in Rome a little while, I was interviewed by an INS officer—the woman's name was McCoy. It was a thirty-minute interview, just this woman and I, no interpreter. They do this to see how your English is. And it's very difficult, even when you translate for a living, because when you use an interpreter, you have a little more time to think. So I was off-balance with this woman. And I didn't have a good persecution story for her—I didn't have a *legend*. The only thing I could tell her was that I had tried to make a circumcision for my son in Leningrad, and the KGB had prevented it. It was harassment; they wanted to know all about the rabbi who was going to perform the ceremony. I finally made a circumcision for him in Rome, when he was seven years old.

"Anyway, this INS woman, McCoy, she was tired of all the stories, and she didn't believe me, anyhow, and—and I was denied permission to immigrate into the U.S.," she says, shaking her head. "Because, from her point of view, *I was not persecuted*—I was simply looking for a better life. By the definition of the United States, a refugee is one who is persecuted.

"It was absolutely subjective on her part. Now there are more criteria for decision. And all my friends who were interviewed by her were also denied. I could make one appeal. If I was turned down then, that's it. There would be only two options—go to Israel, or go to the U.S. as a parolee. For this, you need a sponsor in the States, someone who will sign a paper and lend you money.

"I applied again, and was denied again. Through HIAS, I found an American lawyer in Israel, Arthur Opoleon, who wrote me a great appeal. It went right on the desk of McCoy, and stayed there. Why should she admit she made a mistake?

"So there we were in Italy, with very little money and absolutely no idea what to do. It was a terrible time. I thought maybe we might go to Israel, but there was no job for me in Israel. My languages were Spanish and English and, more and more, a bit of Italian. That wouldn't do me any good in Israel.

"Then I called a friend in Boston who had been here for thirteen years. Could she sponsor me to be a parolee, I asked her. She said yes—she would sign for me, and lend me four thousand dollars.

"And then the Lautenberg amendment was passed, and there were no more parolees. Suddenly, like a miracle, we're approved! I was living in Santa Marinella, about forty minutes outside of Rome, when we heard we were on the list. It was really like a miracle. One day the postman came and said, 'Bella Tserkovskaya, you go and sign papers. Olympic Airlines. Five days.'"

"September twenty-eighth, 1989, was an unbelievable day in Kennedy Airport," Belotserkovsky says. "Two thousand Russian Jews, arriving all at once. Can you imagine it?" Marina and Gyorgi flew Olympic from Rome to Athens to Kennedy, a total of thirteen hours in the air and on the ground, waiting. Waiting, waiting, waiting. "We didn't sleep the whole night before, waiting for the bus to take us to Leonardo da Vinci Airport in Rome. We arrived in the U.S. on a Thursday, at two-thirty P.M.," she says, the moment forever fixed in her mind. "When we were landing, I saw Manhattan out the window. I always thought I would not be surprised—I had seen pictures of New York many times, and I am not a person to be excited."

She takes a deep breath. "But when we looked out the windows, we—Gyorgi and I—were screaming. You have to understand—there were very few Russian Jews on this plane. We were almost the only ones screaming. But we were screaming anyway." She dabs at her eyes, then blinks quickly.

"A—what do you call it?" she asks. "The big bus that drives out to the plane, that moves up and down?"

"Plane Mate."

"Plane Mate." She smiles back, a dazzling sight. "It was the first shock. I had never seen one before. I was not expecting it to go down after we sat in it. All these people sitting there, and Gyorgi and I were staring at each other. And I understood at this moment that *I don't know anything.* How to move. What to do. We got out of the Plane Mate, walked down a hall, got into a giant elevator. We were so shocked when we came out of the elevator—we had no idea what to do.

"But thanks to God, there was a HIAS woman there to meet us. Tina Shulman was her name. She spoke perfect English, and perfect Russian. Tina was telling us what to do, but at the same time, she was so tired. Two thousand Jews! She had been meeting people all day. But she was with us the whole way through Immigration, explaining what to do. We were there for one and a half hours, answering questions, filling out forms.

"Then we got onto another elevator, went down, and we were out on the street at Kennedy Airport. We had no baggage—our baggage had disappeared in Athens. Tina said, 'Stay here and wait.' So we stood—a couple with a kid, and me and Gyorgi. We stood for five hours in front of the International Arrivals Building.

"I was so tired, but what impressed me was the huge size of this airport. Pulkovo in Leningrad, Sheremetyevo in Moscow—they were nowhere near as big. Everything was big, and I was afraid—afraid to let Gyorgi go to the rest room, afraid to go myself. Every step was not easy, because everything—everything—was absolutely new. How to turn on the hot water. How to pull a towel out of the dispenser. And of course I was afraid to ask.

"Since we had no relatives here, we were supposed to go to a hotel. Tina came back from time to time, but she didn't say much—only that we couldn't go yet. Finally another person came and said, 'The problem is, everything is overcrowded today. There is no place for you to go.'

"At last we thought of some acquaintances in Brooklyn, and called them. And they came in a gigantic car and picked up all five of us, and took us back to their place. Driving from the airport in this big station wagon—you have to understand, in the Soviet Union there are basically only two cars. There is the Zhiguly, which is built in partnership with Fiat, and which is like a Hyundai, and there is the Volga, which is Russian-made, and a little bigger. And here we were riding in this enormous station wagon on the Van Wyck Expressway—so exhausted, on this boring road, *but all these big cars around us!*

"We got to Brooklyn. These people lived in two rooms—you can imagine what it was like with five more people stuck in there. But it was OK. Only the kids went to sleep. We were talking and talking. We couldn't stop talking, all night." She smiles. "It's funny," she says. "The other day, some people from Kiev who are staying with another woman who works here came into the office for lunch, and they had no idea what to do—none. What was a can of Pepsi? What was a refrigerator? They were standing there like children."

Then, as is her habit, Marina Belotserkovsky quickly turns serious again. "That was me," she says, shaking her head. "That was me."

❐

Eddie's baggage is always with him, and though he doesn't collect frequent-flier miles, he travels over weeks and days and years, and his tall wire grocery cart contains a world: at least two radios, a couple of Samsonite overnight valises, and many plastic shopping bags containing other treasures. Eddie is tall, like his grocery cart, and small-headed; he looks a little like one of Van Gogh's potato-eaters. He wears his wardrobe, which, like him, doesn't get washed often. He's eating a roll and drinking from a cardboard coffee cup when I catch up with him in the north wing of the IAB, and the other travelers—the more conventional deodorized and ticketed types—are giving him a wide berth. This is more out of fastidiousness than fear: the most dangerous thing about Eddie is his smell. He has a long unshaven face and large gentle eyes, which regard me with full attention, even concern, when I ask if we can talk.

"You wanna talk, Jim," he says, softly. "Sure, we can talk. Sure we can talk."

"Should we sit down?"

"OK." We sit on the last two seats in a bank of plastic chairs. Eddie's cart stands next to him.

"Do you live here, Eddie?" I ask.

"No, no, Jim. I don't live here."

"Where do you live?"

"I live in a home for adults in Canarsie," Eddie says, peering at me intently. "Seaport Manor. It's good weather out today, Jim?"

"Pretty good. How long have you been at the home?"

He nods. "A year, Jim. I've been there a year. Before that I lived with my mother. My mother is German and my father is Dutch."

"Why'd you leave your mother's place?"

"I had a minor fight with my brother Clinton," he says. "Then I went to Creedmore for a while. Then I went to Seaport Manor. That's where I live now. Seaport Manor. Are you married, Jim?"

I tell him I am.

"Do you have children?"

I tell him I do.

"Are they boys or girls?"

"Two boys."

He nods seriously. "How old are they, Jim?"

I tell him.

"What are their names?"

I tell him, and he nods again. He repeats the names. He takes a sip of his coffee and stares at me, awaiting more conversation.

"Do you ever sleep here, Eddie?"

"I sleep here sometimes, Jim."

"Where do you sleep?"

"I sleep near the restaurant or downstairs, Jim. It's nice out today?"

"Pretty nice. Do the cops bother you when you're sleeping near the restaurant or downstairs?"

"Sometimes they tell me to leave if I'm not taking a flight, Jim."

"What do you do?"

"I just move and sleep someplace else, Jim."

"Do you see other people sleeping here?"

Nod. "I see other people sleeping here. Mostly a lot of homeless people, Jim."

"But you come and go?"

"I come here from Seaport Manor, Jim."

"How do you get here?"

"I take the L train to Eastern Parkway at the Broadway junction. Then I take the A train that says Far Rockaway. Then I get off at the stop that says Howard Beach and JFK. Then I take the free bus over here. Then I buy a cup of coffee here. My brother Kenny works here as a porter, Jim. Do you have brothers and sisters?"

I tell him I have two brothers. "How big is your family, Eddie?"

"Five boys and four girls, Jim. My mother's name is Audrey."

"What do you do for money, Eddie?"

"I get a Social Security check every month, Jim. It goes right to the home. Right to Seaport Manor. I get eight hundred fifty-seven dollars a month."

"Does anybody ever bother you here, besides the cops at night?" I ask.

"The cops never bother me during the day, Jim. Nobody ever touches my personal stuff. But I heard that people actually have got robbed here, Jim. It's a nice day out today, Jim?" His blue eyes are wide.

"Not bad. How long do you stay at the home, Eddie? And when do you come here?"

"The most I stay at the home is about a week, Jim. Then I go. They give us ninety-seven dollars a month spending money. My father died in a mugging, Jim. Have you ever been to Israel?"

I tell Eddie I went there about seventeen years ago. He nods gravely. "I'd like to go to Israel sometime," he says.

"Have you ever flown anywhere, Eddie?"

"In 1973 I took Air Canada to Montreal, Jim. That's when the fare was sixty-nine dollars. How tall are you, Jim?"

I tell him. "Do you ever talk to anybody around here?" I ask.

"I talk to mostly people I know, Jim."

"Do you ever talk to any of the homeless people here?"

"No, I never talk to them, Jim. Did you like it in Israel?"

"I did, Eddie. I did. Tell me—have you ever had a job?"

"I did have a job, Jim. I used to work at St. Patrick's."

"The cathedral?"

"Uh-huh. I would take the old candy out and put fresh candy in. And I would scrape the gum off the floors. Is it nice out today, Jim?"

"It is. How long have you been coming to the IAB, Eddie?"

"What's the IAB?" Eddie asks.

20

The Birdman of Kennedy—
Over and Out

South with the Laughing Gulls

"**I**t feels all right in here, doesn't it?" Sammy Chevalier asks, edgily. We're cruising the airport in a four-door, Port Authority–yellow Chevy Custom Deluxe on a hazy September lunch hour at summer's very end. The sun glares hotly from a dirty sky. The warm Jamaica Bay wind blows through the dry reeds along the runways and into the truck's open windows. Sammy looks relieved when I tell him I prefer my climate uncontrolled. Out here, anyway. I like this wind. He tells me scornfully about some people who rode with him over the summer—he won't say just who they were, but his tone hints at Suits—who demanded their A/C. "I drove this vehicle all summer this year and last year," he says, in his glottal Vermont singsong. "And more or less to reinforce my feeling about air conditioning—it's not really necessary."

The Motorola all-facility radio squawks: "Nine Two. Come in. Over." "I just got a signal here from the guy that was drivin' this car in before," Sammy says. "Let me just see what he wants." He picks up the mike and clicks it on. "Yeah, Bill," he says. Incomprehensible static. "Yeah. OK." He puts the microphone back down. "It's nothing," Sammy says.

This has been the texture of his life for thirty-five years: the radios crackling their sound and fury, signifying—usually—not much. Besides the unremitting comings and goings of the airport, the periodic annoyances, alarums, and crises, Sammy's days have been full of light and air and the cries of birds. There has always been the press of business to distract him and draw him back, but out on the runways, under the great dirty sky, amid the fumes of aircraft fuel, a man who couldn't stand to be cooped up in an office for very

253

long could roam freely for a while, in body and mind, while the world gave off its static.

He's leaving in two weeks. It's sheerest coincidence that I've come out to see Sammy today: we've been out of touch over the summer. "The thirtieth of this month I'm outta here," he tells me, as we drive along the inner perimeter road, parallel to taxiway Papa and runway 13 Right. A shiny silver American A300 Airbus is heading down the taxiway toward us. "I've got about nine more days to work, and I'm done. I *could've* retired twelve years ago. But I stuck around—mainly to be point man on this laughing-gull situation."

"That's right," I say. "I heard they were shooting a lot of birds out here." The idea of Sammy shooting birds, or even having anything to do with shooting birds, seems so deeply contradictory that I hardly know how to phrase the next question. "So you were—involved?"

"Well," he says, "I was kinda detached from the Bird Control Unit per se, and I was assigned to the Department of Agriculture shooters. I was kind of the Port Authority liaison man with them. And I worked very closely with them, every day from day one right on through to the end of the season."

But what did you do? I want to ask. *Did you shoot birds?* "Why did the Department of Agriculture come out here?" I ask, instead. "Was there any single incident that provoked it, or was it just slow-filtering legislation of some sort?"

"No—it's not legislation. Let's see. The Department of Agriculture animal-damage-control people are the people who advise airports on bird hazards and animal hazards at airports, such as coyotes and deer—some airports do have that kind of stuff. They work in conjunction with FAA Airport Operations, and they were formerly the Fish and Wildlife Service. Anyway, the laughing-gull bird-strike numbers were rising each summer."

"Oh, there were strikes?"

"Oh, *yeah.*"

"Were any engines or windshields damaged, anything like that?" I ask.

"None that can be directly attributed to the laughing gulls. However, let me put it this way." His voice suddenly becomes authoritative, even tough. "The laughing gulls, as I've told you, are migratory birds. They're only here for six months, and they come up to do their nesting in the national park on Joco Marsh, and then they all leave. During the six-month period that they are here, they accounted for over fifty percent of the total bird strikes for the entire year. So this got to be downright critical.

"And we have not been getting very good cooperation with the Park Service in terms of helping us institute some kind of control measure out at the nesting colony, where it *should* be done. And in fact, they became pretty downright *un*cooperative."

"But didn't you have that blue-ribbon panel come in to convince them? Those four international bird experts?"

We hang a left, parallel to 22 Right. "Yup. That's right," Sammy says.

"So was last summer's gull shooting a result of that?"

"Well, actually, more of a direct result to the fact that the Park Service does not want to even *follow* recommendations of the blue-ribbon panel. Which *they* had impaneled. We funded it, but they invited it."

"So they invited, then ignored it?"

"Exactly," he says. "That's it in a nutshell. The blue-ribbon panel first and foremost said that a nesting colony of birds that size at that location, so close to one of the largest commercial airports in the world, just cannot *exist*. It's an intolerable situation. They all were very surprised that it was occurring, and to a single individual they all said that that would have never been allowed to have occurred in their individual countries. But anyway, certain individuals in the Park Service—"

"Sometimes democracy can be a drawback," I say.

"Exactly. They were being downright muleheaded and stubborn. So anyway, after the study and egg oiling that occurred during the summer of 1990—"

"At that point, how many laughing-gull eggs were there?"

"The survey of the nesting colony that they did that summer was somewhere in the neighborhood of eight thousand nesting pairs. So that's sixteen thousand birds."

"How many eggs would that mean?"

"Well, you're talkin' about eight thousand active nests, and each nest would have anywhere from three to five eggs. On an average, four. Four is pretty much considered a normal clutch."

"So at least thirty thousand eggs. How many of them got oiled?"

"A little under three thousand. Nests."

"Twelve thousand eggs. So that left maybe eighteen thousand to hatch."

"Yeah. The reason that only three thousand nests were oiled is because the Park Service maintained, as a result of a study that was done in *1985,* that there were three thousand nests out there. Not wanting to admit that it was conceivable that the colony grew during the five years."

"More than doubled!"

"Yeah."

"So that was their mandate, and it was a limited mandate," I say. "Limited by ignorance."

"There you are. Exactly. So anyway. At the end of 1990—" He stops. "What are you looking at?"

255

"The radios," I say.

"Oh—OK."

"Why—were you worried?"

"No, I was wondering if there was—well, frankly, I didn't know *what* you were lookin' at. I just noticed that you were."

"I was just noticing that this particular truck has two radios. And I remember the other truck we used to ride around in had three."

"Well, this one here is not in the Bird Control Unit—it doesn't have the tape player, which is probably what you saw in the other. Essentially, the other trucks have—as this one does—ground control radio, all-facility radio, which is our own company frequency, and then the tape player."

A white jumbo is coming out of the sky from the northeast. "Now, here comes a 747," I say. "That's a 400, right?"

"That's correct. Japan Air. See the tiplets, or wing tips, or whatever?"

"Yeah. Now, is he going to land on Two Two Right?"

"No, he's landing on Two Two Left. Parallel." Sammy's voice takes on a weary, pedagogical singsong. "This is the departure runway, and the other one is the landing runway."

I look at a wind sock. "And I see that he's landing into a headwind."

"Yeah."

"Which is nice."

"Well," Sammy says. "That's why they're using the Two Two."

"Beautiful plane."

"Sure is." We drive across the foot of the runway. "All right now," he says. "You've already seen this—" He points over toward the blast fence, where I can see a chartreuse Port Authority pumper truck and several police trainees in fire-fighting suits standing around The Fuselage.

"Right. They're about to light up," I say.

"Anyway," Sammy says, "at the end of the 1990 season, the Park Service came up with a proposal for what would be necessary for any further egg oiling in '91, or thereafter. The bottom line of which was one point eight *million* dollars. Which the Port Authority would have to pay for them to do this additional study, a much more elaborate study than was ever done before.

"Well, we balked at that. We don't *want* any further study. The problem has been identified; it has been studied to death already."

"Why did they want to study it further?"

"Well—foot draggin'. Taking advantage of the Port Authority's generosity and all that. And delaying any control action out at the colony. That was the bottom line, too."

"Like filibustering."

"Exactly. There you go. So as a result of that—"

"I'm sorry," I say. I point to an orange-and-white corrugated-metal shed. "What's this thing here?"

"This is the middle marker for runway Three One Right," Sammy says. "Part of the ILS system. And this instrument right here, on top of this tower, is what gives you the wind shear out at this location." He's shown me this before. I look at the detector for a moment, and think once more of Flight 66, and how this small thing might have prevented it. The cops light The Fuselage. There is the familiar—but never less than startling—billow, then column of red flame, the cloud of thick black smoke.

"There's wind-measuring equipment scattered around at various portions of the airport, to give the tower people a wind indication out near the approach ends of the runways," Sammy says. "To determine not only the wind at the center portion of the runway, where there's *always* been an anemometer, but to give you the actual wind direction and velocity nearer the ends of the runways."

"Because that's where the problem happened with Flight 66."

"That's exactly it, right. Same thing with the transmissometers that give you the visibility out at the ends of the runways. Rather than the one observation point over on the top of the IAB, where it *used* to be. Again, an Eastern Airlines airplane crashed, and killed a bunch of people, because of a three-mile visibility that was being given, measured down there—'

"When was that?" I ask.

"Probably in the sixties. It was a prop job—it was probably a DC-4, or whatever."

Lou Abelson, I remember. *The pea-soup fog.* "So," I say. "They were registering three-mile visibility down at the IAB, whereas—"

"At the end of the runway here it was, uh—"

"Socked."

"Exactly." He peers up through the windshield. "Lemme zap across this runway here—now I've got an airplane comin' in; I want to just beat him across."

We cut south across 31 Right. I look back and see an American DC-10 descending toward 22 Left through the black smoke from The Fuselage. "Of course, those airlines *love* it when the cops light that Fuselage," I say.

"Well, I'll tell you. These guys have to contact the tower and get permission to torch up, for that very reason." He clears his throat. "Now, OK. We hired an adviser—a Ph.D. research biologist in Department of Agriculture— to work with, or against, as the case may be, the National Park Service scientists for the northeast region. His name is Dr. Dolbeer. Richard Dolbeer. Now, when he saw this proposal for spending one point eight million dollars for another *study,* he came up with the concept of using our own depredation permit, to exercise a form of control on the laughing gulls without having to even *deal* with the Park Service—other than letting them know, hey, this is what we're gonna do.

"We did have to go through a certain amount of environmental review, and advising various different agencies that we were gonna be doing this," Sammy says. "Then we went ahead and did it. It started in May through to around August the ninth—roughly a twelve-week period. During that period we killed fourteen thousand eight hundred eighty laughing gulls. I say 'we'; I mean the professional shooters. ADC—animal damage control—people. This was Dr. Dolbeer's recommendation."

"How'd they do it?"

"With shotguns, live ammunition. And the cost of that entire project was—I can't say with complete certainty, but say for instance, somewhere around the area of—well, let's say for instance forty thousand dollars. As opposed to one point eight million."

"But I mean, how do they go about it?" I ask. "Are the gulls easy to kill? I mean, don't they fly away when anybody comes up with a gun?"

"Laughing gulls have not been in the area long enough and have not been shot at long enough to be shy," he says. "This is why there were so many bird strikes in the previous years. They aren't even shy of *airplanes.*"

Now we're driving south on Zulu Bravo, in between and parallel to the two 4-22 runways. "Anyway," Sammy says. "We had a lot of opposition."

"Animal-rights people?"

"Yup. But we succeeded."

"What's that I'm looking at right there?" I ask. Sammy stops the truck. "I've never seen that before," I say. "That thing that looks like a bowling pin sticking up? Is that new?" A giant bowling pin is precisely what the white-orange-and-blue structure looks like—a bowling pin or some kind of stylized fifties burger drive-in.

"Oh, OK. Yeah, that's new. Well, there was one here before—it had to be relocated to accommodate the extension of this taxiway. It's the VOR—the Omnirange. The airport locator beacon for Kennedy Airport. It broadcasts a system out on every cardinal point of the compass. Three hundred and sixty. Those are known as radials. You can pick up a radial that will lead you in from wherever you are, right into that station. It's an airport-locator beacon, essentially.

"There's probably about—I'm not sure if it's three or four or five thousand of 'em, but something like that—at all major airports all the way across the country," Sammy says. "It is the basis for the instrument flying system, nationwide—and worldwide! Yes, of course. Worldwide.

"Now, there's also distance-measuring equipment associated with practically every VOR throughout the country. So that as you tune in the identifiers for this VOR, and if you have the distance-measuring equipment in your aircraft, it will give you a read-out as to how far away you are from this station. And most all commercial airliners, at the very least, have VME—visual measuring equipment. And it's broadcast out of here. Tells the aircraft how far away he is—so how much simpler can it be? You just pick up a radio from wherever you are—you follow it in!"

This is all so beautiful that it makes my chest tight. *The world's best boys' toys.* But how can I say this to Sammy? You can't tell that to another man. "Right," I say.

In comes another white jumbo, with a blue-and-yellow-orange tail. "Lufthansa—*regular* 747," I announce, proudly.

"Right," Sammy agrees.

I can't hold back any longer. "Did you do any of the shooting of the laughing gulls yourself, Sammy?"

"No. No."

"You just drove the people around?"

"Right." But he sounds defensive. "Well—I did shoot, but it was unofficial," he says. "I have a firearms permit, so I'm allowed to *do* it. I just did it to get in on the action. You know, on a Saturday or a Sunday, when I didn't have to monitor the radio, I'd bring the guys out—especially when it was only two shooters—we'd go out to one good prime location, and just—" He pauses, not filling in the terrible blank.

Silence for a moment in the truck. "Now, you're such a bird guy," I say. "I mean, you're so fond of so many different kinds of birds. It didn't bother you to—"

"Not a bit."

"Because they're such a danger?"

"Right. And I'm psyched up to that, and I tell you—I could almost say that I *hate* gulls. I like birds, but I have to exclude gulls. Because of the problems that they've given us, and me, out here. For so many years."

We head down the service road again. I think of those years, and then I think back further, to Sammy's first flights, as a kind of aeronautical prodigy, in Swanton, Vermont, at age fifteen. And then all the years of flying after that—in light airplanes and military airplanes and helicopters—until the flying came to an abrupt halt. "Do you ever miss flying, Sammy?" I ask.

"Well," he says, "as it happens, I'm back flyin' airplanes again. Cessna

150s and Cessna 172s. And in fact, next month I will be going to Texas as a retired person to do as much flying as I can do, and want to do, and am able to do. While I'm still able to fly."

"So you're moving down there?"

"Well, for six months—for the winter months. Then I'll come back up to the Northeast for the summer."

We pull up at the foot of 13 Right. Sammy points to a large, plane-shaped, blue-plastic-shrouded wreck behind Hangar 12, the TWA mainte-nance center. "That's the ONA—no, I'm sorry, the TWA 1011 that crashed in July."

"The Overseas National crash was back in '75," I say.

"Right. But you know, the scenarios were very much the same. Except for the fact that this one was not caused by birds, and ONA was. They ended up in almost the identical same location. It was remarkable."

"What was the cause of this one?"

"Well, that's not known yet, really. The pilot aborted the takeoff—"

"Because it didn't feel right," I remember. "And the ONA pilot also aborted the takeoff, but that was because of a bird strike."

"Yeah. And the engine eventually fell off the wing. Before he ended up—"

"He was on One Three Right?"

"Yeah. As this one was."

"The ONA plane hit a small building—wasn't that the case?"

"The engine that fell off the wing—number three engine—eventually scooted across the outer and inner perimeters and came to rest—yes, up near a building."

"What kind of building was it?"

Sammy shakes his head at his pesky student. "Oh. All right. Just don't let us forget to go get gasoline. Fact, I was gonna go from here now, but I will show you that building." He's a soft touch when it comes to planes. We head off down along 13 Right, on taxiway Papa.

"Now, when you first came here, Sam, after you stopped flying heli-copters, what were your duties then?" I ask.

"I came out here as what is now called the duty manager. What was then called a duty supervisor. This was because of my previous background in avi-ation, and also because of my salary structure at the time. This was a verbal thing with my boss in the helicopter-flying business—from day one we had an agreement: If anything ever happened to me where I couldn't fly anymore, I could stay with the Port Authority if I so desired, and work in a position they would give me where my flying background would be used. And so I came out here in August—about August, I guess—of '57, and I've been out here ever since."

"And what were your duties?"

"The same as a duty manager now. To be in charge of the airport, to represent the airport manager on off-hours, and to be in charge of airport safety. Making sure that the airport can be operated safely both day and night. There is a duty supervisor out here twenty-four hours a day."

"So would you drive around? Would you stay in the office?"

"I drove around. And was in touch with the office."

"And what kinds of things would you be looking at? Lights that were out?"

"Yeah. And reporting that to the proper people, like the electricians. Routine things like that, and then also just making sure that contractors who were tearing up real estate nearby the runways left things in a safe operating condition before they wrapped up for the day."

"Were you sorry not to be flying helicopters anymore?"

"Well—yes and no. As you know, I'd had a sort of difficult incident."

I tell Sammy I do know. For I've finally managed to locate an old newspaper account of the spectacular incident that ended his flying career and brought him to the airport.

It was a clear summer afternoon, Wednesday, July 13, 1955. *Summer afternoon,* Henry James said. *The two most beautiful words in the English language.* Eisenhower was president. Traffic on Ninth Avenue was heavy (the cars were large and rounded); the sidewalks were fairly crowded (men wore hats; women wore dresses). Sammy was about to take an aerial photographer named Arthur Truss aloft in his twenty-three-hundred-pound Bell 47-G Port Authority helicopter—the very plastic-bubbled dragonfly model enshrined, as a paragon of industrial design, in the Museum of Modern Art—for some official picture-taking. For reasons unknown or unsaid, Sammy tried to take off from the PA building while an auxiliary power cord, about an inch in diameter and thirty feet long, was still attached to his aircraft. The incident made the front page of the *Times.*

> A witness in a near-by building said [the *Times* reported] the helicopter rose a short distance and suddenly fell at a forty-five-degree angle. It landed upside down on a wall about ten feet high around the wide sixteenth-floor terrace.
>
> As it hit the wall, its plastic bubble shattered and it began burning.

The pilot and photographer dropped to the terrace, almost uncon-
scious. Employees in the building pulled them away from the helicopter, summoned doctors and turned in a fire alarm.

Just as the pilot and photographer were pulled clear of the tee-
tering craft, it slid over the far side of the wall and fell to the fifteenth floor. There it broke windows and forced employees to
abandon offices. Debris, including parts of a burning gas tank, fell
into Ninth Avenue. . . .

Traffic was rerouted from the avenue. Thousands of people gathered in
the streets and gawked as firemen lashed the helicopter's burned, protruding
skeleton to the building. It was a scene from a disaster movie. The photographer suffered a fractured skull and a broken leg. Sammy had many cuts and
bruises; his skull was also fractured. Both men were extremely fortunate to be
alive, although Sammy Chevalier probably felt anything but fortunate.

"It was a busy day," Sammy tells me, quietly. "I had a lot of flying to do,
and I was rushing, I guess. It was a matter of me forgetting to remove the
cable. I removed that plug up to a dozen times a day for two years, and forgot
once. The removal of the plug was the pilot's responsibility, and I hold to this
day that it just shouldn't have been. There were too many other things to think
about. A simple set of nickel-cadmium batteries would've obviated the need
for the power cord and prevented the whole incident. But that would have
cost three hundred dollars, and the director of the Port Authority didn't want
to spend the money.

"In a typical case of closing the barn door after the cows have got out,
immediately after the accident they mandated that a PA employee had to be
there every time a helicopter took off, to remove the plug and show it to the
pilot before he took off.

"I flew for twenty-three months after the accident," he says. "But then I
began to have what I guess was a kind of psychological reaction to taking off
from that roof on hot summer days with maximum gross load. I just was
thinking more and more about it. So I thought that before I got killed, I'd better stop flying.

"Strangely enough," Sammy says, "my daughter used to be a flight attendant for New York Air and was on both of New York Air's helicopter
crashes—the one in '77, on the Pan Am Building roof, that killed a person
down below, and the one in '79, out at Newark Airport, that finally put New
York Air out of business. So she and I have what I guess you could call the
unique distinction of having been involved in both of the rooftop helicopter
crashes in New York's history."

THE AIRPORT

My mouth is open. The only thing that occurs to me at the moment is that I never knew Sammy had a daughter. I never even knew he had a wife.

"This is the building where that engine ended," Sammy says. We've stopped by a small aluminum-sided structure about three quarters of the way down 13 Right.

"Building Two Ninety-eight," I say. "What kind of building was it in '75?"

"It was a Pan Am—this area was Pan Am at that time—line shack. A utility building."

"What did they keep in there?"

"Oh, oil and grease and spare parts, and stuff like that."

"Did the engine damage the building?"

"No, actually, by the time it got to here from where it fell off back there on the runway, its inertial speed and everything else had slowed down; it dragged—"

"It went a good long way, though," I say. "That's a couple of hundred yards."

"At least. Fortunately, it didn't hit any airplanes, it didn't hit any vehicles. There's a lot of traffic on that road. It just sorta came to rest right up there against that building."

"Traveling roughly in a northeast direction, I guess."

"Yeah. The engine probably fell off somewhere up there." He points back toward the runways. "And of course when the engine fell off the wing, it severed the fuel line, so that caused the fuel to start leaking out, and then you were getting sparks being ignited by blown tires and rims and everything else, so that's how come it caught afire."

Sammy turns the truck around and heads back. Time to get gas. Down at the end of the runway, next to TWA, we're once again alongside the shrouded wreck of the L-1011, Flight 843. "Could you just slow down a little bit?" I say. "I just want to get a gander at this incredible sight." I can see through the blue plastic wrap—it's the same color as the plastic my morning paper comes in—that the plane's tail is white and logo-less. "They took off the plane's markings, I notice."

"Oh yeah. They always do that, first thing."

"That's bad PR, I guess."

"Well, yeah. That's why they do it."

"Now, you said the L-1011 pilot did the same thing the ONA pilot did?"

"Yes. When TWA took off, he had this full runway. Just as ONA did. And as he was approaching the very end of the runway and seeing that heavy-gauge-steel blast fence starin' him in the face, he veered it off to the left. And

263

went out in the dirt, which broke the nose-wheel, and he went up on his nose. Or down on his nose. And of course the airplane was burning. But he avoided going through that blast fence, which would've been far worse."

We drive into the TWA lot to see the wreck's unmasked side. And I see why they've covered the other side: The plane's corpse is black, burned, peeled, and scary-looking. The engines have been removed from the tail and under the wings. "See," Sammy says. "It's pretty much only shielded from the traveling public."

"Unbelievable," I say. "Whew."

"Unbelievable—you might also say miraculous. When you see what you have there, and no one was injured. Rapid evacuation was really one of the things. Everybody had to go out the two front chutes. 'Cause all the other chutes in the back escape areas were burning."

"In the ONA crash, those were all pros on board. But these were mostly civilians."

"Exactly. So probably it's an increased awareness and training of cabin crews to emergency procedures that saved them."

"Where are the engines?"

"They've been sent back—the NTSB is still checking 'em out, or having the manufacturer check 'em out for them. Whatever."

Two TWA maintenance men in coveralls come out of the building. "We ain't gonna touch nothin'!" Sammy calls to them. One of them calls back something I can't hear.

"What'd he say?" I ask.

"'If you can carry it, take it.'"

We fill up the Chevy with gas at an Amoco station outside the runway area, then head back in. "So did the killings of the laughing gulls make a dent in the population?" I ask.

"Yes," Sammy says. "And more importantly, it lowered the number of bird strikes over the same time frame compared to what they were before. It lowered 'em something like sixty-eight to seventy percent—"

"What number of bird strikes are we talking about? Dozens? Hundreds?"

"Dozens. And it decreased down to—well, literally tens instead of dozens."

"So this is likely to be a continuing thing, summer to summer?"

"Yes. Except that we started getting a lot of opposition to it, as you may have read about, and that of course will continue. In fact, one group—the Friends of Animals—have actually initiated a suit against—"

"Is that Pan Am cargo out there?" I point to a big white-and-blue building.

"No, this is a Pan Am hangar. This is where they stored all the equipment that's being sold under Chapter Eleven."

I look into the big empty parking lot. Long dry brown grass is sticking up through cracks in the asphalt. This is the way the world ends.

"Anyway," Sammy says, "the Friends of Animals are suing the New York State DEC"—Department of Environmental Conservation—"for issuing us a permit to do this shooting this past summer. But I'll tell you—the facts and figures that they're using, if the DEC has any kind of a qualified legal staff, it'll be quashed like *that*."

"So you're looking forward to the activities' continuing?"

"Well, not me personally. But conceivably I could be involved in some capacity or other. I told my boss, Gartner, that I foresee being available if he wants me or needs me for anything during the six months that I'm back up here in this area."

"So your being up here will coincide with the laughing gulls' nesting period!"

"Exactly."

I stare at Sammy's raptor profile. "Where do they go in the winter? Do *they* go down to Texas?"

But he doesn't hear me. Two guys in a panel truck, with that lost look on their faces, have stopped to ask directions. "Uh—yeah," Sammy tells them. "Back up if you can, carefully; go down the road to the next exit; follow it right directly to Swissair."

"Where do the laughing gulls go in wintertime?" I ask again.

"As far down as Venezuela," Sammy says. "They go down to the northern one third of South America, both the west coast and the east coast."

"And when they come back up here they'll be shooting them again?"

He shakes his head. "Well, I don't know. We don't even know what we're gonna be allowed to do next year, to tell the truth. To tell the truth, I don't really want to get involved in that—that's one reason I'm retiring. Another reason is that I have forty point two nine years of service. And another is, I want to go flying."

21

Leaving

Terminal One

At the end of September at Kennedy, there is a slowdown in traffic after the summer peak, and late on a weekday afternoon, the airport is relatively quiet. The long, thin clouds in the bright-blue sky are slate-colored; the sun is warm and the wind is cold. The doomed terminal is silent. The terminal used to be Eastern's; by the time you read this, it will be gone, razed, history, soon to be replaced by a shiny new glass-and-steel building, even cleaner than BA's white box, constructed by a consortium consisting of Japan Airlines, Lufthansa, Air France, Korean Air, and Iberia. On this end-of-September afternoon, though, Terminal One still exists, all marble and travertine and onyx and brass and towering windows and dusty gathered drapes and late-fifties-style defunct elegance. October '59 was when they opened the place, and thirty-five years isn't a bad run for a building these days, especially at the airport.

There are ghosts here. This is where the families and friends of the passengers of Flight 66 waited and waited, and found out; this is where a million winter trips down to Miami and the Caribbean, licit and otherwise, began and ended. Pappagallo shoes and Meledandri suits, Ban-Lon and polyester. Sharkskin and blue jaws. Stingy-brim hats. My Sin and Brut and White Shoulders and Aqua Velva. All that's left is the walls and the high, wide space. Doomed. A couple of charter companies are leasing gates here in the meantime, and a carrier called MGM Grand, also doomed as far as regularly scheduled flights are concerned (in January 1993 it would go all-charter), but for the time being a flicker of the past, when flying was for the lucky few. MGM, in its brief history, flew exclusively between New York and Los Angeles, and it was a thing of beauty: The flights were always undersold, and the cheaper seats in the back of the renovated DC-8s were much better than most business-class seats—wide, and upholstered in an ugly but strangely nostalgic

267

pinkish leather. The planes were kept scrupulously clean; each of the large, carpeted lavatories contained gold-colored sink fixtures and flowers in a small vase. All right, it was Vegas; but Vegas in a *good* way. The food was better than passable, the liquor flowed freely, and cruising home in the clear light over the middle of America, sipping Chardonnay and listening to Stan Getz play "Au Privave" on the headphones, you might be forgiven for thinking you had achieved airline Nirvana.

Of course it had to end; all those underbooked flights were wonderful for the nerves but hell on the bankbooks of Kirk Kerkorian, the Las Vegas billionaire and the airline's backer. But this is shortly before the end, and you're on the evening flight to the coast, and just now you've just left your cab, and you're heading for the MGM desk in the expanse of the terminal's main room. Suddenly a guy appears at your side, in a tailored black uniform: he has a baby face, a face out of *Little Archie* comics, and his hair is a flattop sculpture in brown and gold. "MGM Grand Air?" he asks.

"How'd you know?" you say.

He smiles. "Just call it a sixth sense," he says.

You go to a desk where he takes your ticket and checks it against his manifest. A smiling woman in the same black uniform appears, and the *Little Archie* guy says, "Have a nice flight, sir," and pats you on the back.

The woman leads you through the empty halls, her heels echoing on shiny stone, to a set of glass doors, which open into a lounge decorated Vegas-style and unoccupied but for another uniformed woman behind a desk. You smile, sit on the couch, leaf through a magazine, look out the windows at the runways in the clear sunset light; but then you feel restless, as you always do before flying, and you get up and leave.

The hallway is dark. You notice an open newsstand down the way. But before you get there, you see late sunlight streaming out an open doorway, and inside there's a bar, a big room with floor-to-ceiling windows, a television mounted on the wall by the windows, a bored bartender, and four customers. Two of the customers are middle-aged ladies, sitting quietly with their Manhattans and staring at the TV, which is showing the confirmation hearings for a Supreme Court justice. Ted Kennedy's spherical head fills the screen. The other two customers are a middle-aged man and a pretty young woman. "That's *shit,* that's *shit,* that's *shit,*" the man is saying.

You go back out into the hall, buy a *Post,* and return to the bar. Sit down with your beer and the paper at a table with a view of the television and the big windows. Outside the windows, planes taxi by; the electric-colored sky is huge. The disputatious couple leave; you drink your beer. The light coming through the windows is golden, and so is the beer; in a minute the edge is off your flying nerves. Another minute and, your stomach empty, you really feel the alcohol. You read an item on Page Six about a new UFO book, and glance up at the TV screen, where ALF, a puppet alien, is talking with an air force colonel, who is asking ALF if the family, by any chance, has any extraterrestrials in the house.

You glance at your watch. Just past six. You leave some coins and the paper on the table and walk, slightly unsteadily, through the dark hall, which somehow smells like 1964. Back to the lounge. A few people have shown up, and they're gathering their things. Time to board. The people from the first-class lounge across the way emerge, and you all form a line of perhaps a dozen. You show your ticket to the bored security woman, take your keys out of your pocket, put them on the proffered salver, and pass uneventfully through the metal detector as your carry-on gets a half-glance from another weary-looking woman; you walk down the hall to where a slim young man in black, his blond hair as high as a soufflé, smiles brightly and says, "Good evening, sir!" As you stride up the loading bridge to the plane, you notice that the woman in front of you is a well-known television news personality.

She, of course, goes up to the front of the plane. But there's nothing wrong back here. You sit down and stretch out in the wide pink seat. Chopin's *Barcarolle* is playing over the plane's speakers. You buckle your gold seatbelt buckle and accept a Champagne from the attendant—who, in just a few months, will be looking for work. Nor will you ever fly this way again.

Just after 6:30, only three minutes late, the plane pushes back from the gate, past a sign that reads NO INTERNATIONAL TRASH, out taxiway November and onto the outer perimeter road.

Since the weather is fine, and the wind is out of the south and east this evening, and since 13 Right, the usual departure runway, is chockablock with traffic, you've been cleared to take off on 13 Left, at the other side of the airport. So you taxi down past the terminals that were once described as jewels on a necklace: Terminal One and Northwest and what used to be the Pan Am Worldport and is now Delta. The jewels have faded, but in the sunset light, in a Champagne haze, they look magical once more. Then the road turns left, and you roll past the back of the IAB, past the hardstands where the 747s sit, their tails painted with the blazons of international aviation—LOT and Ladeco and Avianca and Lufthansa and KLM and Japan Air. Under their wings, the ramp rats scurry. Beneath the asphalt, the Jet-A flows through singing pipes. A blue-and-white PA cruiser drives by, in no special hurry, the mind of the cop at the wheel on Lotto combinations. Inside the IAB, smiling Colombian killers with phony passports and shy Russian children with wide eyes and quiet Lebanese women with covered heads enter America for the first time. Up in the tower, a controller with a head cold munches a stale doughnut and talks and talks to men and women in the sky.

Left again. Past Eero Saarinen's poem in concrete, TWA International—a poem no longer noticed much, as the airline struggles to survive—and past the more prosaic TWA Domestic and British/United's white box and on to taxiway Alfa. The lights are coming on at the airport: the deep-blue perimeter lights along the taxiway, the red-and-white runway signs and black-and-yellow taxiway signs glowing within, the yellow-and-green in-pavement hold bars, the pink-orange mercury-vapors behind the terminals, the white beacon atop the tower.

You're third in line, behind a United 757 and an American Eagle commuter. To the left, alongside the runway, stand the big cargo buildings of Korean Air and Federal Express and JAL. Crates and containers will vanish into unauthorized hands tonight. You go. Down the runway, faster and faster, up toward 180 knots, as the engines crescendo and you look at your watch: You're up in twenty-five seconds, a light load tonight. Now you're rising, with a slight leftward tilt, the wing blue and orange in the sunset light, and the engines are making that tunneling noise they make as you climb. You cross filthy Thurston Basin, where the SAS plane went into the drink in '84, and Rockaway Boulevard, where Flight 66 smacked down. But you're up, you're safe, and your pilot—who used to work for Eastern, who has white hair in his ears, who is worrying (again) about unemployment and (always) about his prostate—flips the switches that make the gear doors thunk closed, the flaps retract into the wings.

Over the invisible line from Queens into Nassau County, the dense grid of Long Island washed with dying sun and dotted with crime lights. Cars and roads everywhere, dozens of tiny pairs of headlights picking bravely through the rising dark. You pass over Hewlett Bay Park and Woodmere and Hewlett, over my grandparents' old houses, large and small, then turn north and fly over Captain Len Klasmeier's place in Valley Stream. And then up over what they used to call the Hempstead Plains, high above the shopping malls and subdivisions that crowd what once were the quiet potato fields where Glenn Curtiss and Lindbergh and a thousand lost barnstormers flew.

Bank left, into the sun, as the burning towers of the city wheel away. And then, there, two miles below and ten miles to the south, is Kennedy once again, in miniature, with all its lights on, and—seemingly—comprehensible at last. *Working.* And beyond it the oil-dark sea.

Index

Index

Index

Index

Index

Index

Index